SUBJECTIVITY IN ASIAN CHILDREN'S LITERATURE AND FILM

Children's Literature and Culture
Jack Zipes, *Series Editor*

For a complete series list, please go to
routledge.com

Voracious Children
Who Eats Whom in Children's Literature
Carolyn Daniel

National Character in South African
Children's Literature
Elwyn Jenkins

Myth, Symbol, and Meaning in
Mary Poppins
The Governess as Provocateur
Georgia Grilli

A Critical History of French Children's
Literature, Vol. 1 & 2
Penny Brown

Once Upon a Time in a Different World
*Issues and Ideas in African American
Children's Literature*
Neal A. Lester

The Gothic in Children's Literature
Haunting the Borders
Edited by Anna Jackson, Karen Coats,
and Roderick McGillis

Reading Victorian Schoolrooms
*Childhood and Education in
Nineteenth-Century Fiction*
Elizabeth Gargano

Soon Come Home to This Island
West Indians in British Children's Literature
Karen Sands-O'Connor

Boys in Children's Literature and
Popular Culture
*Masculinity, Abjection, and the
Fictional Child*
Annette Wannamaker

Into the Closet
*Cross-dressing and the Gendered Body
in Children's Literature*
Victoria Flanagan

Russian Children's Literature and Culture
Edited by Marina Balina and
Larissa Rudova

The Outside Child In and Out of the Book
Christine Wilkie-Stibbs

Representing Africa in Children's Literature
Old and New Ways of Seeing
Vivian Yenika-Agbaw

The Fantasy of Family
*Nineteenth-Century Children's Literature
and the Myth of the Domestic Ideal*
Liz Thiel

From Nursery Rhymes to Nationhood
*Children's Literature and the Construction
of Canadian Identity*
Elizabeth A. Galway

The Family in English Children's Literature
Ann Alston

Enterprising Youth
*Social Values and Acculturation in
Nineteenth-Century American
Children's Literature*
Monika Elbert

Constructing Adolescence in
Fantastic Realism
Alison Waller

Crossover Fiction
Global and Historical Perspectives
Sandra L. Beckett

The Crossover Novel
*Contemporary Children's Fiction and Its
Adult Readership*
Rachel Falconer

Shakespeare in Children's Literature
Gender and Cultural Capital
Erica Hateley

Critical Approaches to Food in
Children's Literature
Edited by Kara K. Keeling and
Scott T. Pollard

Neo-Imperialism in Children's Literature
About Africa
A Study of Contemporary Fiction
Yulisa Amadu Maddy and Donnarae
MacCann

Death, Gender and Sexuality in
Contemporary Adolescent Literature
Kathryn James

SUBJECTIVITY IN ASIAN CHILDREN'S LITERATURE AND FILM

Global Theories and Implications

EDITED BY
JOHN STEPHENS

Routledge
Taylor & Francis Group
NEW YORK AND LONDON

First published 2013
by Routledge
711 Third Avenue, New York, NY 10017

Simultaneously published in the UK
by Routledge
2 Park Square, Milton Park, Abingdon, Oxon OX14 4RN

First issued in paperback 2017

Routledge is an imprint of the Taylor & Francis Group, an informa business

© 2013 Taylor & Francis

The right of John Stephens to be identified as the author of the editorial material, and of the authors for their individual chapters, has been asserted in accordance with sections 77 and 78 of the Copyright, Designs and Patents Act 1988.

All rights reserved. No part of this book may be reprinted or reproduced or utilised in any form or by any electronic, mechanical, or other means, now known or hereafter invented, including photocopying and recording, or in any information storage or retrieval system, without permission in writing from the publishers.

Trademark Notice: Product or corporate names may be trademarks or registered trademarks, and are used only for identification and explanation without intent to infringe.

Library of Congress Cataloging in Publication Data
   Subjectivity in Asian children's literature and film : global theories and implications / edited by John Stephens.
        p. cm. — (Children's literature and culture)
   Includes bibliographical references and index.
   1.   Children's literature—History and criticism—Theory, etc. 2.   Children's literature—Asia—History and criticism. 3.   Children's films—History and criticism. 4.   Children's films—Asia—History and criticism. 5.   Children—Books and reading. 6.   Children—Asia—Books and reading. 7.   Subjectivity in literature. 8.   Subjectivity in motion pictures.   I. Stephens, John, 1944–
   PN1009.A1S877 2012
   809'.89282—dc23
   2012018661

ISBN 13: 978-1-138-10898-1 (pbk)
ISBN 13: 978-0-415-80688-6 (hbk)

Typeset in Minion
by IBT Global.

Contents

Figures

Series Editor's Foreword

Dedicated to furthering original research in children's literature and culture, the Children's Literature and Culture series includes monographs on individual authors and illustrators, historical examinations of different periods, literary analyses of genres, and comparative studies on literature and the mass media. The series is international in scope and is intended to encourage innovative research in children's literature with a focus on interdisciplinary methodology.

Children's literature and culture are understood in the broadest sense of the term children to encompass the period of childhood up through adolescence. Owing to the fact that the notion of childhood has changed so much since the origination of children's literature, this Routledge series is particularly concerned with transformations in children's culture and how they have affected the representation and socialization of children. While the emphasis of the series is on children's literature, all types of studies that deal with children's radio, film, television, and art are included in an endeavor to grasp the aesthetics and values of children's culture. Not only have there been momentous changes in children's culture in the last fifty years, but there have been radical shifts in the scholarship that deals with these changes. In this regard, the goal of the Children's Literature and Culture series is to enhance research in this field and, at the same time, point to new directions that bring together the best scholarly work throughout the world.

Jack Zipes

Naming Conventions

The general practice in this book is to use the normal order of family name + given name for Chinese, Korean, and Japanese names, with two exceptions: the names of contributors are transposed to the English language order, given name + family name; and given name + family name order is used when the person concerned is publically known by the transposed form—for example, the picture book author-illustrator Satoshi Kitamura.

Chapter One

Introduction

The Politics of Identity:
A Transcultural Perspective on
Subjectivity in Writing for Children

John Stephens

Experiencing interdependence entails seeing oneself as part of an encompass-
ing social relationship and recognizing that one's behavior is determined, contingent on, and, to a large extent organized by what the actor perceives to be the
thoughts, feelings, and actions of *others* in the relationship.

Markus and Kitayama

Over recent years, it has become usual in Western literary criticism to talk
about literature for children in terms of its representations of subjectivity.
Given a prevailing concern in the literature with identity and individual
development, it is easy to slip into a habit of thinking that the literature is
about subjectivity, and then principally about the nature and enhancement
of agency, and the kinds of circumstances that frame an individual's decisions and capacities to make choices and act upon them. Starting with one
or other of the conceptions of subjectivity that are available to us and which
seem to predominate in children's literature, we can then go on to examine
how this subjectivity is represented in texts. This has been the case for almost
twenty years now, since the concept of subjectivity was first discussed in the
field of children's literature in John Stephens's *Language and Ideology in Children's Fiction* (1992) and in an article by Roberta Seelinger Trites, "Claiming

the Treasures: Patricia MacLachlan's Organic Postmodernism" (1993). Like a lot of conceptual thinking about children's literature, however, it works well mainly because both the literature and the criticism are informed by the same cultural metanarrative. The literature, in most cases, is only *about* subjectivity to the extent that the producing culture is preoccupied with it, whether or not it is named as such.

There have been very few dedicated studies of subjectivity in relation to children's literature, and these have either explicitly or implicitly shaped discourse in the field. In her study of the textual formulations of a "confrontation between humanist and postmodernist approaches to subjectivity" in Terry Pratchett's *Nation* (2010, 112), Blanka Grzegorczyk grounds her argument on the truism that humanist assumptions about the uniqueness of the individual and the idea of selfhood as essential are to be rejected, and have been replaced by "a sense of a dialectical relationship between subjectivity and sociality, and between self-representations and the social constructions of self" (113). She then turns to the work of Paul Smith (1988), John Stephens (1992), and Robyn McCallum (1999), who share this sense of a dialectical relationship, and derives her analytical method thence. In doing so, Grzegorczyk has made explicit what has long been implicit in the criticism. In addition to Smith, key influences on the formulation of conceptions of subjectivity in children's literature scholarship have been Mikhail Bakhtin's *The Dialogic Imagination*, Jacques Lacan (see Coats, 2004), and Linda Hutcheon's works on postmodernism (1988, 1989). Two position statements at the beginning of McCallum's *Ideologies of Identity in Adolescent Fiction*, in which all of the above theorists are discussed, encapsulate what is implicit in subsequent criticism:

> [I]deas about and representations of subjectivity pervade and underpin adolescent fiction. Conceptions of subjectivity are intrinsic to narratives of personal growth or maturation, to stories about relationships between the self and others, and to explorations of relationships between individuals and the world, society or the past—that is, subjectivity is intrinsic to the major concerns of adolescent fiction. (1999, 3)

> [S]ubjectivity is an individual's sense of a personal identity as a subject— in the sense of being subject to some measure of external coercion—and as an agent—that is, being capable of conscious and deliberate thought and action. And this identity is formed in dialogue with the social discourses, practices and ideologies constituting the culture which an individual inhabits. (4)

How quickly these positions have become naturalized in children's literature criticism is well illustrated by Maria Nikolajeva's *Power, Voice and Subjectivity in Literature for Young Readers* (2009): even though this work aspires to be a general theory for children's literature, there is no perceived need to define *subjectivity* here, and the term itself rarely appears, although readers should now know it is implicit in conceptualizations such as, "how writers can empower and disempower fictive children" (57). What has perhaps been forgotten is a question posed by Paul Smith: given that subjectivity was attributed with "a privileged position in contemporary discourses" (1988, xxviii), "what epistemological and political effects might have been produced as a result of this privilege"?

The problematic question of privileged theory may be seen in an acute form in the more specific and less eclectic Lacanian paradigm of subjectivity that grounds Karen Coats's *Looking Glasses and Neverlands* (2004), a work available in Chinese and Korean translation. On the assumption of a particular theory of the unconscious, the subject is always split, "a construction of both natural and cultural influences, of conscious and unconscious processes" (6), and the unconscious "is deeply implicated in the Other; its verbal and visual representations come from culture, from outside the subject, so that what is most uniquely 'ours' is in fact not native to us at all" (4). When a child reads, s/he uses books to activate this split, "to fill his unconscious with representations and images, shape his reality, and define the parameters of his possibilities" (4). Coats argues that this process depends on repetition of "structures, images, and values" across a range of books. It is uncertain whether this formulation allows for agentic capacity in McCallum's terms, that is, a capacity for conscious and deliberate thought and action, although the further description of the process of reading seems to imply that it doesn't:

> [A]s her books have a definable structure, so structure becomes a psychic necessity for the child. As her books depict a whole world, the child seeks nothing less than a whole world. As her books operate under an oedipal configuration, the child will become structured under an oedipal configuration. As her books value closure, the child comes to desire closure. (7)

The "Lacanian poetics" (32) that produces this position is arguably a specifically Western construction. The symbolic order that it presupposes is derived from European cultures, and the behavioral structure that grounds it may well be, as Kay Stockholder argues, a metaphor based on circular logic: Lacan's description of what children do when first confronted with their mirror images is simply accepted, although it is no more verifiable than the conclusion that it constitutes a moment of alienation of inner being from a subsequently acquired conscious sense of self (1998, 362). In Coats's description, this is the moment of splitting. Looking in the mirror, and seeing an image that is both herself and not herself, the child concludes that "she must not be wholly in either place—she must be lacking" (2004, 47). It is not my purpose here to dispute either what Coats elsewhere refers to as the "overdetermined 'truths' of psychoanalysis" (174) as such, or the applicability of the approach to Anglo-American children's literature,[1] but to suggest that such a theory and approach are not portable. They do not simply transfer to the narratives of non-European cultures, so with the rapid development of children's literature and its scholarly discourses in Asia, it is becoming increasingly desirable to seek a basis for dialogue about the crucial concepts of subjectivity. And, after all, the cultural Other "not native to us at all" in Coats's formulation does not encompass an Other that is outside the subject's specific geographically defined culture.

A good example of how understandings of self in society have been shaped across much of Asia is Buddhist thought. Its influence has been, and still is, felt across most of the region, and it has in its own right made an impact on many areas of Western thought—for example, the concept of *mindfulness*, derived from Buddhist contemplative traditions, is widely utilized in clinical psychology. What the concept—to some degree a program for cultivating subjectivity—means in Western practice is defined in a widely cited summary by Bishop et al., who identify two components: "the self-regulation of attention so that it is maintained on immediate experience, thereby allowing for increased recognition of mental events in the present moment," and "adopting a particular orientation toward one's experiences in the present moment, an orientation that is characterized by curiosity, openness, and acceptance" (2004, 232). As Christopher et al. have demonstrated, Western conceptualizations of mindfulness are framed and validated by Western psychological constructs, and may not generalize to Buddhist cultures (2009, 607). The practice of mindfulness is analogous with some Buddhist ideas about the cultivation of subjectivity (emotional, ethical, and aesthetic), especially through awareness of the interconnectedness of each subject (Bodhakari, 2008). Bodhakari observes that "The self is really part of a continuum, a network of processes, locked in interdependence and constantly affected by everything around us, within and without. . . . However, though we have little or no influence over many events in our lives or in the world, Buddhism teaches that we have a lot of choice in how to relate to what occurs, and how this relating influences experience." The principle of choice in how to relate to events in a Buddhist culture is explored in Chapter 8, this volume, in which Salinee Antarasena demonstrates how karmic law undergirds a bundle of Thai films for teenage audiences and limits choice in precisely this way. Similarly, the Naikan contemplative practice developed in Japan within Shin Buddhism turns on a concept of subjectivity similar to, but different from, those developed in the West. Cultivation of this subjectivity involves, "the learning of new ways of thinking, perceiving, feeling, attending, aspiring, and remembering (changes in the subject's modes of experiencing). Attention to subjectivity enables us to study the cultivation and reorientation of values, the balancing, cultivation, and tempering of emotions, processes of maturation, the development of emotional and social intelligence, and the transformation of experiences of suffering" (Ozawa-De Silva and Ozawa-De Silva, 2010: 158). Questions that contributors to this volume continually pose are, "What does interconnectedness imply for subjectivity in different cultures? What similarities and differences are there between different versions of subjectivity in East and West? Are concepts of subjectivity global, local, or glocal?"

In 1997, shortly after the concept of subjectivity had begun to appear in the scholarly discourses of children's literature, a crucial intervention into the theorizing of subjectivity was made by Sakai Naoki in *Translation and Subjectivity*, although this argument was to remain unnoticed by children's literature scholars. In Chapter 4, Sakai addresses the problem of subjectivity in relation to "Asian Studies" in general, with particular reference to Japan. He argues that the acceptance of "theoretical approaches" across cultures has taken place without interrogation of the political implications of social and epistemic formulations that are profoundly ethnocentric and Eurocentric (1997, 118).[2] Hence to ground conceptions of subjectivity in any of the competing Western theories is to accept the authority of those theories across a wide range of differing cultures and to import conceptions of subjectivity which do not in practice work. The propensity of cultural and literary theories to flow from West to East is largely unremarked in the field of children's literature, although it is effectively visible in the substantial number of graduate students from Asia who complete MA or PhD degrees in Western countries. It is also present in three other ways: in literary or pictorial representations of the East by means of Western paradigms; in Western critical discussions of Eastern literature; and in the criticism written by scholars educated in the West who have subsequently returned to their home countries. One might dare to say that as a "problem" this situation is exacerbated by a reluctance of the West to be open to dialogue with "other" discourses. In what follows, I consider some symptomatic examples of theory flows.

A simple example of representation through Western paradigms is afforded by the oppositional discussion that focuses on Eleanor Coerr's "classic" narratives, *Sadako and the Thousand Paper Cranes* (1977) and *Sadako* (1993). In an article discussing representations of the bombing of Hiroshima in Western and Japanese books, Makito Yurita and Reade W. Dornan adduce various criticisms (such as the absence of moral questions), but here I wish to concentrate on an issue of representation cited from the work of Sakuma Aki:

> Sakuma objects to the value that North Americans place on one individual as heroine, when many thousands of children in Japan died of radiation poisoning. For example, Coerr suggests that the monument in the Hiroshima Peace Park is dedicated to Sadako, whereas Sakuma notes that the Children's Peace Memorial is named for *all* the children who died in the war, not just a few. (Yurita and Dornan, 2009: 231)

The literary structure in which an individual stands for a group or is the pivot of narrative action is the most common structure in children's literature, and is not particularly peculiar to the West, although the rise of first person narration and single character focalization in the years following World War II has endowed it with distinction (and ideological impact) as a self-as-subject or self-as-agent which initiates or responds to action. When these strategies are employed to tell an Eastern story, a Western paradigm of self inevitably intrudes. Sadako's agentic action—to ward off death by making a thousand paper cranes—is tragic because death cuts short her process of individuation. Tragedy is mitigated, Sakuma further argues, because of an orientalist move in the text: "dying beautifully is one of the happiest things in Japanese culture, and Sadako's is a beautiful and romanticized death, a portrait of love and warmth and peace" (Apol et al., 2003: 442). A key distinction implicit in Sakuma's analysis is a contrast between identity-with and difference-from as a basis for subjectivity (see Miyuki Hisaoka's deployment of this contrast in Chapter 4, this volume). In Chapter 3, this volume, Seemi Aziz analyzes how when such Western narrative structures are used to represent Muslima characters, cultures are again falsified in novels positively received in the West.

There is not a substantial body of critical attention to Eastern children's literature in the major children's literature journals, and the bulk of it deals with picture books and, increasingly, manga, anime, and film. It is probably a reasonable judgment that few Western children's literature scholars master the principles of East Asian visual arts or the narrative conventions of manga, and film tends to be a globalized medium and hence generally accessible to viewers used to indie films. Transcultural authors and illustrators, such as Satoshi Kitamura, Allen Say, or Junko Morimoto, have successfully blended Eastern and Western styles and forms, and because such blending is apt to become more common in future and to produce particular glocal forms (see Katrina Gutierrez's discussion of blending in Chapter 2, this volume), Western scholars will need to develop better understandings of Eastern styles because of their implications for represented subjectivity. It is refreshing to observe that, as early as 1991, Jane Doonan has begun to discuss this potential in the picture books of Satoshi Kitamura:

> Kitamura's use of perspective is eclectic. He readily juggles between the Western Renaissance convention, which dictates that parallel lines should converge in the distance, and a system of perspective widely used in China and Japan which may be related to the concept of the "traveling eye." The beholder is assumed to be scanning the painting in different directions rather than maintaining one fixed viewpoint and is not looking at a scene so much as wandering about in it. (110)

Doonan's comment on the different ways a beholder may be positioned by different representational conventions is another perspective on the distinction between difference-from (Renaissance perspective) and identity-with (Eastern planar perspective and "negative space"), and points to a challenge to consider different processes by which viewer subject positioning is shaped and other subjectivities might be presented.

A reciprocal exchange of literary theories and methodologies between Eastern and Western scholars of children's literature is still nascent and remains hampered by Western dominance of the discourse and by the absence or invisibility of local Eastern traditions as applied to the field. In a brief report on "Children's Literature Research in Japan" (2003–2004), Hayashi Michiyo and Kawabata Ariko comment that research "tends to focus on bibliographical and historical research" and little attempt has been made to adapt critical theories, such as postmodernism, feminism, and reader-response theory, to children's literature (245). They suggested that translation of some English-language books might "contribute to the development of study by being applied to Japanese texts" (245), although of the books named only Roberta Seelinger Trites's *Waking Sleeping Beauty* would conceivably have such an impact. Elsewhere in the article, reader-response criticism is designated as a prime desideratum, and although it is a long time since there has been any significant theorizing of this area, recent developments in cognitive narratology could be of great interest, in that they could enable exploration of reading processes grounded in "identity-with" conceptions of subjectivity and contemporary research into empathy, for example. As any academic culture takes on board theories that originate and circulate within other academic cultures, it seems to me important that such theories are returned with difference added. Because models of subjectivity are, as Deborah Knight puts it, "artifacts of theory" (1995, 50) and over-schematic binarisms, it seems obvious that constructions of subjectivity within, for example, postmodernist, feminist, or reader-response theories need to be evaluated within specific sociohistorical contexts and not taken up willy-nilly. For instance, as is observed in chapters by Suchismita Banerjee (Chapter 11, this volume) and Sung-Ae Lee (Chapter 6, this volume), representations of female subject positions within patrifocal Hindu and Confucian institutional structures, respectively, may not be simply dealt with by means of a feminist interrogation of patriarchy (or poststructuralist psychoanalysis, for that matter). Islamic feminists make much the same point (see Chapter 3, this volume). Or, as Tran Quynh Ngoc Bui's practice illustrates (Chapter 9, this volume), a blend of local and global methodologies is an effective means to compare subjectivities across ethnic groups.

To begin to redress these problems in the critical discourses of children's literature, this volume of essays brings together contributors who are culturally and/or academically situated within a particular Asian society. They were asked to investigate what local, often implicit concepts of subjectivity exist and in what ways they are distinct from and influenced by Western theories. They follow Sakai's lead and a direction articulated some years ago by Shlomith Rimmon-Kenan, that is, a direction that resists "impositions of theoretical models on literary texts or reductions of literary texts to the status of examples" (1996, 125).

By using texts as the ground for theory, contributors argue that subjectivity is like ideology and inheres in texts as something immanent in narrative forms and language. Thinking about subjectivity in children's texts might be better served by inverting the process followed in the past few years and taking a more bottom-up approach: that is, by beginning with the question, how is something we might think of as subjectivity or selfhood represented in a focus text, and only then moving to the question of what subjectivity is, of how contingently it can be defined.

A very good example of how this bottom-up approach works can be seen in Ngarmpun ("Jane") Vejjajiva's *The Happiness of Kati* (2003). The text is an English translation of the Thai original (the author is named as collaborator on the translation—she is herself a translator, translating into Thai from French and English).[3] *The Happiness of Kati* has sold 250,000 copies in nine languages, so is something of an international phenomenon. Vejjajiva's intellectual horizons seem to have been shaped by diverse worldviews, and so it is possible that the instantiation of subjectivity in her novel may be interpreted according to emphases that accord with a Western reader's concept of subjectivity as a superordinate term with a specific meaning. The book seems to play with this possibility. At the beginning of the final chapter, it almost brazenly states what readers normally expect of a young adult novel:

> Once Mother had said that we were all like characters in a story who encountered various challenges, which, once passed, conferred a new depth of emotional experience and made you a fuller person for having experienced them. You looked at the world differently from then on. Mother liked to use big words with Kati. They sounded good, even though they were sometimes hard to understand, but at this moment Kati felt that she really had grown up a lot more. (131–132)

This formulation looks like a schematic development trajectory common in children's fiction. It will border on cliché for many English-language readers, but is unlikely to be perceived as such in Thailand, where social hierarchy and respect for authority is stronger, nor in some other countries where the novel is read. The passage seems to advocate the development of subjective agency through a familiar individuation process: the subject finds the emotional and mental resources to deal with the challenges she encounters and develops a more mature, complex, and agentic subjectivity as a result. But by attributing understanding of the process to Kati's now deceased mother, the novel avoids the kind of individualistic subjectivity evident in Western fiction, as in, for example, Michael Gerard Bauer's *Don't Call Me Ishmael*. This Australian novel presents a familiar depiction of adults (parents and most teachers) as generally incompetent in comparison with children, who must therefore forge their subjectivities from their own resources. Kati's adult community is able to offer both guidance and the freedom to choose. To read *Kati* as if it were a Western novel, then, is to impose a foreign conception of subjectivity upon it.

This different understanding clarifies what might otherwise appear to be a contradiction suggested by the novel's close, where it is revealed that a letter Kati was given by her mother to send to her father, who doesn't know she exists, was never sent, as Kati had chosen to shape her life differently and saw no need to justify her decision to others:

> Sometimes life did not lend itself to explanations. Hadn't Mother said that? As for Kati and Mother, Kati knew her mother understood, and there was no need for explanations.
>
> Kati bowed to the Buddha before she went to bed. Tomorrow morning she would have to wake early for school. Everything was the way it always had been. Nothing had changed. And tomorrow the clatter of Grandma's spatula would wake Kati from her slumber to greet the world again. (139)

The possible contradiction is between Kati's earlier sense that she "had grown up a lot" and her affirmation at this point that "Everything was the way it always had been. Nothing had changed." This is not a contradiction; however, I would suggest that my habits of reading in terms of oppositional structures—a characteristic of my academic culture—prompt me to see a contradiction here, and might further induce me to perceive a fragmented subjectivity. One way to overturn that impulse is to invoke the understanding offered by Salinee Antarasena and Bodhakari that "though we have little or no influence over many events in our lives or in the world, Buddhism teaches that we have a lot of choice in how to relate to what occurs, and how this relating influences experience." A further resource is something like Takie Sugiyama Lebra's argument, in *The Japanese Self in Cultural Logic* (2004), that concepts of the self (or, broadly speaking, subjectivity) vary between cultures depending on whether the self is construed as oppositional or contingent. Lebra cites Clifford Geertz's (1984) characterization of the "Western self" as "a bounded, unique, more or less integrated motivational and cognitive universe, a dynamic center of awareness, emotion, judgment, and action organized into a distinctive whole and set contrastively both against other such wholes and against its social and natural background" (4), and argues that these assumptions are grounded in a metalogic of opposition (I am I because I am not you). Certainly Western notions of the self have embraced other versions since 1984—especially a postmodern self, decentered and fragmented, and (eco-)feminist subjectivities—but, Lebra argues, such concepts are still enmeshed in the metalogic of opposition, dependent on new binary oppositions to overthrow older oppositions. Contingent selves, on the other hand, are more akin to what we think of as intersubjective selves, called into being by interaction with others, grounded in randomness, uncertainty, unpredictability, and enmeshed in their social and environmental background.

The close of *The Happiness of Kati* is an affirmation of a Buddhist self, in tune with the Buddhist practices which have pervaded the novel since its opening paragraphs. The cognitive communication of this subjective consciousness is articulated here, as generally through the text, by the drifting of narrative perspective between narrator report and character perspective, a mode familiar in third-person limited narration in English novels when it cannot always be determined whether the discourse is narrative report or free indirect thought. Such indeterminacy is characteristic of the narrative mode Andrea Schwenke Wyile terms "restricted third-person engaging narration." She argues that its effect is to present "a fuller and more sophisticated explanation of events and feelings than the character would be capable of, without explaining more than the character knows" (2003, 117). Within this mode, it is possible to plot the drift between narration and character perception, although not all readers will necessarily agree with my assignment to categories at every point. The English translation, and my analysis of it, are precisely equivalent to the discourse of the original Thai text:[4]

> Sometimes life did not lend itself to explanations. [Narr or FIT] Hadn't Mother said that? [FIT] As for Kati and Mother, Kati knew [Narr/FIT → IT] her mother understood, and there was no need for explanations.
>
> Kati bowed to the Buddha *before* she went to bed. [Narr] *Tomorrow morning* she would have to wake early for school. [Narr/FIT] Everything was the way it *always* had been. Nothing had *changed*. [FIT] And *tomorrow* the clatter of Grandma's spatula would wake Kati from her slumber to greet the world again. [Narr] (139; my italics)
>
> [Narr = narration; FIT = free indirect thought; IT = indirect thought]

Here at the close of the novel, the text enacts Kati's cognitive processing of this particular moment of her young life. The two text segments which are most clearly free indirect thought—"Hadn't Mother said that?" and "Everything was the way it *always* had been. Nothing had *changed*"—bring together her recognition of maternal authority with a Buddhist concept of time—the concept of tomorrow is encompassed by a conception of time not limited by space or distance or the units of clock-time. The heavy use of temporals in the second paragraph expresses this temporal paradox that "tomorrow" and "always" are much the same thing. This perception of the self within time and society is not the mind-frame of the individualistic Western subject whose subjectivity unfolds over linear time.

The forms of subjectivity may thus be invisible in a book which reproduces beliefs and assumptions of which readers are largely unaware, because they exist as a structure deeper than the everyday manifestations of subjectivity familiar in, for example, English-language young adult fiction. Even though such a book may openly advocate forms of subjective agency as desirable for readers to espouse, insofar as fictive actions are broadly isomorphic with actions in the actual world, readers may readily assimilate fictive actions to scripts and schemas already present in memory, although such schemas and scripts must of necessity remain fluid. It is possible, needless to say, for a single text to incorporate multiple versions of subjectivity, as Mio Bryce argues in Chapter 10, this volume, with reference to the Japanese manga series, *Inuyasha*, and as Christie Barber argues (Chapter 7, this volume), subjectivity can shift depending upon context, such as levels of formality or informality appropriate to situation and the degree of agency possible for each actor. Further, Markus and Kitayama remind us that conceptions of subjectivity may be specific to a particular historical time, so that, for example, "the *individual*, in the sense of a set of significant inner attributes of the person, may cease to be the primary unit of consciousness. Instead, the sense of belongingness to a social relation may become so strong that it makes better sense to think of the *relationship* as the functional unit of conscious reflection" (1991, 226). In Chapter 5, this volume, Lifang Li identifies such moments as she maps the relationship between movements in Chinese culture and politics and conceptions of subjectivity in children's literature over the past century. In their reading of Huang Chunming's postcolonial short fiction, Suh Shan Chen and Ming Cherng Duh identify various subject positions into which characters are interpellated by Taiwan's colonial and postcolonial history, from the agentic to erased individual consciousness.

As I mentioned earlier, *Don't Call me Ishmael* offers a good example of subjectivity represented as an agentic development of awareness, emotion and judgment through processes of contrast and conflict. Named after the narrator of *Moby Dick*, and one of the primary targets of the school bully, the hapless narrator sees himself as abjected—as a loser and a victim—but with the example of a new-found friend who is intelligent, resourceful, and marked by a physical disability, he ends up confident, able to deal with conflict, and friends with the girl of his dreams. That much of Ishmael's confidence comes from his unwilling involvement in the school debating team foregrounds how central oppositional engagement can be in formulating subjectivity. The book is largely comedic, so doesn't readily yield up brief examples, but I will cite a couple.

[Scobie tells Mr. Barker that Bagsley, the class bully, has just explained the school policy on bullying. Barker replies:]

"Everyone should feel safe at St. Daniel's. I'm sure Mr. Bagsley pointed that out to you, because that's what our bullying policy is all about, Mr. Scobie. No one should be afraid here. Are you clear on that, Mr. Scobie?"

"You don't have to worry about me in that regard," replied James Scobie. "I have every faith in the school's bullying policy, and after talking with Mr. Bagsley here, I also have a great respect for the quality of education that the school provides."

"Really?" said Mr. Barker cautiously.

"Absolutely. Mr. Bagsley has just given us all a demonstration of how he can count to five . . . ,"

Jab!

" . . . and he didn't use his fingers once."

Upper cut!

The class laughed. Mr. Barker frowned. James Scobie twitched. Barry Bagsley smouldered.

BRIIIIIIIING!

"All right, move out, you lot. I'll check those exercises tomorrow and that is a threat." (73)

In this dialogue, Ishmael's friend Scobie, having just faced down the bully, uses logic and irony to humiliate and disempower him after a teacher, Mr. Barker, arrives on the scene. Ishmael both interpolates jargon from a boxing match commentary, in which it is presumed one participant is knocked out, and as narrator identifies the responses of all participants: "The class laughed. Mr. Barker frowned. James Scobie twitched. Barry Bagsley smouldered." By exploiting the ready complicity of the class and the authority of the inept teacher, Scobie transforms Bagsley's illusory agency into abjection.

In another scene, Ishmael is in conversation with Kelly Faulkner, a girl he finds so beautiful that he thinks there should be a law against it. Having decided that, "It just wasn't possible for eyes as beautiful as that to see anyone as ordinary as me," he relaxes and together they build a joke about Ishmael's friend Orazio:

"Do you want to know a secret? That guy's really a superhero."

"Is that right?" Kelly Faulkner said, raising her eyebrows and looking impressed.

"Yes, but the thing is, in order to keep his identity hidden, he has to pretend that he's a complete idiot."

"He's doing a wonderful job."

"Nobody does it better."

She pushed up her bottom lip and nodded thoughtfully.

"I've never seen a real-live superhero before. How come you know his identity?"

"Well, I shouldn't really be telling you any of this . . . but I'm his sidekick."

"Wow, pretty impressive. So you guys go around solving crime, rescuing babies from burning buildings, saving damsels in distress, regular stuff like that?"

"We do what we can."

"And I suppose that you have cool costumes, like Spider-Man or the Phantom?"

"Not really—neither of us can sew."

"That's a shame. Any superpowers, then? You know, to help you combat all those evil villains?"

"Well, I don't have any, personally, but he has the power to talk people to death . . . and I know from personal experience that his jokes can make you want to throw yourself under a train." (209–210)

This genuinely funny conversation models how subjectivity can be enhanced by conversational pragmatics, especially tight cohesion in turn-taking as the two speakers unfold a comic version of a modern folktale schema, the superhero (concealed identity; companion/ assistant/ "sidekick"; action clichés; cool costumes; superpowers). In fictive representation, two of the key aspects in the constitution of (inter)subjective agency are point of view and intentionality, as narratives model subject positions by depicting characters in relationship with other characters within social structures, and imply particular positions for readers to take up in relation to what is depicted. This tightly scripted dialogue, with only minimum narrative interruption and speaker tagging, performs a process of subjective fashioning through its intersubjective playfulness, although in making Orazio the focus of the joke it still depicts agency as a function of verbal power.

The role played by opposition in Western subjectivity is thrown into still sharper relief if we consider the function of conflict in two texts from India: Ruskin Bond's novel, *Binya's Blue Umbrella* and Vishal Bhardwaj's film adaptation of this novel (in which the main character is renamed Biliya). The source of conflict is the eponymous blue umbrella, which is an exotic object from outside the cultural experience of the small subsistence farming community into which it is accidently introduced. The umbrella is not only perceived as an object of unparalleled beauty but functions as a marker of distinctiveness. It comes from elsewhere: in Bond's novel, it is brought by a party of picnickers, "holiday-makers from the plains. The women were dressed in bright saris, the men wore light summer shirts, and the children had pretty new clothes" (13). The novel is third-person omniscient narration, with minimal character focalization, so that point of view and attitude lie with the narrator. Thus Binya's first sighting of the umbrella has the form of character focalization but expresses a narrator judgment on the umbrella's lack of intrinsic value: "And then her gaze came to rest on a bright blue umbrella, a frilly thing for women, which lay open on the grass beside its owner" (13). The (American) illustrator reinforces this impression of frivolity by drawing the scene as a version of Manet's *Lunch on the Grass*.

Like Western concepts of subjectivity, the umbrella becomes a cultural imposition, which changes the culture by introducing individualism. This point is more strongly emphasized in the film, where the umbrella is from Japan, as is its original owner, one of a mixed group of European and Japanese tourists. In both versions, however, the behavior of the intruders is imperious

Figure 1.1   Shot-reverse-shot sequence from *The Blue Umbrella.*

and overbearing as they try to buy the necklace (or amulet) that Binya/ Biliya wears. In the film, this imperiousness and Biliya's lack of agency in the exchange is emphasized by shot-reverse-shot sequences, with close-up, low-angle shots of the tourists and more distant centered shots of Biliya. The protective amulet, the claw of a dangerous animal (variously leopard or bear), has value for the tourists as an exquisite "native" artifact. Biliya's parting with it in exchange for the umbrella signifies a potential loss of cultural self, and her possession of the umbrella threatens both herself and others who desire to possess it with social abjection.

Despite living most of his life in India, Bond still seems to have a Western concept of oppositional subjectivity. Where the novel begins with Binya alone in the hills with the family cows ("Binya liked being on her own, and sometimes she allowed the cows to lead her into some distant valley" [10]), the film substitutes a strong sense of community, as the village children sing and dance (Bollywood style) while they extract money for sweets from the village adults who pretend to flee rather than contribute to their fund. Only the miser, Nandkishore, is set apart, comically attempting to disguise himself as not belonging, and thus foreshadowing his abjected and solitary state after he attempts to steal the umbrella. The opening montage also includes a scene in a Hindu temple—irrelevant to the plot, but an evident cultural icon, and symptomatic of the way Bhardwaj is transforming Bond's Anglo-Indian novel into a Hindu film.

The amulet foregrounds a key difference between the Anglo-Indian novel and the Hindu film, in that in both a bear's claw is found and made into an amulet necklace, but only in the novel is this given to Binya as a symbolic restitution and reward. Bhardwaj's film seems to tease its audience with the possibility of this narrative symmetry, especially when its owner, Nandkishore, attempts to give the amulet to the son of a local dignitary as a way of gaining re-entrance to society. But the pattern of reward is subtler than this, and would be obscured by a merely material exchange. Rather, it returns the community to a state of harmony in which subjectivity is neither individualistic nor abjected.

Finally, the discourse of *The Blue Umbrella* (film, rather than the book) is consonant with that of *The Happiness of Kati* in premising subjectivity on the existence of social, ideological, and cultural codes and conventions which shape a person's actions, speech, thoughts, or sense of their own identity. These codes and conventions imply that the construction of subjectivity is communal, so that a person's sense of identity as agent is established by contingent communal experience, rather than by conflict or opposition.

The chapters in this collection present a diverse range of approaches to the representation of subjectivity in fiction and film from nine countries across the Asian region. Each has undertaken a delicate and groundbreaking task, especially because of the countries represented only Japan has a theoretical literature concerning *subjectivity* and the *subject*, and, as Naoki Sakai remarks in Chapter 4 of *Translation and Subjectivity*, there are no directly equivalent terms. Nor has the concept been applied to children's literature or film. It seems straightforward enough to write *in English* about the various national literatures, but even then the meanings ascribed to the term will inevitably slip. Because subjectivity is formed within sociality, people hold divergent views about the self both within and across cultures, so the meaning of *subjectivity* will be forever unstable. Whereas for purposes of argument, it is tempting to fall back on apparent binaries—the independent self versus the interdependent self; difference-from versus identity-with; individuated versus collectivist—such contrasts are, to borrow a useful descriptor from Markus and Kitayama, *construals*. When we examine representations of the self in fiction of film, we are concerned to see what particular construal is at work in *this* particular text. We may identify a familiar schema, functioning within a familiar script. For example, much Western young adult fiction is underpinned by processes of individuation, as characters are represented as identifying their unique qualities and becoming more fully developed human beings. We might contrast this construal of the self with construals in Bhardwaj's *The Blue Umbrella* or Yang Hongying's stories about *Ma Xiaotiao* (Chapter 5, this volume), where meaningful behavior and desirable subjectivity are delineated by reference to the thoughts, emotions, and actions of others. Various construals may seem surprisingly similar, but the determining question is then likely to be, what understanding of the self is the reference point that grounds this construal? I think the contributors to this volume will give its readers much food for thought in answering this question.

Notes

1. Because the meaning of a text changes according to the interpretative frame brought to bear on it, taken-for-granted theories may have a propensity to produce readings that are arguably misreadings. Coats's reading of Brown and Hurd's *Goodnight Moon* (1947) is an example which seems to me to cross the border into misreading. The book is removed from its context in social practice, and the clinching argument is marked by the circularity of untestable assumption pointed to by Stockholder: "If it is true that the child will 'recognize himself in the other, and . . . discover his own attribute in the equivalence of their respective times' (Lacan, *LT*, 14), then what the child subject will recognize in this logical time of undefined reciprocity is his smallness and isolation" (Stockholder, 1998: 47). Other readings (from other psychological, interpretive frames) seem more adequate accounts of this elusive story about bedtime anxiety, where a sense of "smallness and isolation" is something to be overcome (see, e.g., Dresang, 2009: 100; Robertson, 2000: 206). If assumptions about subjectivity can preempt interpretation of a well-known American book, how wide of the mark might they be if brought to bear on, let us say, Akiko Hayashi's *Kon to Aki* (1989; in English as, *Amy and Ken Visit Grandma*)? (See Chapter 4, by Miyuki Hisaoka, this volume.)
2. With regard to children's literature, the epistemic subject is a kind of Piagetian formulation, whereby subjectivity is grounded in a common universal rationality which develops. This is a version of the traditional humanist subject.
3. Some work has been done on this translation. Wimonwan Aungsuwan "The problems of non-equivalence at word level and translation strategies applied in the children's literature named *The Happiness of Kati* by Prudence Borthwick," *Journal of Language and Culture* 26.1–2 (2008) concludes, "the problems arising from the non-equivalence at word level can be divided into two groups—omission in the target text, and words in the source text which have a different meaning from the target text. In order to solve these problems, the translator applied the translation methods through the use of borrowing, borrowing plus definition, paraphrasing, specific terms, words with broader meaning, omission and superordinates."

4. My Thai consultant, Todsapon Suranukkharin, advises that the translation precisely reproduces the style of the original Thai text, where the shift from narrative voice to free indirect thought and indirect thought is already present. He further comments that it is also very difficult to tell even in the Thai original version whether it is the narrator's voice or Kati's free indirect thought:

บางทีชีวิตก็ไม่มีคำอธิบาย [Narr or FIT] แม่เคยบอกไว้อย่างนั้นไม่ใช่หรือ [FIT] และระหว่างแม่กับกะทิ กะทิก็เชื่อว่า [Narr/FIT → IT] แม่เข้าใจได้ โดยที่ กะทิ ไม่ต้องอธิบาย กะทิกราบพระก่อนนอน [Narr] พรุ่งนี้ต้องตื่นแต่เช้าไปโรงเรียน [Narr/FIT] ทุกอย่างเหมือนเดิม ไม่มีอะไรเปลี่ยนแปลง [FIT] แสงเสียงตะหลิวของยายก็จะปลุกให้กะทิตื่นขึ้นมาพบกับโลกใบนี้อีกครั้ง [Narr]

Ngarmpun Vejjajiva has also confirmed the accuracy of the translation and the analysis (personal communication).

Works Cited

Primary Texts

Bauer, Michael Gerard. *Don't Call Me Ishmael* (2006). New York: HarperCollins, 2007.
Bond, Ruskin. *Binya's Blue Umbrella*. Illustrated by Vera Rosenberry. Honesdale: Boyds Mills Press, 1995.
Coerr, Eleanor. *Sadako and the Thousand Paper Cranes*. New York: Puffin, 1977.
Vejjajiva, Jane. *The Happiness of Kati* (2003). New York: Atheneum Books, 2006.
The Blue Umbrella. Directed by Vishal Bhardwaj, 2005.

Secondary Texts

Apol, Laura, Aki Sakuma, Tracy M. Reynolds, and Sheri K. Rop. "When Can We Make Paper Cranes? Examining Pre-Service Teachers' Resistance to Critical Readings of Historical Fiction," *Journal of Literacy Research* 34.4 (2003): 429–464.
Bishop, Scott R., Mark Lau, Shauna Shapiro, Linda Carlson, Nicole D. Anderson, James Carmody, et al. "Mindfulness: A Proposed Operational Definition," *Clinical Psychology: Science and Practice* 11.3 (2004): 230–241.
Bodhakari. "The Prison of the Self," *Therapy Today* 19.6 (2008): unpaginated. http://www.therapytoday.net/article/show/317/. Accessed October, 12, 2010.
Christopher, Michael S., Sukjai Charoensuk, Brennan D. Gilbert, Timothy J. Neary, and Kelly L. Pearce. "Mindfulness in Thailand and the United States: A Case of Apples versus Oranges?," *Journal of Clinical Psychology* 65.6 (2009): 590–612.
Coats, Karen. *Looking Glasses and Neverlands: Lacan, Desire and Subjectivity in Children's Literature*. Iowa City: University of Iowa Press, 2004.
Doonan, Jane. "Satoshi Kitamura: Aesthetic Dimensions," *Children's Literature* 19 (1991): 107–137.
Dresang, Eliza T., and Bowie Kotrla. "Radical Change Theory and Synergistic Reading for Digital Age Youth," *The Journal of Aesthetic Education* 43.2 (2009): 92–107.
Grzegorczyk, Blanka. "'All I Can Be Is Who I Am': Representing Subjectivity in Terry Pratchett's *Nation*," *Children's Literature Association Quarterly* 35.2 (2010): 112–130.
Hayashi, Michiyo, and Ariko Kawabata. "Children's Literature Research in Japan," *Children's Literature Association Quarterly* 28.4 (2003–2004): 241–246.
Hutcheon, Linda. *A Poetics of Postmodernism: History, Theory, Fiction*. London: Routledge, 1988.
———. *The Politics of Postmodernism*. London: Routledge, 1989. Knight, Deborah. "Women, Subjectivity, and the Rhetoric of Anti-Humanism in Feminist Film Theory," *New Literary History* 26.1 (1995): 39–56.
Lebra, Takie Sugiyama. *The Japanese Self in Cultural Logic*. Honolulu: University of Hawaii Press, 2004.

Markus, Hazel Rose, and Kitayama Shinobu. "Culture and the Self: Implications for Cognition, Emotion, and Motivation," *Psychological Review* 98.2 (1991): 224–253.

McCallum, Robyn. *Ideologies of Identity in Adolescent Fiction: The Dialogic Construction of Subjectivity.* New York: Garland, 1999.

Nikolajeva, Maria. *Power, Voice and Subjectivity in Literature for Young Readers.* New York: Routledge, 2009.

Ozawa-De Silva, Chikako, and Brendan Ozawa-De Silva. "Secularizing Religious Practices: A Study of Subjectivity and Existential Transformation in Naikan Therapy," *Journal for the Scientific Study of Religion* 49.1 (2010): 147–161.

Rimmon-Kenan, Shlomith. *A Glance beyond Doubt: Narration, Representation, Subjectivity.* Columbus: Ohio State University Press, 1996.

Robertson, Judith P. "Sleeplessness in the Great Green Room: Getting Way Under the Covers with *Goodnight Moon*," *Children's Literature Association Quarterly* 25.4 (2000): 203–213.

Sakai, Naoki. *Translation and Subjectivity: On 'Japan' and Cultural Nationalism.* Minneapolis: University of Minnesota Press, 1997.

Smith, Paul. *Discerning the Subject.* Minneapolis: University of Minnesota Press, 1988.

Stephens, John. *Language and Ideology in Children's Fiction.* New York: Longman, 1992.

Stockholder, Kay. "Lacan versus Freud: Subverting the Enlightenment," *American Imago* 55.3 (1998): 361–422.

Trites, Roberta Seelinger. "Claiming the Treasures: Patricia MacLachlan's Organic Postmodernism," *Children's Literature Association Quarterly* 18.1 (1993): 23–28.

Wyile, Andrea Schwenke. "The Value of Singularity in First- and Restricted Third-Person Engaging Narration," *Children's Literature* 31 (2003): 116–41.

Yurita, Makito, and Reade W. Dornan. "Hiroshima: Whose Story Is It?," *Children's Literature Association Quarterly* 34.3 (2009): 229–240.

Chapter Two

Metamorphosis

The Emergence of Glocal Subjectivities in the Blend of Global, Local, East, and West

Anna Katrina Gutierrez

The impact of globalization and the shifts in global culture on the development of subjectivities in children's and young adult literature is a topic of great interest for critics in the field, and yet critical discourse for non-Western texts has mainly been grounded on Western theories of subjectivity. One of the reasons for this orientation is that the non-Western texts that flow into Western culture are read and analyzed through a multicultural lens, which manages cultural anxieties and tensions within the idea of the Other as another Self, and in doing so appropriates difference through a focus on global values. Shaobo Xie points out that the promotion of such an ideology of reassurance represses the distinct qualities of the Other in favor of an "imperialism of the same," wherein hegemonic "white mythology" dictates what is globally valued (1999, 139).

As Gilles Fauconnier and Mark Turner explain, the search for sameness is an automatic cognitive process used to make sense of the world. They contend that the mind is made up of a network of conceptual spaces (called input spaces) connected by similar elements. Connected by similarities, spaces are able to integrate unconsciously through a fundamental cognitive operation described as "conceptual blending" (2002). The blending of elements from several input spaces forms a new conceptual space from which emerges a new meaning, called an "emergent structure" (42–44; 48). The emergent structure is not copied from any of the input spaces but arises from the conversation between spaces, made possible by the intersection of similar elements.

Globalization is a manifestation of the conceptual integration network on a global scale and is even described by Francesco Loriggio as a "network society" (2004, 55–57) grounded on similar patterns (such as scripts and schemas) through which occurs the exchange of information between global and local spaces. Increased attention on globalization as a network of exchanges coincides with the recognition that although global, local, Western, and Eastern spaces are related by sameness, the spaces themselves are not the same. The elements that connect these spaces are then similar and yet also different from one another because of the spaces they come from, and cultural enrichment comes from the dialectic between diversity and similarity. The movement toward diversity throws light on a generally disregarded phase of globalization, in which the threat of global homogenization and the fear of local isolation seek resolution through the establishment of a middle ground. This process of penetration-integration of the global with the local, or *glocalization*, allows global and local spaces to interact with and enrich one another through the blending of shared elements and vital relations. Glocalization, then, is an example of conceptual blending and the new conceptual space created by the blending of elements from global and local spaces is what I call a glocal heterotopia.

That globalization is often thought of in terms of the West infiltrating and colonizing the East forms analogous connections with the application of Western theories of subjectivity on non-Western children's literature. Both hinge on identifying likeness between the Other and the Self, or more commonly, transforming the Other into another Self. Such critical discourses reflect the most commonly held notion of globalization as a proponent of homogeneity rather than as a process that makes possible intercultural dialogue and exchange. The resurgence of diversity through glocalization allows previously repressed or ignored non-Western strands to be included and to add new dimensions to ideologies of subjectivity. The conversation between global, local, Eastern, and Western notions of subjectivity in the glocal heterotopia gives rise to an emergent structure. This structure is a glocal subjectivity able to give new meaning and contribute to all spaces. Contemporary children's literature consequently reflects the effect of the dialectic between global and local systems on a regional scale (Stephens and McGillis, 2006: 364–367), with particular attention to the impact of globalizing processes upon ideologies that underpin metanarratives and schemas, the development of global subjectivity and local subjectivities, and the possibility of blending subjectivities to create glocal subjectivities (Stephens and McGillis, 2006: 367; Gutierrez, 2009: 159–176).

In this chapter, I will explore the interactions of global and local processes on constructions of subjectivities in Western and Eastern versions of Otherworldly Maiden tales, with a focus on two major conversations: the conversation between global and local subjectivities and the conversation between Western notions of subjectivity and Eastern notions of subjectivity.

My analysis of these conversations will be anchored in metamorphosis motifs discerned in Otherworldly Maiden tales and whose interactions result in glocal subjectivities: a blend of global, local, East, and West that is significant across cultures.

Glocalization As an Example of Collaborative Conceptual Blending

The ability to find relations between seemingly incompatible concepts is the basis for imaginative thinking and inventiveness and is "as indispensable for basic everyday thought as it is for artistic and scientific abilities" (Fauconnier and Turner, 2002: vi). In conceptual blending, the combination of two or more conceptual spaces through the identification of similar elements and relations is instantaneous, unconscious, and intuitive. Fauconnier and Turner explain how conceptual blending works by pointing to the operation of computers as an example of a generally unconscious and immediate blend. When we first learned to use the computer, we had to blend the concept of a "technological device" with the concept of "work we do on a real desktop," such as pushing a button twice to "open" a "folder," or clicking on the icon of an arrow hovering over a "folder" to "lift" it into view (2002, 23). The blend of a computer desktop with work on an actual desktop is "an imaginative mental creation" that allows us to operate the computer, and we can only manipulate the computer when we are running this particular blend or "live in the blend" (23; 83).

In the globalization process, blending is also experienced as unconscious and immediate through "time-space distanciation," a phenomenon wherein space and time are compressed so that there is no need to physically cross borders to form global relationships (Giddens, 1990: 21). Global networking devices such as television, cellular phones, and the Internet facilitate a culture of connectivity. Connectivity impacts upon the development of a culture, which in turn transforms the development of subjectivity within that culture, because transcultural relationships not possible before are now accessible. The fear that global connectivity might result in global homogeneity is counterchecked by glocalization, a blending process that occurs when the resurgence of the local culture disrupts the tendency of global culture toward homogeneity (Robertson, 1997: 30; Gutierrez, 2009: 160). The hegemonic global culture contaminates and is appropriated by local culture, and the transformative transaction results in an integrated glocal product that is significant both globally and locally. The network society formed by the exchange of information between spaces depends on patterns that exhibit sameness, yet the use of the word "sameness" to describe these connections tends to focus on the notion of universal values. "Sameness" leans too much on the side of global homogeneity, whereas "sharedness," a term that Strauss and Quinn use to explain the timeless quality of elements that are similarly valued by several cultures (1997, 118–123), more accurately describes the connections in the glocal network. The distinction between sharedness and universal values is that the former foregrounds differences rather than subsumes them within similarities. Fauconnier and Turner emphasize that although the blend is initially created by compatibilities, "the point of the blend is not to obscure incompatibilities but . . . to have at once something and its opposite" (2002, 29). The glocal space formed by the connections of similar elements from global and local spaces is then further enriched by the qualities that make these elements distinct from one another.

As a form of conceptual blending, glocalization then exhibits several key factors. Global and local spaces are connected by shared elements that are both compatible and incompatible; the compression of global and local spaces both enables global relationships and creates a "third mental space" (Yoshida); and interaction of global and local within the glocal space is generally automatic and spontaneous and results in global insight that emerges as an imaginative glocal product. Further, glocalization and conceptual blending share another feature, which is that a blend is often the result of inputs that are themselves blends. The combination of global and local spaces thus contains multiple global relationships characterized by contamination-syncretism (Gutierrez, 2009: 162), which, in turn, creates multiple glocal spaces that stimulate the growth of the network. This continually expanding network of glocal spaces is the glocal heterotopia. The glocal heterotopia is not composed of just one blend; rather, it is a complex web of blends wherein blends interact with one another.

Eastern and Western versions of Otherworldly Maiden tales constitute an example of a global tale type, which is a narrative that makes use of symbols and images shared by a significant number of cultures so that the script is considered global. Because shared connections include "connections of identity or transformation or representation, analogical connections, metaphoric connections" (Fauconnier and Turner, 2002: 47), versions of this tale can be connected by similarities in scripts, schemas, or functions. These shared connections create the global metanarrative, a skeletal framework that influences and is influenced by local scripts. The interactions of the Otherworldly Maiden and the man who captures her represent complications that arise in transcultural relationships. When the pattern of metamorphosis and capture in a Western tale intersects with an analogous pattern in an Eastern tale, the relations between them have implications for the development of global, local, Eastern, and Western subjectivities. A glocal subjectivity may also emerge from this intersection as a blend that reminds us that in a globalized world subjectivity is created at the meeting point of global and local domains.

Two Conversations: Global and Local, East and West

Before we can even begin to imagine glocal subjectivity, we must distinguish and define the different flows that contribute to the emergence of this hybrid.

In the network society, a "generalized mutual interaction" (Giddens, 1990: 64; Bayart, 2007: 24) occurs in which local events are affected and shaped by global signs (Harvey, 1990: 240; De Block and Buckingham, 2007: 3). The appropriation of the global sign does not transform the appropriator into its image and likeness; rather, it is the global sign that is transformed by the appropriator's unique qualities. Global subjectivity, then, is characterized by its neutrality and fluidity. This is not to say that global signs and symbols have no meaning but that "sharedness" allows these meanings to become generalized. The fluidity of the global sign is given substance when grounded on what Heise calls local rock: local landscape, local bodies, and the ideologies embedded in them (2004, 125–141). This does not eliminate stereotypes but conveys the possibility of multiple identities, or multiple dimensions to national identity, that break free from the rigidity of stereotypes. The hybrids created are recognized as both global and local citizens, able to dialogue with and influence events across spaces. Globalization develops subjectivities that are "dispersed and integrated" (Bradford et al., 2008: 42) and above all intersubjective, in that subjectivity "exists within interrelationships with others and with the world" (McCallum, 1999: 25). Intersubjectivity includes the impact of cross-cultural encounters on the development of global and local subjectivities and sustains the cycle of contamination-syncretism seen as global and local influencing one another to create the glocal, which in turn influences both global and local. The neutrality of the global symbol, then, is what allows it to be a shared element that can be charged with local meaning. The superimposition of global culture on local culture produces a glocal vocabulary that suggests culture is a "combination of operations" shaped by the "construction of one's own phrased with a received vocabulary and syntax" (De Certeau, 1988: 15).

The idea that global culture is a reflection of Western culture (as represented by the U.S.) makes way for ideas of a blended culture formed by Western and Eastern cultures influencing one another in significant ways. The fragmentation of global subjectivity into Eastern and Western subjectivities within a glocal heterotopia makes possible a cross-cultural analysis wherein the East and West are seen as *equal* contributors. The challenge is to move away from Western theories of subjectivity by focusing on the useful negotiation between East and West rather than on the assimilation of or identification with the Other.

Western subjectivity theories are based on binary logic, wherein the subject is the central processing system within a subject-object opposition (Geertz, 1984: 126; Lebra, 2004: 3). The need for the Western concept of the unified subject to have an opposition to a non-self or an "other" therefore automatically moves the Western subject in opposition to any construction of subjectivity that is not integrative (Lebra, 2004: 3). Imperialism and colonialism find their roots in opposition logic, wherein the Western subject occupies a position of power over the exotic and irrational non-selves of the non-West. However, the strategic concept of a unified Western subject breaks down when applied to non-Western subjects. Studies made by Marcel Mauss of constructions of subjectivity in Hindu and Chinese ethnographic literature, and Michelle Rosaldo's studies of Philippine tribal constructs, argue that the Western notion of a constant "I" cannot be applied to non-Western cultures in which subjectivities are relationally negotiated in context (4).

The movement of Western thought toward postmodernism transformed the subject into a "disintegrating play of selves" (Heller et al., quoted in Day, 2007: 21) created through the intersubjective relations of its multiplicities with other subjects. Eugene Chen Eoyang, however, critiques postmodernity as still being deeply rooted in binary oppositions (2007, 108), stating that postmodern discourse "vaunts pluralism but sees separateness rather than unity. It promotes the fragmentary, but envisions fragmentariness as wholeness truncated. It claims to be revolutionary in its eclecticism, but is ignorant of East Asian syncretism" (109). He suggests that Western postmodernism should adopt East Asian syncretism, which he describes through the Chinese concept *maodun* (矛盾: spear-shield). *Maodun* most closely translates to the English word "contradiction" and comes from a story about an impenetrable shield and an invincible spear. The combination of both assertions into a phrase that stands for contradiction creates dimensions of meaning not available in a binary opposition (27–28). According to Western logic, only one of two dichotomous assertions can be considered true, but *maodun* includes within the world of contradiction the paradoxical possibility that both assertions are true, that one is true and the other false, and that both assertions are false. Eoyang describes this facet of Chinese thought as "four-cornered logic," the incorporation of all possible states neutralizing the power struggle inherent in binary oppositions. *Maodun*, like the glocal space, encourages us to live in the blend and focus on the emergent meaning created by compatibilities between seemingly incompatible concepts (which are themselves blends) rather than on these concepts as separate input spaces. Eoyang states as an example the way Asians do not intentionally seek to form an "Asiatic Imaginary" but a sense of community is formed by similarities in values and interpersonal relationships that predisposes integrative attitudes toward superficially contradictory values. Eastern and Western concepts of subjectivity can blend in a similar way when contained in the glocal space.

The need to preserve identities in order to remain relevant to global and local cultures pushes the global, local, and Eastern and Western identity formation processes to blend together in seemingly incompatible ways to introduce new vocabularies that lead to new narratives and new kinds of human beings (Turner, 2007: 118; Howell, 2010: 73; Stephens and Geerts, 2013). In the Otherworldly Maiden tales, the interactions of diverse constructions of subjectivity make the emergence of glocal constructs possible. The tales analyzed here do not speak for an entire Western culture or an entire Eastern culture, but they exemplify how the conversations between Eastern and Western subjectivities in a glocal heterotopia construct glocal subjectivities.

Glocalizing the Otherworldly Maiden

To perceive the Otherworldly Maiden as a global tale type is to assume a metanarrative that links not only to the timeless and transcendent but also crosses ethnic and national boundaries, fostering a sense of "sharedness" between East and West, although instruments such as the Aarne–Thompson *Motif Index* do not assume sharedness. The original *index* did not include Eastern tales,[1] which were subsequently added when the index was updated by Hans-Jörg Uther to include tales from non-Western cultures, such as Asia, South America, Africa, and American Indian. That the index is constructed according to tales important to Western culture (the hegemony of "white mythology") and that the inclusion of Eastern tales depends on whether they are *versions* of Western tales implies that the categories arise from Eurocentric preoccupations, and hence have further implications for conceptions of subjectivity. Multiple versions of a global tale type, however, show that it contains within it hundreds of different, overlapping images of the Otherworldly Maiden, her metamorphosis, and the opportunities for action that metamorphosis makes available, all of which are ideologically charged and fragment global symbols into Eastern, Western, and local symbols.

Wilt L. Idema reminds us "We can make no greater mistake than to assume that these stories embodied a single, unchanging, essential meaning, even though many modern and contemporary scholars write about these stories as if they did" (2009, ix). Idema's study of versions of the *Legend of Dong Yang and the Weaving Maiden*[2] and of how the functions of this tale in Chinese society transformed through time, establishes that meaning is fluid not only from a global perspective, but locally as well. Hayao Kawai lists many versions of the "non-human wife" and characterizes the heavenly maiden as the one that stands between "the animal wife stories of Japan and the Western stories" (1996, 116). Barbara Fass Leary, in her extensive study of swan maiden and Selkie girl tales, avers that:

> Folktales are only one dimensional when taken one at a time (and not always then); once the stable elements and variants of a folktale or related group of tales are understood to interact, they form layers of meaning that imbue the narrative pattern with complex significance. Even seemingly contradictory versions of the same story are enlightening, *since the contradiction is likely to reflect the strife depicted in the narrative situation* (italics mine) . . . Variations in the tale make possible a deepening perception of [the maiden's] dilemma. Thus a Japanese swan maiden who barely pauses as she makes her escape is complemented by an Icelandic seal maiden, who oscillates between earthly home and sea, until the call of the ocean proves irresistible and she plunges into her native element. (1994, 38–39)

That Leary's book, which includes hundreds of variants of the tale type, is hardly comprehensive attests to the contradictory nature of fairy tale as both stable and fluid and accentuates that literary metamorphosis is constant. When examined through the interpretative lens of *maodun* within the glocal heterotopia, meaning is revealed through the dynamic and often contradictory connections between variants of the tale type on the global, local, and glocal levels.

Metamorphosis in the Otherworldly Maiden Tales

Otherworldly Maiden tales follow a narrative script through which runs the metamorphosis motif. Writing of the imbrication of metamorphosis and conceptual blending in tales about metamorphosis between humans and nonhuman animals, Asker argues that, "The idea of 'blending' fits well the cross-species muddling that goes on in metamorphosis literature, as if a heightened objectification of human beings is rendered more easily through projecting ourselves into nonhuman animals" (2001, 11). In Otherworldly Maiden tales, the nonhuman includes supernatural beings stranded in human form, but as with movement between animal and human, the blending has deep implications for representations of subjectivity, in that it evokes alterity and fluid personhood and pivots on crises of choice and agency. There are key moments or points of metamorphosis within the narrative script that mark physical transformation, boundary crossing, the beginning or ending of a transcultural relationship, and the product yielded by such a relationship. Components of these metamorphosis points, such as schemas of the Otherworldly Maiden, the man who captures her, and the events that lead to metamorphosis, connect variants of the tale, creating a network wherein their interactions and combinations construct a glocal heterotopia which discloses the ideologies that underpin notions of Eastern and Western subjectivities. Below is an outline of the script and the points at which metamorphosis can occur:

A. A man catches sight of the Otherworldly Maiden in human form and covets her (Metamorphosis 1).
B. The man steals the item that grants the maiden powers of metamorphosis. The theft traps her in human form. He domesticates her (Metamorphosis 2).
C. The maiden, now a wife, finds the item or her children find the item and present it to her. She is faced with a choice to metamorphose back to her original form and return to her world (Metamorphosis 3) or to remain with her husband and children. Her actions prompt the man who captured her to either accept their separation or to try to win her back.
D. If the man goes after her, the maiden is faced with a second choice to either stay in her world or return with him as a willing partner (possible Metamorphosis 4).

These metamorphosis points represent visually and narratively negoti- ations between worlds: the world of man and the world of the maiden, and, because the contact is in effect transcultural, between the global and the local, the East and the West. The transcultural relationship puts pressure not only on the individuals but threatens the worlds they come from. The coming together of two beings from different worlds also constructs a glo- cal heterotopia wherein both beings negotiate in an effort to restore bal- ance between the global and the local, with the hope of the blend emerging as a significant glocal product. Whether or not the global and/or the local benefit from glocal subjectivities reveals the ideological underpinnings of the variant being discussed.

My main focus shall be on *Ah! My Goddess The Movie*, a full-length fea- ture *anime* directed by Hiroaki Gohda (2000), and *Stardust*, written by Neil Gaiman and illustrated by Charles Vess (1998). These reversions of the folk- tale exemplify visual and narrative representations of glocal space from an Eastern and a Western perspective. Other variants shall be referred to in order to show that the metamorphosis motif is ideologically charged in contradic- tory ways and that these contradictions contribute to the blend. The variants from Asia include: *Oh My Goddess!*, the *manga* created by Fujishima Kosuke (translated into English by Dark Horse Manga), on which the movie and the television series is based (Volume 1, 2005; Volume 4, 2007); Episodes 1 and 2 of the *Ah! My Goddess* TV series, also directed by Hiroaki Gohda; *Ang Alamat ng Bahaghari (The Legend of the Rainbow)*, a retelling in picture book form from the Philippines by Rene O. Villanueva and Frances C. Alcaraz (2002); and *The Heavenly Spinning Maid* from the anthology *Chinese Folk and Fairy Tales*, chosen and retold by Leslie Bonnet (1963). The versions from the West are the picture books *The Selkie Girl* as retold by Susan Cooper and Warwick Hutton (1986) and *The Seal Mother* by Mordicai Gerstein (1987).

Ah! My Goddess and *Stardust*: Creating Glocal Spaces

Retellings and reversions of the Otherworldly Maiden tale type almost always specify local space: a fishing village for the Selkie girl tales, rice terraces in *Ang Alamat ng Bahaghari*, a farm in *The Heavenly Spinning Maid*, and so on. This specification is an important move because it instantiates the premise that subjectivity is grounded in the local but may transform as intersubjective fields expand. In *Stardust* and *Ah! My Goddess*, local space is described in ways that create a contrast with global space, emphasizing how neither is mutually exclusive. The inevitable interactions between global and local set conditions ideal for subjective metamorphosis. Both fantasies are anchored in versions of England and Japan respectively, and both authors deliberately include ele- ments of realism (or elements that allude to realism) to add texture to their fantastic texts. The effect of the mixture of elements creates a sense of a world that exists both within and without time and space, whereas the blurring of lines further allows for interactions between spaces.

Gaiman simultaneously draws borders and pushes them when he begins *Stardust* with a description of the monocultural ordinariness of the English town of Wall and then compounds it with the explanation that it is named for a grey rock wall that marks the boundary between our world and Faerie (1998, 6). Borders become even more fluid when the tale of a young man from Wall "who wished to gain his heart's desire" (6) is both situated within history and narrated in a discourse that sporadically picks up the Victoriana register typical of the fairy tale genre, the effect of which widens and at the same time compresses the sense of time and space:

> Queen Victoria was on the throne, but she was far from being the black-clad widow of Windsor; ... She was, as yet, unmarried, although she was very much in love.
>
> Mr. Charles Dickens was serializing his novel *Oliver Twist*; Mr. Draper had just taken a photograph of the moon, freezing her pale face for the first time on cold paper; Mr. Morse had just announced a way of transmitting messages down metal wires.
>
> . . .
>
> People were coming to the British Isles that spring ... men and women with skins as pale as paper, skins as dark as volcanic rock, skins the colour of cinnamon, speaking in a multitude of tongues ...
>
> At that time, Dunstan Thorn was eighteen, and he was not a romantic. (7–8)

The historical figures chosen are representative of the atmosphere of wonder associated with a specific time in British history, the early Victorian period (when Victoria herself was a vibrant figure of romance), and a blend of human inventiveness with the magic of fairy tales through the use of the Victoriana register[3] even when droll and comical as in "the black-clad widow of Windsor." Vess adds another dimension to the space in his approximation of the style and color palette popularly used in illustrated versions of early Victorian fairy tales, which situates *Stardust* within both the historical period and "Within the Realms of Faerie."[4] Gaiman's self-reflexive note that Dunstan is unromantic comments upon the way the Victoriana register romanticizes history and shifts alignment toward the scientific, technologically advanced, and unromantic world imputed to the implied reader. The blending of fairy tale magic and (historical) human magic generates connections between the input spaces "Faerie," "Wall," "Victorian England," and the reader's "England," that trigger relational thinking in the glocal heterotopia.

Furthermore, the connection of Dunstan, an ordinary young man from a provincial town, to people of historical consequence foreshadows the importance of his actions both locally and globally. When it is revealed that just as people are traveling from all over the world to visit the British Isles and others flock to Wall with the intent of crossing into Faerie to visit the market that occurs once every nine years, communities real and imagined form a network with intertextual links as the points of intersection wherein the global and the local actively negotiate. These negotiations constitute a glocal heterotopia, which, in *Stardust*, is not only an abstract space but also an actual space: the Fairy Market. The market is the rare occasion when the people of Wall and Faerie come together to trade. In Vess's illustration, the market is a mixture of English fair and Oriental exoticism, which he describes in detail in an interview for *Stardust: The Visual Companion*. Cross-cultural encounters occur underneath a red canopy reminiscent of medieval fairs. On the left-hand side immediately behind the fabric is Beethoven listening to a fairy fiddler. Behind Beethoven and the fiddler are Chinese merchants, their servants bearing goods. At the top with their backs to us are Vess's favorite Japanese *anime* characters, Kiki and Totoro, entering the tent of a goblin palm reader. To the right and below, Prince Valiant chooses a new helmet. Below him are Vess himself, wearing a Tintin sweatshirt, in the company of a musketeer and an anthropomorphic fox, and beneath them, a woman from the British comic strip *Rupert the Bear* walks her dragons (Jones, 2007: 15) (see Figure 2.1).

Figure 2.1   Stardust The Fairy Market.
Source: © Neil Gaiman and Charles Vess

The Fairy Market represents the glocal heterotopia created by intersecting and unique elements from "Wall/England," "Faerie," and the reader's "England," as well as from a new input space: the reader's idea of "East/Orient." Embedded within the latter two input spaces are ideologies that impact upon the first two input spaces. The interaction between spaces positions readers to reflect upon the ways ideologies are mirrored or interrogated in the scripts and schemas present in the first two input spaces. The use of real and imagined characters to represent cultural exchange in both the illustration and description creates a self–other, East–West dynamic (Curry, 2010: 22–23) that reveals the depth and breadth of these negotiations and their impact upon subjectivities. The Fairy Market, like the glocal market, illustrates *maodun* in that information from all spaces (global, East, West, Wall, Faerie) are on equal footing, and thus affect the construction of subjectivity equally.

Representation of subjectivity in *Ah! My Goddess* is fluid and intersubjective as the narrative visualizes the universe as a network society in a simultaneously literal and metaphoric way, drawing connections between Heaven, Earth, and other planets into a system loosely based on the Internet and communication and surveillance systems merged with mythology. The combination of technology and magic compresses space and time in a similar way to the compression described in *Stardust,* and similarly constructs subjectivity as emerging from the interplay of materiality and imagination. Keiichi, the abjected protagonist of the *manga* on which the movie is based, is bullied into taking phone messages for an upperclassman and accidentally makes a call to the Goddess Technical Helpline (Fujishima, 2005: 2–3; Gohda Episode 1). A direct connection between the global and the local is established, wherein the surveillance of the local through mystical and technological means presupposes the symbiosis between the two spaces. Belldandy, then, acts as a cipher or a personal computer that enables access to the global network. That the more powerful character—the goddess Belldandy—is captured by Keiichi's inadvertent wish that she might stay with him always, and, in a common paradox of agency, subsequently chooses to be subordinate to Keiichi suggests the investment the global has in the local and the need the local has of the global. Belldandy provides all of Keiichi's needs, in order to give him room to develop a stronger sense of self, so that eventually the local can contribute to the global. The service she provides conforms to the traditional roles men and women in Japan fulfill even today. Anne Allison, in her examination of the gendered construction of identity in Japan, asserts that gendered roles are ideologically guided by the state and that "Labor from males, socialized to be compliant and hard working, is more extractable when they have wives to rely on for almost all domestic and familial management" (2000, 102–103). The interpellation of subjects into gendered social roles is apparent in both *manga* and *anime* through Keiichi's desire to have a nurturing woman like Belldandy be with him, and by Heaven's compliance to his wish that one of their finest goddesses become Keiichi's personal domestic goddess.[5]

Metamorphosis: The Need to Break Forms and Cross Borders

A border is first breached when the Otherworldly Maiden crosses into the world of man and is captured (Metamorphosis 1). In cultures across the East and West, at this point of the script, she is stripped of subjective agency and becomes an object of desire. The Otherworldly Maiden schema is a blend of woman and nature, wherein nature takes different forms, often a bird or a seal. The blend is considered magical and invaluable, whether or not the schema includes any magical characteristics, such as flight or the power to grant wishes. In *Stardust* and *Ah! My Goddess*, both maidens are associated with images that represent wish-fulfillment. Belldandy is a goddess sent to Keiichi to grant his wishes, and possession of the star Yvaine grants her captor his or her heart's desire. The men in these tales are positioned as active subjects in a state of lack, and so readers are induced to empathize with them. It is the men who wish, who desire, and who capture. Readers first see Yvaine through Tristran's point of view:

> She was sprawled, awkwardly, beneath the hazel tree, and she gazed up at Tristran with a scowl of complete unfriendliness.
> She hefted another clod of mud at him, menacingly, but did not throw it.
> Her eyes were red and raw. Her hair was so fair it was almost white, her dress was of blue silk which shimmered in the candlelight. She glittered as she sat there. (1998, 99)

The description and the accompanying illustration (Figure 2.2) bring to mind an image of a cornered, exotic animal. The illustration of a dirty and disheveled Yvaine, hemmed in by a tree trunk and branches, supports the allusion, and furthermore, signifies a loss of subjectivity. The angry demand gaze she throws Tristran/the reader from below eye level heightens the sense of entrapment, which is then materialized when Tristran binds Yvaine to him with an unbreakable chain. The reader is positioned to see her through Tristran's eyes, and this induced focalization solidifies her position as object. Tristran sees that she is a woman but does not ask for her name until midway through the book. Until then, the narrative labels her as "star" or "girl," the refusal to blend star and girl through a name is a deliberate reminder of her status as object.

In imposing a master–slave relationship, Tristran seems heartless in his behavior, but the first half of the book establishes him as the exact opposite. Indeed, many modern retellings of this global tale type emphasize that the men who capture the Otherworldly Maiden do so because they are effectively abjected: they are lonely or in need of a woman to help them organize their lives so that they might fulfill their potential. Tristran is described as a "gangling creature of potential" (Gaiman and Vess, 1998: 40), and Keiichi is introduced in the television series and *manga* (the movie does not show the

She was sprawled, awkwardly, beneath the hazel tree, and she gazed up at Tristran with a scowl of complete unfriendliness.

She hefted another clod of mud at him, menacingly, but did not throw it.

Her eyes were red and raw. Her hair was so fair it was almost white, her dress was of blue silk which shimmered in the candlelight. She glittered as she sat there.

Figure 2.2 Stardust. Yvaine.
Source: © Neil Gaiman and Charles Vess.

beginning of Keiichi and Belldandy's relationship) as a kind college student bullied by his seniors. In these and the following examples, readers empathize with the men and experience how hardworking, gentle, and alone they are: Bulawan, the "gallant . . . farmer" who "happily" plants (Villanueva, 2002: 4);

Chen-li, a cowherd ill-treated by his brother's wife and chosen by the Celestial Empress to be a "suitable husband" for the Heavenly Spinning Maid (Bonnet, 1963: 90); Donallan, a lonely fisherman who "would listen to the wind singing in the chimney, and wish it were a human voice" (Cooper, 1986: 1). Alignment with these male characters highlights an ideology wherein the Self needs an Other to be complete, and the need for completion through a self–other dialectic drives even nice men to a travesty of intersubjectivity.

Leary comments that it is ironic "that the swan maiden is not ordinarily held to be the main character in her own story" (1994, 40). Hans-Jörg Uther lists the Heavenly Maiden and Selkie girl tales under the tale types "The Man on a Quest for His Lost Wife" (2004, 400) and "The Magic Flight" (313, 313A, 313B, 313C, 313H). The general descriptive label points to the tale as a transnational, male-focalized experience of loss, which implies that global subjectivity is anchored in representations of masculine hegemony and the imperialist, colonialist, and Orientalist notions that characterize them.[6] Tristran travels to the East (Gaiman and Vess, 1998: 47) to take a star from Faerie to win the hand of the most beautiful girl in Wall, much as the imperialists colonized the Orient and brought her treasures to the Queen (Curry, 2010: 21–22). As an archetypal passage to manhood juxtaposed with hegemonic globalization, Tristran's journey to the East normalizes both the global and local experience of the West conquering the East and the global conquering the local for the benefit of the subject to which the reader is aligned. The Otherworldly Maidens are, or represent, a path toward the heart's desire of men in all variants of the tale, symbolizing that the yearning toward the Other and its subsequent domination is necessary for maturation. Indeed, some of the first words that Belldandy utters to Keiichi in the *manga* are "What is your desire?" (Fujishima, 2005: 4), whereas the television version asks specifically "What is your heart's desire?" (Episodes 1 & 2). The theft of the item that grants the maiden powers of metamorphosis is a literal stripping away of subjectivity and entraps the maiden in the world of man. The loss of her true form equates with a loss of agency and allows the man to transform her into the form that best meets his needs (Metamorphosis 2). Stripped of her skin, wings, or heavenly garment, the symbol of her subjectivity and agency, she is made to wear clothing that forces her to perform acts of domesticity. While Bulawan (*Ang Alamat ng Bahaghari*) hides the maiden-star's wings in a jar, she gets fully dressed and puts up her hair in a bun as a sign that she has become a civilized Filipina maiden ready to be "taught how to cook and do household chores"(opening 10). In *The Selkie Girl*, Donallan tells the captured Selkie, "Come with me and be my wife, and I will work for you and love you well, and we shall be happy all our days!" (17). He names her Mairi and dresses her in a shawl that belonged to his mother, signifying her future as wife and mother of his children (18–19). The unbreakable chain Tristran uses to bind Yvaine to him alludes to the unbreakable ties of marriage, the exchange of the star for his ideal woman's hand in marriage a guarantee for the domestic life he believes he desires. Belldandy, on the other hand, does not consider herself trapped by Keiichi's wish that she stay forever, but sees it as an opportunity to use her powers for the service of others. Moreover, although Belldandy and Keiichi's relationship is begun as a compulsion, Keiichi's trust and respect for Belldandy transforms their relationship into one based on love.

The Heavenly Spinning Maid is made of a similar mold. When she caught sight of Chen-li seizing her clothing, she turned around and:

> With a welcoming smile, said, "Young sir, if you will give me back my clothes, I will come with you and see to the cooking."
> "And the washing?" Chen-li stuttered.
> "And of course the washing," said the Heavenly Spinning Maid. (93)

In these East Asian versions, the maidens go willingly and even gladly with the men in an understanding of mutual need. Indeed, the Heavenly Spinning Maid is known as a tale of filial piety in China. She is rewarded for her dutifulness by being given a husband for whom she could keep house. Like Chen-li, Keiichi needs Belldandy to help him put his life in order. She magically changes into clothes that mark her as the perfect girlfriend, her deepest desire to bring happiness to Keiichi, and in doing so, to all humankind. She and Keiichi become responsible for one another, but she takes on this duty cheerfully: "My name is Belldandy and I came from the Goddess Relief Office. I am here to grant you your wish, which I hope will let you realize your dream. However, you are allowed one wish only . . . It is our mission to help troubled people, such as yourself" (*Ah! My Goddess The Movie*) (also see Episode 2 of the series). Unlike the other heavenly maidens, wearing domesticated clothing does not completely rob her of her power,[7] but rather the disguise grants her agency in Keiichi's world, and this agency allows her to develop a "new" subjectivity. This domestic, local subjectivity negotiates with her global, goddess subjectivity and creates Belldandy as a glocal product: the conservative Japanese girl combined with the magical girlfriend schema made popular in the American series *Bewitched*, given the name of the Norse goddess of the present (Verðandi).

The literal binding between Tristran and Yvaine is a visual representation of a self–other, nature–culture, East–West and global–local opposition. It is later revealed that the stone that knocked Yvaine from the sky is an emblem of the Lords of Faerie and Tristran's birthright, binding them twice to one another. Tristran, like Yvaine, is considered Other. An important element in his journey toward maturation is his discovery of his transcultural heritage and the reconceptualization of his ethnicities into a glocal subjectivity. When Tristran trades his suit and bowler hat for a colorful costume in an effort to blend in, it is observed, "There was a swagger to his steps . . . a glint in his eye that he had not possessed when he had worn the bowler hat . . . Tristran felt quite at home with his new garb" (95). Just as being forced to wear clothes from the world of men transforms the Otherworldly Maidens, the exchange of his clothes for those from Faerie triggers a metamorphosis in Tristran. The change in clothing that subjugates the women empowers Tristran.

When Tristran eventually unchains Yvaine out of pity, the beginning of his recognition of her as a person rather than as an object is signaled. Yvaine's first agentic act is to run away, but events transpire so that Tristran saves her life from a witch, binding her to him a third time. By saving her life, he returns her life to her, and this act fully restores her agentic subjectivity. It is then that she gives him her name, fully realizing her existence as a subject rather than an object:

> "Now that you have saved my life, you are, by the law of my people, responsible for me, and I for you . . ."
>
> " . . . Perhaps we could start all over again . . . my name's Tristran Thorn, pleased to meet you." He held out his un-burned hand to her . . .
>
> "Aye," said the star. "It is a mighty joke, is it not? Whither thou goest, there I must go, if it kills me . . ." Then, momentarily, she touched her hand to Tristran's. "My sisters called me Yvaine," she told him. "For I was an evening star." (152–153)

The archaic language points to the Book of Ruth and alludes to the binding vows of marriage.[8] The binding words are analogous to the unbreakable chain, yet the difference is that it is Yvaine who speaks and thus binds herself to him. Although Tristran still intends to take her to Wall to win Victoria's hand, it is no longer as an object to be handed over but in the context of a mutual responsibility for the quality of life of the other.

In many variants of the Otherworldly Maiden tales, the dialectic relationship between nature and culture is expressed as marriage between the maiden and the man. The integration of two different yet complementary individuals through the marriage ritual is a structure that emerges through cause and effect, wherein the performance of the vows is the cause and the effect is the marriage (Fauconnier and Turner, 2002: 80–81). In *Ang Alamat ng Bahaghari*, the maiden-star, unaware that Bulawan stole and hid her wings, marries and falls in love with him. Their marriage is depicted as fruitful by the healthy plants that surround them and the child they cradle. The portrait of the family is a happy one, with Bulawan and the maiden-star turned toward one another, smiling as they cook rice together and contemplate their child (opening 10). The family as a blessed unit is highlighted by their placement within a circle in a manner reminiscent of Byzantine mosaics of the Holy Family. The illustration style adds glocal flavor to the text for the walls of the rice terraces that Bulawan farms (his clothing marks him as a member of the Igorot tribe) are built of blocks of soil and dirt that form a pattern described as a mosaic, creating a mixture of ethnic and Catholic spirituality to a story that has elements of both. The glocal heterotopia opened up by their marriage points to the need for culture to interact with nature and the divine in order to flourish, yet the fact that their union came about due to Bulawan's trickery puts their marriage in a tenuous position, which reflects an imperialistic hegemony that robs the maiden of an agentic subjectivity.

Becoming Glocal: How Intersubjective Dialogues Blend to Create Balanced Subjectivities

Glocal subjectivities are formed within glocal heterotopias when the multiple flows of information from the network of input spaces negotiate to create a blend that contributes to all parties. In the same way that glocal children gain power when information from shared connections intersects and combines in ways that grant agency, those not born glocal become glocal when the dialogue between input spaces becomes based on mutuality rather than opposition. The intersubjective relationship increases freedom and agency and creates glocal subjectivities relevant in global, local, and glocal worlds. When the otherwordly maiden finds her magical garment, there is a resurgence of the local, dominated, and silenced flow that restores her capacity to choose whether to stay or flee. The Otherworldly Maiden's flight opens opportunities for action for the men to either accept separation or to pursue her (Metamorphosis 3). The story may end with flight, such as in *The Selkie Girl* and *The Seal Mother*, pointing to an ideology that sees value in glocal children yet underpinned by the need for global and local spaces to remain separate. Stories that continue with pursuit value the growth gained through the sustained interactive dialogue between worlds underscored by mutual responsibility and love. In the pursuit, the women are no longer viewed as objects of desire but as subjects with the right to choose separation or union (possible Metamorphosis 4). The woman's choice to stay or return with her husband/lover marks their metamorphosis into glocal subjects: beings who have agency across worlds.

In most variants of the tale, glocal heterotopias are abstract spaces still within either the global or local worlds, but, as demonstrated earlier, there are physical spaces between worlds in *Stardust* and *Ah! My Goddess* that exist for the purpose of negotiation and dialogue. In *Stardust*, The Fairy Market is the only space and time where the inhabitants of both worlds are allowed to interact and trade, and it is also the liminal space wherein Tristran and Yvaine take stock of the transformations that have occurred through their interactions with one another and choose to either remain in interactive dialogue or to separate. What is at stake is their subjective agency, more so for Yvaine than for Tristran. In her desire to make him happy, she does not mention that when they cross from the market into Wall, she would metamorphose into a rock, a possibility which is both a potential story catastrophe and a metaphor for loss of the subjectivity she has formed in conversation with him. As they approach the gap that would take them out of Faerie and into Wall, she echoes the words that bind her life to his: "She looked at him, and she smiled, gently and ruefully. 'Whither thou goest . . . ' she whispered" (183). Whereas in the earlier excerpt this active choice signaled a shift from object to subject, the choice made here is to give up her life to become a literal object, paradoxically signifying the highest level of subjective agency. Furthermore, this second allusion to the Book of Ruth shows how the dialogue between Tristran and Yvaine (and the elaborate blends they each represent) has shifted from obligation to love.

Tristran's pursuit of Yvaine when she ran away from him marked the beginning of his recognition of her as a subject and the beginning of an intersubjective dialogue between them that moved their relationship away from domination toward partnership and triggered a mutual transformation.

> He could no longer reconcile his old idea of giving the star to Victoria Forrester with his current notion that the star was not a thing to be passed from hand to hand, but a true person in all respects and no thing at all. (183)

Their intersubjective development and maturation could not have happened if Yvaine hadn't allowed him to engage with her in interactive dialogue. Tristran's journey into manhood is completed by his choice to dwell in Faerie with Yvaine when he recognizes that she is his true heart's desire and thus secures her position as subject. Tristran discovers that he is a glocal child and even born of the Fairy Market when his mother, a Princess of Faerie, exchanged a magical glass flower with his father, a citizen of Wall, for a kiss, which led to a midnight tryst. Just as Tristran created Yvaine as subject by interacting with her as such, Yvaine completes Tristran's journey into manhood when she gives him the stone emblem of the Lords of Faerie and installs them both in positions of the highest power, able to contribute to both worlds. The mutual metamorphosis instigated by the negotiations that occurred between them in the Fairy Market culminated in their becoming glocal subjectivities empowered by partnership and love.

In *Ah! My Goddess,* an actual negotiation between worlds occurs when Celestine, Belldandy's former mentor and now the principal source of discord in the universe, sends Keiichi and Belldandy to the Judgment Gate to test their love for one another, believing that their partnership will be judged lacking and the forced separation will cause a surge of emotion from Belldandy that will quicken the spread of a virus he has implanted that rides on her emotional rhythms and finally shut down Heaven's connection with all worlds. He also believes that the separation will force Belldandy to see the truth of the hegemonic rule of the gods and move her to join his cause for a borderless universe, and in doing so, eliminate Otherness and promote harmony. One of the effects of the virus was to erase all of Belldandy's memories of Keiichi and her time on Earth, and the loss of ties deconstructed her subjectivity. In an effort to stop the spread of the virus, her sisters and the Goddess Technical Helpline attempt to reboot her (strengthening the personal computer analogy). Doing so deconstructs Belldandy further into what looks like digital code. The deconstruction is metafictive and emphasizes that Belldandy is both a mystical and computer construct of the perfect goddess and the perfect girlfriend. Indeed, when Belldandy loses her memories, she seems to become two-dimensional. The lack of depth highlights that she is a glocal construct—an emergent structure that arises from the perfect blend of traditional Japanese girl, magical girlfriend, Norse goddess, hologram, creator, and destroyer. She is built from global and local signs, but intersubjective dialogue between global and local is essential to gain a glocal subjectivity. That Belldandy is a projection of perfection both womanly and transcendent points to a dialogue within the global–local dialogue: the intersubjective relationship between human and divine.

The need for balance between human and divine is also a central theme in *Ang Alamat ng Bahaghari* and *The Heavenly Spinning Maid*. As mentioned earlier, filial piety is at the heart of the Chinese variant of the Otherworldly Maiden tale type. The maiden as a child of the heavens stands for two kinds of relationships: filial piety toward elders and parents and respect toward the divine. In the Chinese variants, a balance must be maintained between mundane and domestic duties and duties to the divine. The Emperor and Empress of Heaven, angered that the Heavenly Spinning Maid forgot to return to her heavenly tasks, turn her and Chen-li into constellations separated by the Milky Way. The gods allow them to come together once a year on the seventh night of the seventh month, which emphasizes the need for all unions to be orchestrated by and be to the benefit of the gods, and thus to all worlds. In *Ang Alamat ng Bahaghari*, the god Lumawig takes pity on Bulawan when the wife, upon the discovery that it was he who stole her wings, takes their child and leaves him. Lumawig aids Bulawan in his quest to win his wife back and, in the end, even creates the rainbow as a sign "of the great love that a father has for his wife and child" that has the power to bridge worlds (25). Bulawan's efforts, advocated by Lumawig, eventually convince his wife of his devotion, and she chooses to return to Earth to live in partnership with him. She dresses once more as an earthly wife, yet leaves her hair unbound to signify the integration of her two worlds in her shift from object to agentic subject. She and Bulawan have become glocal subjectivities able to move between worlds through intersubjective relationships with the global, local, domestic, and divine.

Keiichi's relationship with Belldandy deepens when he is transported into Belldandy's world and made to see her past. His observation of how her life had been in heaven makes him aware of her multiple subjectivities (as magical girlfriend, goddess, etc.) and adds another dimension to their intersubjective relationship. This deeper knowledge of Belldandy enables him to empower her in the same way that she has empowered him (the local contributes to the global). His experience of her as a child of heaven allows him to interact with the gods as Belldandy knows them, and this window into her relationship with the divine enables him to remind her of who she is as a goddess, who she is to their friends on earth, and who she is in their partnership. She comes into her full power when Keiichi tells her, "Even if the entire universe comes between us, I would find you" and she, in turn, declares "I consider myself so fortunate that Heaven has seen fit to grant my selfish wish to remain here by Keiichi's side." Their dialogue transforms Belldandy's multiple selves from a construct into a glocal subject. Their time in one another's worlds and the multiple flows that make up their intersubjective relationship give their partnership the authenticity needed to pass the test of the Judgment Gate (Figure 2.3). Agency comes not only from the love they bear one another, but from their relationships with their communities (global and local, domestic and divine, East and West, virtual and real, and so on) and the support their relationship garners from the community. Their union wipes out the virus that threatens the system, thwarts Celestine, restores harmony to the universe, and receives the blessing of the gods. Their triumph over Celestine's vision of a borderless universe emphasizes the importance of balance maintained through the existence of borders, the former leaning toward chaos and the latter advocating dynamic dialogues. The Judgment Gate is no longer a space of threat, but a place where intersectionality is possible.

In this comparison of Otherworldly Maiden tales, Eastern and Western versions yearn toward syncretism in different ways. The concept of *maodun*

Figure 2.3   Ah! My Goddess. The Judgment Gate: Negotiating Subjectivities.

allows syncretism to contain all possibilities, whether based on multidimensional and multileveled intersections as in *Ah! My Goddess* or an intersubjective dynamic based on oppositions as in *Stardust*. Either way, the metamorphoses triggered by dialogues made possible by connections between global and local, East and West, human and divine, culture and nature, and the blends that compose each of these concepts, emerge as glocal subjectivities and glocal children able to contribute to all worlds.

Notes

1. In *The Folktale*, Stith Thompson acknowledges "very ancient strata of folk narrative" in the regions that lie east of India, where "native story" is a mixture of local traditions and borrowings from India. He nevertheless excludes the East from the Index and outlines his reasons, among which is the "free give and take of theme and motif that binds all these lands together [westward to the Atlantic and southward to the Sahara] by a multitude of common traditions" (1977, 14).

2. Dong Yang is the most common name given to the cow herd in *The Cow Herd and the Weaving Maiden*, a Chinese narrative of the Otherworldly Maiden tale type.

3. The blending of Victoriana with contemporary elements is not unique to *Stardust*. Cora Kaplan remarks that there exists a long tradition of "pastiche Victoriana" that can be traced back to the late 1960s (2008, 42).

4. The full title of the Gaiman and Vess comic book is *Stardust, Being a Romance within the Realms of Faerie*. The tale originally appeared in this form and as such approximates the way novels were serialized in the Victorian period. The novelizations and the film version that followed do not include this subheading.

5. Anne Allison structures her argument around the strict parameters Japanese mothers need to comply with when preparing the customary *obentō* (a boxed lunch) for their children's first day of school. The ritual symbolizes the sacrifice expected of a mother and the discipline required by the child when he or she enters into the educational system (2000, 81–103). Belldandy is often shown preparing a meal for Keiichi, and the act of preparation and the food she provides sustains him physically and emotionally (Volume 1, 108; Episode 4).

6. In *Off With Their Heads!*, Maria Tatar points out the unequal treatment of men and women in the Aarne–Thompson *Motif Index* through a comparison of the titles AT 400, "The Man on a Quest for His Lost Wife", with AT 425, "The Search for the Lost Husband." She argues that all the tale types are described such that the man is always the subject of the titles and the first themes, whether or not the protagonist of the tale is a woman (1992, 159).

7. On Earth, Belldandy's powers are capped so that if she overuses them, she is drained until they rebuild. The happiness and contentment Belldandy shows throughout the *manga* and television series and in the movie indicates that it is more of an inconvenience than a loss.

8. In actuality, Ruth speaks the words to her mother-in-law, Naomi, after the death of her husband and indicates that the marriage bond includes a separation from one's own family and a commitment to the husband's family.

Works Cited

Primary Texts

Bonnet, Leslie, and Maurice Brevannes. "The Heavenly Spinning Maid." In *Chinese Folk and Fairy Tales*. New York: G. P. Putnam's Sons, 1963.

Cooper, Susan, and Warwick Hutton. *The Selkie Girl*. Hong Kong: Hodder and Stoughton Children's Books, 1986.

Gaiman, Neil, and Charles Vess. *Stardust: Being a Romance within the Realms of Faerie*. New York: DC Comics, 1998.

Gerstein, Mordicai. *The Seal Mother*. London: Methuen Children's Books, 1987.

Gohda, Hiroaki., Dir. *Ah! My Goddess The Movie*. Kodansha/Ah! My Goddess Partnership, 2000.

———. *Ah! My Goddess Complete Collection TV Series*. Based on the manga by Kosuke Fujishima. Kodansha/Ah! My Goddess Partnership, 2009.

Fujishima, Kosuke. *Oh My Goddess!*, Vol.1 and Vol. 4., translated by Dana Lewis, Alan Gleason, and Toren Smith. Milwaukee, OR: Dark Horse Manga, 2005 and 2007.

Villanueva, Rene O., and Frances C. Alcaraz. *Ang Alamat ng Bahaghari (The Legend of the Rainbow)*. Manila: Lampara Publishing House, 2002.

Secondary Texts

Allison, Anne. *Permitted and Prohibited Desires: Mothers, Comics, and Censorship in Japan*. Berkeley: University of California Press, 2000.

Asker, D. B. D. *Aspects of Metamorphosis: Fictional Representations of the Becoming Human*. Amsterdam: Rodopi, 2001.

Bayart, Jean-Francois. *Global Subjects: A Political Critique of Globalization*, translated by Andrew Brown. Cambridge: Polity Press, 2007.

Bradford, Clare, Kerry Mallan, John Stephens, and Robyn McCallum. *New World Orders in Contemporary Children's Literature: Utopian Transformations*. Basingstoke: Palgrave Macmillan, 2008.

Curry, Alice. "'The Pale Trees Shook, although No Wind Blew, and It Seemed to Tristran That They Shook in Anger': 'Blind space' and Ecofeminism in a Post-colonial Reading of Neil Gaiman and Charles Vess's Graphic Novel *Stardust* (1998)," *Barnboken—tidskrift för barnlitteraturforskning* 33.2 (2010): 19–33.

Day, Tony. "'Self' and 'Subject,' in Southeast Asian Literature in the Global Age." In *Asian and Pacific Cosmopolitans: Self and Subject in Motion*, edited by Kathryn Robinson. New York: Palgrave Macmillan, 2007.

De Block, Liesbeth, and David Buckingham. *Global Children, Global Media: Migration, Media and Childhood*. Basingstoke: Palgrave Macmillan, 2007.

De Certeau, Michel. *The Practice of Everyday Life*, translated by Steven F. Rendall, 1984. Berkeley: University of California Press, 1988.

Eoyang, Eugene Chen. *Two-Way Mirrors: Cross-Cultural Studies in Glocalization*. Lanham, MD.: Lexington Books, 2007.

Fauconnier, Gilles, and Mark Turner. *The Way We Think: Conceptual Blending and the Mind's Hidden Complexities*. New York: Basic Books, 2002.

Geertz, Clifford. "'From the Natives' Point of View': On the Nature of Anthropological Understanding." In *Culture Theory*, edited by Richard A. Schweder and Robert A. LeVine. Cambridge: Cambridge University Press, 1984.

Giddens, Anthony. *The Consequences of Modernity*. Stanford, CA: Stanford University Press, 1990.

Gutierrez, Anna Katrina. "*Mga Kwento ni Lola Basyang*: A Tradition of Reconfiguring the Filipino Child," *International Research in Children's Literature* 2.2 (2009): 159–176.

Harvey, David. *The Condition of Postmodernity: An Enquiry into the Origins of Cultural Change*. Cambridge, MA: Blackwell, 1990.

Heise, Ursula K. "Local Rock and Global Plastic: World Ecology and the Experience of Place," *Comparative Literature Studies* 41.2 (2004): 125–141.

Howell, Tes. "Conceptual Blends and Critical Awareness in Teaching Cultural Narratives," *L2 Journal* 2.1 (2010): 73–88.

Idema, Wilt L. *Filial Piety and Its Divine Rewards: The Legend of Dong Yang and Weaving Maiden with Related Texts*. Indianapolis, Indiana : Hackett Publishing Company, 2009.

Jones, Stephen. *Stardust: The Visual Companion*. London: Titan Books, 2007.

Kaplan, Cora. "Fingersmith's Coda: Feminism and Victorian Studies," *Journal of Victorian Culture* 13.1 (2008): 42–55.

Kawai, Hayao. *The Japanese Psyche: Major Motifs in the Fairy Tales of Japan*, translated by Hayao Kawai and Sachiko Reece. 2nd ed. Woodstock, CT: Spring Publications, 1996.

Leary, Barbara Fass. *In Search of the Swan Maiden: A Narrative on Folklore and Gender*. New York: New York University Press, 1994.

Lebra, Takie Sugiyama. *The Japanese Self in Cultural Logic*. Honolulu: University of Hawaii Press, 2004.

Loriggio, Francesco. "Disciplinary Memory as Cultural History: Comparative Literature, Globalization and the Categories of Criticism," *Comparative Literature Studies* 41.1 (2004): 49–79.

McCallum, Robyn. *Ideologies of Identity in Adolescent Fiction: The Dialogic Construction of Subjectivity*. New York: Garland Publishing, 1999.

Robertson, Roland. "Glocalization: Time-Space and Homogeneity-Heterogeneity." In *Global Modernities*, edited by Mike Featherstone, Scott Lash, and Roland Robertson. London: Sage, 1997.

Stephens, John, and Roderick McGillis. "Critical Approaches to Children's Literature." In *The Oxford Encyclopedia of Children's Literature, Vol.1*, edited by Jack Zipes. New York: Oxford University Press, 2006.

Stephens, John, and Sylvie Geerts. "Mishmash, Conceptual Blending and Adaptation in Contemporary Children's Literature Written in Dutch and English." In *Never-ending Stories*, edited by Sara Van den Bossche and Sylvie Geerts. Ghent: Academia Press, 2013.

Strauss, Claudia, and Naomi Quinn. *A Cognitive Theory of Cultural Meaning*. Cambridge : Cambridge University Press, 1997.

Tatar, Maria. *Off With Their Heads! Fairy Tales and the Culture of Childhood*. Princeton, NJ: Princeton University Press, 1992.

Thompson, Stith. *The Folktale*. Berkeley: University of California Press, 1977.

Turner, Mark. "The Way We Imagine." In *Imaginative Minds*, edited by Ilona Roth. London: British Academy and Oxford University Press, 2007.

Uther, Hans-Jörg. *The Types of International Folktales: A Classification and Bibliography, Based on the System of Antti Aarne and Stith Thompson*. Helsinki: Suomalainen Tiedeakatemia, Academia Scientiarum Fennica, 2004.

Xie, Shaobo. "Rethinking the Identity of Cultural Otherness: The Discourse of Difference as an Unfinished Project." In *Voices of the Other*, edited by Roderick McGillis. New York: Garland, 1999.

Yoshida, Kaori. "Issues in Children's Media in Glob/calized Cultural Industry," presented at the Graduate Student Research Conference, *Asia Pacific: Local Knowledge versus Western Theory*, The University of British Columbia, Canada, February 2004. http://www.iar.ubc.ca/centres/cjr/publications/grad2004/index.htm. Accessed September 25, 2007.

Chapter Three

The Muslima within American Children's Literature

Female Identity and Subjectivity in Novels about Pakistani-Muslim Characters

Seemi Aziz

Within the context of the current global and geo-political landscape and the 'war on terror,' competing imaginaries—Western imperialist, Orientalist, imperialist feminist as well as transnational feminist, anti-colonial and Islamic—form a contested terrain of knowledge production upon which the lives, histories and subjectivities of Muslim women are discursively constituted, debated, claimed and consumed through a variety of literary, academic and visual forms of representation.

Zine, Taylor, and Davis, "Reading Muslim Women and Muslim Women Reading Back"

A particular problem of representation in recent young adult fiction is discernible in the depiction of female Muslim characters, or Muslimas. This is all the more a problem because it is frequently unrecognized as such, especially in terms of an endemic slippage between forms of representation, between depicting a character and presuming to speak for the society in which that character is located. Clare Bradford points directly to the problem of representation in noting the preponderance of "first-person and character-focalized narratives thematizing the identity formation of Muslim girls" (2007,

48), because such narrative strategies assume that the character's interiority, and hence her subjectivity, can be made unproblematically accessible to readers. In her often-cited essay, "Can the Subaltern Speak," Gayatri Chakravorty Spivak argues that academic disciplines that strive to retrieve information from the "silenced areas" of culture—the disciplines of anthropology, political science, history, and sociology—are apt to be sustained by constructions of consciousness or subjectivity that "cohere with the work of imperialist subject-constitution, mingling epistemic violence with the advancement of learning and civilization." She concludes that in such a context, "the subaltern woman will be as mute as ever" (1988, 295). Bradford recognizes a form of this mingling of "epistemic violence" and "advancement of civilization" in young adult fiction when she observes, with reference to Suzanne Fisher Staples *Shabanu*, that the deployment of first-person, present tense narration forecloses the possibility of representing any subject position other than that of Shabanu, the narrator, and her subjectivity "is represented according to the liberal humanist paradigms of individualism and personal growth that dominate texts featuring Western protagonists" (2007, 51). Through the narrator's tenure of the discourse, a female Muslim subjectivity is rendered mute.

Published in 1989, *Shabanu* marked the onset of a continuing flow of books about Muslim girls and young women, but with the 1990–1991 Gulf War and especially the events of 9/11, these representations quickly became imbricated with what Minoo Moallem terms the "feminine iconography" (2008, 107) of the reified idea of "the Muslim woman": "Muslim women have become the material evidence (the body) upon which racial, religious, and cultural notions of authenticity and otherness are framed to give meaning to civilizational thinking as well as religious and secular forms of nationalism and fundamentalism." A pivotal cultural text for children's literature was Disney's *Aladdin* (1992), in which commentators quickly identified a neocolonialist discourse, whereby, as Erin Addison puts it, "Jasmine, the Arab woman, is the locus at which the colonial catalysis occurs, through whom the narratives of naive individualism, romance, and secularism pass into and unravel the fabric of Islamic culture. To save Jasmine from her own culture, *Aladdin* dismembers that culture and replaces it with ours" (1993, 6).

As part of a roundtable symposium on "the Muslimwoman" in 2008, Jasmin Zine mapped the politics of identity that shape how the body and subjectivity of a Muslim woman are narrated. In an encapsulation that has a strong suggestive resonance for the representation of Muslim girls in recent fiction, she remarks: "The narrow discursive boundaries that frame the articulation of our identities limit the agency of Muslim women to locate our sense of subjectivity and identity outside the parameters that have been determined for us" (110). This form of the tyranny of representation finds inexplicit reinforcement in the fiction and in the reception of that fiction, both of which are grounded in the particular politics of identity articulated by Zine, Moallem, and Addison, among others, and which, in the fiction, assumes that "progress," whether perceived as what is gained or what is to be desired, entails replacing "that culture" with familiar Western paradigms.

Muslim women within literature for children are characteristically represented as abject subjects, comprising a discomfiting mixture of the dehumanized, oppressed, and exotic (Whitlock, 2005; Bradford, 2007; Raina, 2009), as in books such as Latifa's *My Forbidden Face* (2003); Ellis's trilogy, *The Bread Winner* (2000), *Parvana's Journey* (2002), and *Mud City* (2003); Bunting's *One Green Apple* (2006); or Lofthouse and Ingpen's *Ziba Came on a Boat* (2007). The impression of exoticism stems not only from the images on the covers and unusual titles but also from the customs and artifacts described within the novels, the inclusion of words from languages other than English, and occasional uses of more formal language to hint at the mental structures of people from another culture (Bradford, 2007; Aziz, 2011). Overt versions of the exotic are exploited in, for example, Kim Antieau's *Broken Moon* (2007), in which versions of South and West Asia are an external, Western construction (Antieau has never been to the region). Thus at the beginning of the novel the protagonist, referring to life before her family became outcast and impoverished, mentions that, "Ami had several saris and dupattas then—made from the softest silks, with most becoming colors" (2). Saris are not a common dress worn by Pakistani women, and only very few upper-class families may wear saris as party wear. She mentions "the bangle woman came . . . the women kept slipping (or pushing) on bangle after bangle: orange, blue, maroon, red, purple, gold . . . her arms covered in bangles, her hair laced with jasmine" (13). Reference to ornate silks, bangles, and bright color combinations evokes accepted 'Oriental' images of Third World Muslim women—adorned, eroticized, and never quite adult.

The exotic is more than a hook for readers, however: it establishes the essential otherness of the people depicted and suggests that, constantly interpellated by the practices of a rigid culture, they suffer from a lack of the kind of subjective agency assumed as a matter of course in the West. For example, when early in *Shabanu* the narrator is thinking about the weddings arranged for herself and her sister, she remarks:

> Mama says it's a good match, because Hamir and Murad have land. Dadi will give us each ten camels with our dowries.
> "Don't worry," I say, smoothing Phulan's hair and kissing her tears. But both of us know that their ways are strange, and there are unimaginable things to cry about. (1989, 6)

The extract is dense with signifiers of otherness: the arranged basis of the wedding; its underpinning economic exchange; the paying of a dowry (which includes a gift of camels); the valuing of the match by the parents, not the bride; and the shift to a slightly more formal register to emphasize the character of arranged exogamy ("their ways are strange," "unimaginable things"). The effect is that the girls are simultaneously exotic and oppressed, subaltern women who lead imperiled lives and are devoid of any possibility of agency or voice.

The setting of *Shabanu* within a tribal society in Pakistan may exacerbate such effects, but two other examples set in Pakistan which I discuss in this chapter—*Broken Moon* (Kim Antieau, 2007) and *Beneath My Mother's Feet* (Amjed Qamar, 2008)—likewise illustrate how the structure and epistemology of fictive representation which narrates and interprets Asian societies are implicated with regimes of hegemony that form, reinforce, and circulate accepted stereotypes. Stories written by authors who are outside of the culture or have been disconnected from it for a substantial time can misrepresent and silence significant groups of people and their values through a lack of inclusion (Young, 2003). The significance of this analysis is not so much to do with the impact of an individual book but the impact of a collection of books depicting a particular region of the world that is dominated by colonialist perspectives. Commonly classified as multicultural literature, they provide neither a mirror which reflects a mainstream of insiders nor a window that provides glimpses of authentic subjective experiences of people within the region and its cultures. Thus discourse about Pakistan becomes one with an implicit postcolonial epistemology that goes unchallenged.

Children's literature can play a critical role in either giving voice or silencing the "other," particularly within the previously colonized world in which authors from both inside and outside of the culture write from Eurocentric perspectives that erase and transform the ways of living and thinking of peoples belonging to that region (Said, 1978, 1981, 1993; Mills, 1997). Children's literature also provides the children perceiving the world with various lenses. The existence of a multiplicity of books may help counter misconceptions and stereotypes about other regions, as Freeman and Lehman argue (2001, 26), but the possibility that readers may thereby "gain their own sense of what is authentic" will be limited if a common process of subject-constitution underlies these books. As Zine et al. contend, "Since 9/11 and the ongoing 'war on terror,' narratives by and about Muslim women have been increasingly commodified, circulated, and uncritically consumed, particularly in the West" (2007, 272). The plight of Muslim women as oppressed beings is a continuing discourse that constructs the perception as an epistemic reality (Mohanty, 1997; Bradford, 2007; Raina, 2009). Central to the iconography of the Muslim women is the hijab, both as an object and a symbol interpreted in specific ways. Through popular discourse and images in pop culture, women in Muslim countries are deemed inaccessible and backward *because* they are veiled. There seems to be a struggle among Western countries to "free" and "unveil" the Muslim women through passing laws such as the 2004 French law, which banned the wearing of overt religious symbols, and the subsequent 2010 law which was specifically directed at the niqab and burka.

Mohanty categorizes three analytic presuppositions that describe the manner in which the West views and represents women from Third World countries and through which their experiences and reactions are universalized. The first presumes that these women form "an already constituted, coherent, group with identical interests and desires, regardless of class, ethnic or racial location, or contradiction"; the second constitutes "the uncritical way 'proof' of universality and cross-cultural validity are provided"; and the third presumes she "leads an essentially truncated life based on her feminine gender (read: sexually constrained) and her being 'Third World' (read: ignorant, poor, uneducated, tradition bound, domestic, family oriented, victimized, etc.)" (1997, 258–259). This frame contrasts directly with the manner in which Western women view themselves. Each of these presuppositions informs the three novels discussed in this chapter.

Representations of Pakistani Muslim
Female Identity in Young Adult Fiction

The female protagonists of the three novels—Shabanu (*Shabanu*), Nadira (*Broken Moon*), and Nazia (*Beneath My Mother's Feet*)—weave in and out of the boundaries and pressures placed on them by their family, society, religion, and above all by their unique circumstances. They seem to be caught within an endless web of lies and deceit from which they try to break free. The inevitable resolutions of their circumstances are through either giving up their fight or taking it to the extreme, finding a way out, and hence developing an agentic subjectivity. The authors present each of the female protagonists as freethinking and upright characters in contrast to many of the peripheral characters through whom readers are shown how the society constrains female subjectivity by interpellating women and girls into narrowly defined spheres.

According to popular (Western) perception, Muslim females are "supposed to" present a particular outward appearance, with the "hijab" as a necessary head covering within most Muslim cultures. Because hijab is assumed to be an overt sign of interpellation, being "Muslim" is transparent and immediately recognizable as such. These women are also required by the tradition and religion to behave in a certain manner that has modesty and humility at the forefront. Within these perceptions, the *hijab* or headcovering is depicted as a necessary evil imposed upon Third World Muslim females, even though hijab in varied forms has been and is being worn by many Muslim women within their various cultures and regions and is usually adhered to through a personal choice rather than a dress code enforced by men or complicit women. Thus Shabanu is depicted as angered by her aunt's insistence that she wears a *chadr* (a cloth that covers not only the head but most of the body as well), and the implied reader endorses her resistance: "The dark blue cloth slips to my shoulders. I push back my clean and newly plaited hair and make no effort to adjust the *chadr*" (1989, 33). As the camel she is sitting on stands up, its motion naturally displaces the *chadr* and displays Shabanu's femininity, which is encapsulated in "clean and newly plaited hair": the implication is that this should not be hidden away. In a comparable way, when Nadira in *Broken Moon* is first disguised as a boy to begin her quest to find her kidnapped brother, she experiences an unusual sense of liberty: "I left and walked freely through the streets—as I never had before—and no one noticed me! I got lost twice and had to stop and ask someone for directions" (2007, 81). Dropped in between her meeting with Bashir, a man who can give her some information, and her encounter with the kidnappers, Nadira's observation is narratively redundant and functions rather as an element of texture, a reminder that in this world girls' lack of freedom and agency is coded by dress.

The female protagonists of the three novels are depicted as characters that take their clothes and *hijab* as a necessary boundary and work with that to the best of their ability although rebelling against it through their actions. The assumption that hijab is an overt sign of interpellation seems to be reinforced by the various covers of each of the novels, which represent the protagonist in various postures but always with a head covering. As Bradford points out, "The women on these covers do not look at viewers in a way that constructs a relationship of affinity with viewers" (2007, 48). Even the 1991 Knopf edition of *Shabanu* in which, Bradford contends, the figure on the cover "looks directly out to the viewer in a manner that appears confrontational or angry" doesn't establish a reciprocal gaze, but plays on a being-looked-at structure. A viewer looks at Shabanu, but her eyes pass over the viewer's shoulder. In each case, the figure that appears on the cover is *Muslimwoman*.

Questions of agency are in such ways central to the fictive constitution of Muslim females as subjects. Shabanu is depicted as a twelve-year-old belonging to a nomadic family living in a tent and tending camels, who is forced by her parents to marry Rahim, a man who is between fifty-five and sixty, merely to settle a family and land feud. The marriage will entail a radical change to her sense of self. As she does not have a male sibling all the "male" duties of managing the outside fall on her, and so there has been no possibility that she will be confined within the home. Hence from the beginning of the story, she is presented as different from other everyday characters. The lack of a male child as a negative is frequently mentioned in conversations between Shabanu's mother and aunt (her father's sister). Shabanu and her sister wear a *chadr*, but as her sister is thirteen and ready for marriage, she has to cover up more than Shabanu, who rebels against this forced covering, as it seems to hinder her duties that make her close to her animals and father. Social conventions, family structure, and dress codes are thus all factors that limit agency.

Shabanu is a female growing up in a male dominant society; the images, settings, dialogues, and sequence of events are all structured in a way that creates a strong sense of reader empathy with Shabanu's struggle. At the same time, this empathy is not rewarded with an outcome whereby Shabanu overcomes her obstacles and transforms her life. Rather, the teleology of the novel, which represents her as *bought* by a future husband—"[Rahim] has paid more than a fair price for a troublesome girl like you" (1989, 196)—and confined to domestic tasks as a wife-in-training (230), affirms that this is immutably the way things are in this culture. The teleology of *Shabanu* reinforces most of the typical stereotypes a Western reader would have about women from Pakistan: they follow men's lead all the time, they don't have a say about their future, and if they challenge the traditional role assigned to them, they may be killed by men. The story also re-creates that image of the Islamic world as consisting of nothing but desert, tents, and camels. Staples encapsulates the conceptual/ ideological position within this first volume, and subsequent volumes extend the story from within the same set of assumptions. The series does not show Shabanu's subjectivity taking new Muslima forms, and when she expresses moments of agency, these are perceived from the perspective of European values and outlook. The final chapters of the novel include several conversations about *choice* between Shabanu and her older mentors, Sharma and Fatima, who lead lives as independent women. The available choices are of two kinds. The first is set out by Sharma:

> The choice is, you try to make [your husband] so happy he can't bear to be away from you a single moment. If he treats you badly, come stay with us. (1989, 209)

In Western terms, this is a choice dependent on limited agency: one chooses to do what one has no choice other than to do and willingly makes it work. The alternative is potential abjection. The second choice is to cultivate a form of subjective agency that depends on maintaining an essential self that negates the first choice. This position is set out in the closing sentences of the novel in which Shabanu redefines Sharma's advice:

> "The secret is keeping your innermost beauty, the secrets of your soul, locked in your heart," Sharma's voice whispers in my ear, "so that he must always reach out to you for it."
> Rahim-*sahib* will reach out to me for the rest of his life and never unlock the secrets of my heart. (240)

This resolution pivots on the concept of resistance to relations of subordination and structures of male domination. Such a situation, Saba Mahmood argues, is a product of Western (feminist) thinking, whose project is both *analytical* and *politically prescriptive* (2001, 206). Having discerned a problem in Islam from a Western perspective, a Western mode of behavior is proposed as the solution.

The protagonist of *Broken Moon* (2007), Nadira, is a conservative, poor, "small" female who has been made abject prior to the beginning of the novel, when, as a twelve-year-old, a village council *fatwa* permitted her to be gang raped, beaten, and branded to settle a dispute blamed upon her older brother. Compelled to leave her village, she works at a rich woman's house in the city. The story elements thus position her as the most abject of Muslim females, but when her younger brother is abducted and taken by a Middle Eastern group to be forced to become a notorious camel rider, she asserts an agentic subjectivity by dressing as a boy and going in search of him. As Victoria Flanagan points out, female-to-male cross-dressing is the most common form of cross-dressing in children's literature, in which it functions as "a clever strategy for the interrogation of traditional gender categories" (2008, 20). When the cross-dressing heroine is a Muslima, who thus eludes the practical and symbolic confinement of hijab, the interrogation will be understood as even more subversive.

Moreover, because a core aspect of Nadira's agency is that she is a storyteller, inspired by the legendary Shahrazad, and she tells stories to negotiate a way out of unusual and impossible circumstances, agency is combined with voice. Whereas a fantastical story is woven from homologies between the legendary *A Thousand and One Nights* and the social issue of enslaved juvenile "camel riders," as a male storyteller, Nadira attains the freedom required to be herself as an intelligent woman and to help her brother escape the barbaric Middle Eastern practice of tying very young camel jockeys to the camel until they win or die. In short, in *Broken Moon* Nadira's life and quest are framed by Islamic atrocities conventionally assumed within Western notions of "Oriental barbarism," and her subjectivity is shaped by her capacity to oppose that barbarism.

The first-person narration of these two novels positions readers to align or empathize with the narrator/protagonist and with the attitudes and concepts she develops. Ideas such as self-fashioning and resistance against all odds are, as Sensoy and Marshall put it, "ideas firmly rooted in mainstream U.S. ideals of exceptionalism and Western values of individuality" (2009–2010). The same effect of reader alignment can be achieved in third-person narration focalized through the principal character, as in Amjed Qamar's *Beneath My Mother's Feet*. As Stephens observes, the majority of children's fictions employ only one focalizing character (2010, 56), and this is again the case with *Beneath My Mother's Feet*. Nazia, the protagonist and focalizer, is present on every page of the novel, and although her perceptions often express puzzlement or lack of specific knowledge, such gaps are part of her process of evolving understanding and subjective agency. Although the narrative effect is very close to first-person narration, the more complex representation of perceptions and responses maps a more complex subject-construction. Nazia is depicted as an independently thinking, intelligent girl who is a "good" daughter to a mother who takes her from a settled life of lower-middle-class existence to work as a housecleaning maid to support the family after they have been failed or betrayed by the male members of the household. She is fourteen but is soon to be married to her cousin in the village, which is a prospect the novel consistently depicts as undesirable. Her mother has been collecting her *jehez* (dowry) since she was born, but her older brother steals it and runs away. Her father feigns illness in order to avoid work and then steals from the family that shelters them when they lose their home due to nonpayment of rent. Her mother exploits Nazia by compelling her to work in her stead.[1] Given such negative circumstances and a family which seems to have no regard for her welfare, Nazia seems to have little prospect of making choices on her own behalf.

However, Nazia's subjectivity evolves across a trajectory from innocent schoolgirl through abjection to agentic subjectivity. At the opening of the novel, she is represented as a typical Third World woman who loves clothes and is surrounded by the exotic, although this does not include *hijab*. She does wear a *dupatta*, which is a necessary part of Pakistani attire, but seldom wears it over her head. She goes to school bareheaded, with her hair scented with mustard oil and tightly braided (2008, 1). The colorful clothes in the bazaar between school and home tempt her, "it was nearly impossible to walk by day after day without getting drawn in by enticing apparel" (1). Rather than the forms of religion, her subjectivity is constrained by a social practice that has no concept of female agency, and so assumes a girl is always subject to her parents and to males. Her mother's fatalism is not only a constant barrier to her dreams and ambitions but also a motif in the novel that generates consistent reader resistance. Thus when her mother dismisses her hopes with utterances such as, "All you can hope for is to get married to a good man and pray that he treats you well. That is your fate" (112), readers align strongly with any alternative perspective, especially because the novel makes it clear that there is no such thing as a good man in that society. Nazia's hard life as a cleaning maid has prompted her to challenge parental "wisdom": "Was there some unwritten law that said even when things were going wrong, when the choices that her parents made led to one disaster after another, she had to ride the waves, holding her breath?" (113). The more Nazia asks such questions and contemplates the possibility of making her own choices, the more she moves toward choices that will lead to agency. Her growing resolve eventually promotes a reluctant transformation in her mother, who finally assists Nazia to evade the marriage and choose her own destiny.

In the novel's closing pages, Nazia and her mother transgress against the codes of their society. Such transgression is pivotal in all three novels discussed in this chapter and acts as a fulcrum for the ideological opposition between a represented "Pakistan" and Western social ideology. Of the three authors, Amjed Qamar is closest to having an insider perspective, having been born in Hyderabad (an Indian city in which Muslims have a substantial presence) and having lived for many years in Pakistan. Most of her life has been spent in America, however, so she is only marginally an insider, and her conception of subjective agency does seem to be Western. Transgression proves to be the conduit by which Western ideology frames these novels. As Robyn McCallum argues, fictional characters who are displaced from familiar social, cultural, or family contexts are situated within alienated subject positions as the socially marginal other in relation to their own society (1999, 100). In the process of achieving an agentic subjectivity, such characters may be employed both to represent and interrogate the structures of their society. Novels such as *Shabanu*, *Broken Moon*, and *Beneath My Mother's Feet* offer a special perspective on Western representations of Asia, in that the closest thing to representations of a "South Asian Subjectivity" appears in the parents in *Beneath My Mother's Feet* as the abject fatalism of the mother and the (equally abject) irresponsible self-regardingness of the father. And yet, these are Orientalist clichés, against which Nazia's other-regardingness and intersubjective reaching out are highlighted as components of a rich and agentic subjectivity which is an ideal of Western young adult novels. McCallum further argues that to displace a character out of his/her familiar surroundings can destabilize his/her sense of identity, that such a displacement can offer ways to explore sociocultural influences on cognition and the formation of subjectivity, and that "representations of transgressive modes of behavior or being in fiction can construct interpretative positions from which to examine and interrogate the limitations that the dominant cultural and social discourses and practices of a given society or culture place on experience, action, and subjectivity" (1999, 100–101). The novelistic formula that might produce such a complex of ideas proves ideal for the varying degrees of cultural imposition in novels about Pakistani society and religion, in that the dominant cultural and social discourses are invariably found wanting, and the protagonist must find another (Western) form of subjectivity if she is to survive as an agentic human being. To conclude this chapter, I will consider some themes common to all three novels which bear on the constructions of subjectivity which emerge within them.

As noted above, Muslim feminists identify a tendency in Western feminism to compound analysis and political prescriptiveness when they focus attention on Asian societies, and the prescriptive element impacts upon the ways in which female subjectivity is constructed in fiction. When a Western audience reads narratives about life and gender viewpoints that are alien to them, their reactions may be varied, but principally they are positioned to recoil in revulsion. In the following example, reader positioning is determined by a combination of the focalizer's bewilderment and presuppositions implicitly attributed to an implied reader. Nazia is attempting to respond to her younger sister's suggestion that Nazia's impending marriage is just an excuse to escape the family:

> "That's not true!" Nazia protested. "Why would I want to leave all of you? My life was planned when I was younger than you, chotti. No one asked me what I wanted." How could she explain the traditions of matrimony to her sister when she barely understood the cultural requirements herself?
>
> Amma had never sat her down and explained what would happen in all the years of growing up. Anything that happened in their lives was always seen as inevitable, as Allah's will. There was never any room in their tiny existence to entertain the possibility of other choices, other dreams. (2008, 83)

The shift from direct speech to FIT (free indirect thought: "How could she explain . . .") indicates that discourse represents the character's inner thoughts, but the register shifting within the FIT between the over-formal language of "traditions of matrimony . . . cultural requirements . . . entertain the possibility" and more demotic "never any room in their tiny existence," and the formal doublets of "inevitable, Allah's will" and "other choices, other dreams," disclose a narrator shaping of the discourse designed to evoke a critical response from readers: child betrothal is wrong; the cultural practice of child subjection is wrong; belief in destiny is a false ideology; to be fully human is to dream and have choices. In her bewilderment, Nazia is reaching toward a Western concept of subjectivity that interrogates the whole principle of her "tiny existence." In other words, the sequence both identifies a problem and asserts a solution in the form of a particular kind of subjective agency. As the protagonist in these novels evolves into an empowered female, the female society left behind is perceived by Western readers as at best surviving under conditions that render them inferior and unable to make a meaningful contribution to their own lives or to society within the (Islamic) nation.

The reified idea of "the Muslim woman" which underpins these novels, and those about other countries in the region, has appeared, Margot Badran argues, "at precisely the moment when the West is intent upon containing Islamists" (2008, 102), and she goes on to ask whether "Western embrace of the Muslim-woman [could] be the gendered equivalent of a penchant for backing repressive (patriarchal) regimes" (102). A pervasive focus in young adult fiction on girls from regional, rural, tribal, or underclass societies risks creating the impression that these are metonymic of entire countries, whereas there have been many empowered women in Pakistan, for example, and there has been a strong international Islamic feminism for the past couple of decades. As Badran further writes:

> As we move further into the twenty-first century, in both the East and the West, growing numbers of Muslim women are being energized and emboldened by the new Qur'anic discourse of gender equality and justice and becoming part of the Islamic feminist surge as women increasingly decide for themselves how to be Muslims and how to be women within their diverse contexts. (2008, 104)

In a very informative study of the development and diversity of feminisms in Islamic countries in an earlier article, Badran makes a point with significant resonance for Western young adult fiction dealing with Islam:

> The West is not the patrimonial home of feminisms from which all feminisms derive and against which they must be measured. Indeed, Middle Eastern feminisms generated a critique of Western "imperial feminism/s" as they brought the insights and activist modes of their own secular/national feminisms to the table of (Western-dominated) international feminism during the twentieth century. (2005, 12)

The protagonists of the three novels become empowered even as they face the worst times of their lives and their very existence is in peril. Their struggle is against not only circumstances over which they have no control but also the regimes of oppression that purpose to suppress women in particular. A common strategy in Western young adult literature is to portray teenagers as transgressing any kind of rules by adults, and in Antieau, Qamar, and Staples's books, transgression by young girls against patriarchal rules is evident. Transgression is not an entirely isolated experience, however, and each of the girls finds support, to varying degrees, from strong and influential adult females. Such influential characters are role models because they have resisted the interpellation of patriarchal (that is, Islamic) society and have chosen their own paths. What has not been incorporated into their representation, however, is a clear sense that it is not Islam which they must resist, but the structures of family and society that prevent women from enjoying the rights held out to them by Islam (and see Badran, 2005: 21–22). Islam as a religion is part of the life of inhabitants in Pakistan, but fiction written by outsiders and drawing upon popular Western conceptions of Islam may easily misrepresent it through the depiction of events and of actions performed by Muslim characters that impact upon the protagonist. When, for example, Nadira (*Broken Moon*) tells the complete story of her rape and mutilation, it concludes thus: "When they were finished, they took out their knives and left a mark on me. The father, the two brothers, and the holy man. He left the one on my cheek. That is the story" (2007, 74). The sequencing of the actions, to culminate in "the holy man" who makes the scar that renders her visibly unmarriageable, attributes the entire event to religious sanction and creates the possibility that, in the absence of any representations of everyday religious life, the complicity of a village cleric in a barbaric act typifies the whole religion.

The part is also seen to stand for the whole in that protagonists in these novels conform to a pattern which gives them a low socioeconomic standing and limited or no education. That is, they reflect the presuppositions about Third World women identified by Mohanty: their interests and desires are uniform, and they lead abject lives because they are female. The authors thus reproduce audience expectations about actions and events set in this region, and so foreground issues of social justice such as child marriage, bonded and child labor, and the plight of Muslim females. The heroines, in particular, are then represented as unusual and unlike other real-life females in Pakistani society because they are independent and resist societal constraints. Their experiences are perceived as distinctly alien and often in breach of human rights, and such representations in turn reinforce common perceptions about the lives of women in Pakistan. Their unusual nature and inconceivable circumstances portrays them as distinctly "other" from the Eurocentric audiences who read these stories. In short, as Sensoy and Marshall point out, the marketing of "Save the Muslim Girl" stories by major publishers, favorable reviews by "literary and educational gatekeepers," award citations (*Shabanu* received a Newbery Honor and a *New York Times* Notable Book of the Year citation), and achievement of bestseller status suggest "an intimate connection to the current ideological climate within which these stories are told, marketed, and consumed" (2009–2010).

The brief essay by Sensoy and Marshall is unusual in setting out a negative review of what the "Save the Muslim Girl" label suggests is a subgenre of young adult fiction, although Isaac reports some negative comments from Islamic groups (2010, 86–87), who criticize *Shabanu* for "colonialist" tendencies, for its "extremely narrow and stereotypical view of Islam and Muslim cultures" (ING, http://www.ing.org/index.php/k-6/61-tips-for-teaching-about-muslims), and because if this is a book "about Muslims" taught in schools, "the nomadic people that live in the desert of Cholistan" will be a metonym for all Pakistani Muslims and Muslims in general. Reviews and discussions of *Shabanu*, the earliest published of my group, were otherwise generally enthusiastic, and major forums published interviews (Sawyer, *The New Advocate*, 1993) or commissioned essays by Staples (*Bookbird*; 1997). The reviews are apt to take the book on its own terms and reflect the current ideological climate both in their assumptions about authenticity and their implied notions of subjectivity. Hearne, for example, accepts that the novel has a "Pakistani setting" and that within it "the binding rites of the Muslim faith are vividly related" (1989, 45). She does not question if this setting deals with the whole of the society in Pakistan or what actually are the rites of the Muslim faith. McDonald's reaction toward such a literary piece is typical of the Muslim Third World stereotype when she says, "Tending camels. Arranged marriages. Living in thatched mud huts. Thirst. Moving from place to place. Monsoon rains. Enter the world of Shabanu" and more specifically when she comments on a "society that permits women to be beaten for disobedience, enslaved in marriage, or stoned to death for looking at another man" (1990, 63–64), when no such societal norm exists in Islam let alone Pakistan.

A more revealing approach to *Shabanu* is implicit in Jinx Watson's comparison of it with a later Staples novel, *Dangerous Skies* (1996), now set on the coast of Virginia. Despite "the obvious external differences in the setting of these novels," Watson observes that they are similar "coming of age" narratives in which the protagonists "successfully craft new identities and learn to compromise with their communities as they negotiate for acceptance and affirmation" (1999, 28). The parallel is underscored by a specific assumption, drawn from Erik Erikson's *Childhood and Society* (1964), that adolescence is a universal stage that entails a search for identity. A still deeper (unarticulated) level of assumption is that subjectivity is the same in all places and cultures, and this is no doubt an assumption discernible in the novels themselves as well as in the process of comparison.

The assumption that there is a universal form of subjectivity links with a further issue in the fictive representation of other cultures, the question of what is an authentic representation. A realist narrative characterized by thick descriptive detail may readily convince readers of its authenticity. *Shabanu*, for example, opens with such a thick description:

> Phulan and I step gingerly through the prickly gray camel thorn, each of us balancing a red clay pot half filled with water on our heads. It was all the water we could get from the *toba*, the basin that is our main water supply.
> Our underground mud cisterns are infested with worms. We'll dig new ones when the monsoon rains come—if they come. (1989, 1)

The accumulation of detail, along with a large number of modifiers (step *gingerly*; *prickly gray camel* thorn; *red clay* pot), creates a dense semantic load here that conjures an exotic, often romanticized scene, especially in the opening sentence that places two figures in a landscape: females carrying water pots on their heads in an arid country dependent on monsoon rains. Names and social practices are strange (*Phulan, toba, mud cisterns*) and made stranger by the addition of a gloss ("the basin that is . . ."). In a work of fiction, this landscape does not need to be real, provided that it seems real. The opening has already been preceded by a map, so the overall reality effect is high, and questions of authenticity may not subsequently arise. Mingshui Cai, for example, arguing that in order to write about another culture an author needs to have developed "a culturally specific sense of its reality" (2003, 178), identifies *Shabanu* as an example where the author has made "earnest effort to get inside a culture"—and the novel's opening does convey "a culturally specific sense of its reality," except that the scene is also generic.

A literary work might to a certain degree be accurate in depicting a segment of a certain society, but it takes a lot more to make it authentic. Weimin Mo and Wenju Shen, who explain the comparison between authenticity and accuracy and its significance in writing multicultural literature from an "insider" or "outsider" authorial perspective, argue that a work might be considered accurate but may lack authenticity:

> Authenticity is not just accuracy or the avoidance of stereotyping but involves cultural values and issues/practices that are accepted as norms of the social group. Although there is conceptual overlap, the various aspects of cultural accuracy do not constitute an appropriate definition for cultural authenticity. Strictly speaking, accuracy basically focuses on cultural facts instead of values. (2003, 200)

These distinctions have important implications for a consideration of the representation of subjectivity which may underpin the coming of age narrative in diverse cultures and periods. Elusive as it may be, there cannot be authenticity without authentic representations of subjectivity.

Because of a lack of resources, literature for children is almost nonexistent in Pakistan (Mughal, 2000), and hence there is a distinct lack of insider perspective on female subjectivity. Islam as a religion provides women with a lot of respect and power. Muslim women can hold their own property, be educated, make decisions for themselves and their families, and be their own person and have had this capacity since the inception of Islam. Muslim women throughout the world are speaking out about their right of choice in how they dress in particular and live their lives in general. We see more examples of educated, forward thinking women deciding to wear the *hijab* than ever before. A recent visit to Pakistan brought this to the fore when I saw a lot of women working in offices *and* wearing *hijab* in the Middle Eastern manner, something that my mother and I would probably never do. Pakistani Muslimas are articulating for themselves the parameters within which they locate their own sense of subjectivity and identity.

Notes

1. The title of the book stems from a saying by the Prophet Muhammad (PBUH) which affirms the significance of and respect for mothers by reiterating that paradise is beneath the Mother's feet. The saying is repeated at times within the novel, but mostly functions to question whether Nazia's mother, or other mothers depicted in the novel, merit such respect. The worst example is Parveen, who regards her ten-year-old son, Sherzad, as a mere economic resource and consigns him to virtual slavery.

Works Cited

Primary Texts

Antieau, Kim. *Broken Moon*. New York: McElderry Books, 2007.
Qamar, Amjed. *Beneath My Mother's Feet*. New York: Atheneum Books, 2008.
Staples, Suzanne Fisher. *Dangerous Skies*. New York: Farrar, Straus and Giroux, 1996.
Staples, Suzanne Fisher. *Shabanu: Daughter of the Wind*. New York: Random House, 1989.

Secondary Texts

Addison, Erin. "Saving Other Women from Other Men: Disney's *Aladdin*," *Camera Obscura* 11.1 [31] (1993): 4–25.
Aziz, Seemi. "Issues within Picturebooks Representing Pakistan and Afghanistan," *Childhood Education* 87.6 (2011): 444–445.
Badran, Margot. "Between Muslim Women and the Muslimwoman," *Journal of Feminist Studies in Religion* 24.1 (2008): 101–106.
Badran, Margot. "Between Secular and Islamic Feminism/s: Reflections on the Middle East and Beyond," *Journal of Middle East Women's Studies* 1.1 (2005): 6–28.
Bradford, Clare. "Representing Islam: Female Subjects in Suzanne Fisher Staples's Novels," *Children's Literature Association Quarterly* 32.1 (2007): 47–62.
Cai, Mingshui. "Can We Fly Across Cultural Gaps on Wings of Imagination? Ethnicity, Experience, and Cultural Authenticity." In *Stories Matter*, edited by Dana L. Fox and Kathy G. Short. Urbana, IL: National Council of Teachers of English, 2003.

Flanagan, Victoria. *Into the Closet: Cross-Dressing and the Gendered Body in Children's Literature and Film*. New York: Routledge, 2008.

Freeman, E., and B. Lehman. *Global Perspectives in Children's Literature*. Boston, MA: The Allyn & Bacon Press, 2001.

Hearne, Betsy. "A Review of *Shabanu: Daughter of the Wind*," *Bulletin of the Center for Children's Books* 43.2 (1989): 45.

Isaac, Megan Lynn. *Suzanne Fisher Staples: The Setting Is the Story*. Lanham, MD: Scarecrow Press, 2010.

McCallum, Robyn. *Ideologies of Identity in Adolescent Fiction*. New York: Garland Publishing, 1999.

Mahmood, Saba. "Feminist Theory, Embodiment, and the Docile Agent: Some Reflections on the Egyptian Islamic Revival," *Cultural Anthropology* 16.2 (2001): 202–236.

McDonald, Megan. "Review of *Shabanu: Daughter of the Wind*," *The Five Owls* 4.4 (1990): 63–64.

Mills, Sara. *Discourse*. London and New York: Routledge, 1997.

Mo, Weimin, and Wenju Shen. "Accuracy Is Not Enough: The Role of Cultural Values in the Authenticity of Picture Books." In *Stories Matter*, edited by Dana L. Fox and Kathy G. Short. Urbana, IL: National Council of Teachers of English, 2003.

Moallem, Minoo. "Muslim Women and the Politics of Representation," *Journal of Feminist Studies in Religion* 24.1 (2008): 106–110.

Mohanty, Chandra Talpade. "Under Western Eyes: Feminist Scholarship and Colonial Discourses." In *Dangerous Liaisons: Gender, Nation, and Postcolonial Perspectives*, edited by A. McClintock, A. Mufti, and E. Shohat. Minneapolis: University of Minnesota, 1997.

Mughal, R. "Five Decades of Children's Literature in Pakistan," *Bookbird* 38.4 (2000): 10–15.

Raina, Seemin A. "Critical Content Analysis of Postcolonial Texts." Diss., University of Arizona Press, 2009. ProQuest (3379604).

Said, Edward. *Covering Islam*. Library of Congress, 1981.

Said, Edward. *Culture and Imperialism*. Library of Congress, 1993.

Said, Edward. *Orientalism*. Library of Congress, 1978.

Sawyer, Walter E., and Jean C. Sawyer. "A Discussion with Suzanne Fisher Staples: The Author as Writer and Cultural Observer," *The New Advocate* 6.3 (1993): 159–169.

Sensoy, Özlem, and Elizabeth Marshall. "Save the Muslim Girl!," *Rethinking Schools* 24.2 (2009–2010). http://rethinkingschools.org/index.shtml. Accessed February 7, 2012.

Spivak, Gayatri Chakravorty. "Can the Subaltern Speak." In *Marxism and the Interpretation of Culture*, edited by C. Nelson and L. Grossberg. Basingstoke: Macmillan Education, 1988.

Staples, Suzanne Fisher. "Writing about the Islamic World: An American Author's Thoughts on Authenticity," *Bookbird* 35.3 (1997): 17–20.

Stephens, John. "Narratology." In *The Routledge Companion to Children's Literature*, edited by David Rudd. London: Routledge, 2010.

Watson, Jinx Stapleton. "Individual Choice and Family Loyalty: Suzanne Fisher Staples' Protagonists Come of Age," *ALAN Review* 27.1 (1999): 25–28.

Whitlock, Gillian. "The Skin of the Burqa: Recent Life Narratives from Afghanistan," *Biography* 28.1 (2005): 54–76.

http://chronicle.com/article/A-Fourth-Wave-Gathers-Strength/126302/.

Young, R. *Postcolonialism: A Very Short Introduction*. New York: Oxford University Press, 2003.

Zine, Jasmin. "Lost in Translation: Writing Back from the Margins," *Journal of Feminist Studies in Religion* 24.1 (2008): 110–116.

Zine, Jasmin, Lisa K. Taylor, and Hilary E. Davis. "Reading Muslim Women and Muslim Women Reading Back: Transnational Feminist Reading Practices, Pedagogy and Ethical Concerns," *Intercultural Education* 18.4 (2007): 271–280.

Chapter Four

Cooperation and Negotiation

Formation of Subjectivity in Japanese and Australian Picture Books

Miyuki Hisaoka

Children develop and are socialized according to the social conventions and cultural practices of the society they belong to, so it is inevitable that literary works produced for young audiences will represent explicitly or implicitly those conventions and practices, and be shaped by the ideologies of self and society which inform them. As a child's subjectivity unfolds over time, it will do so in participation with a cultural community (which is itself subject to flux and change), and hence whatever we might think of as "subjectivity" will take many forms. Sakai Naoki has pointed out that "one cannot perceive cultural difference unless as an already determinate object of description" (1997, 121), and this offers a cue to consider how notions about subjectivity can be discerned. According to James et al., a consideration of the dichotomy of identity and difference entails "a process of establishing identity-with and difference-from as a continuous issue of self and status definition and redefinition" (1998, 202). They argue that this distinction is more delicate than the earlier binary between self and other, which "depended on a strong sense of interiority and identity and postulated a locatedness and constancy for categorical systems that enabled the fixity of the other" (202). Identity-with and difference-from are pivotal concepts in children's picture books, and are discernible both within a particular culture and in comparison between cultures. In this chapter, I explore how subjectivity is represented in Japanese picture books and draw some comparisons with thematically parallel Australian picture books. Differing understandings of subjectivity can be observed in the representations of performativity and cooperation.

Barbara Rogoff argues that human development in a particular community is guided by local goals and can be understood only in the light of the cultural practices and circumstances of the community (2003, 3). The kinds of behavior and competences expected of children differ between communities depending on circumstances and traditions which includes the economic, educational, and political conditions of their society, family system and child care institutions, and the kinds of domestic responsibilities and routines. As an example, Rogoff raises the question of when children are trusted enough to take care of infants. Whereas middle-class U.S. families think only children of 10 years and up can take responsibility for younger siblings, many other communities around the world give that responsibility to 5- to 7-year-olds, or sometimes even to younger children. This difference is because those communities are organized by different social institutions. Children in the U.S. are segregated from adult society and put into educational institutions where children are divided by ages and given activities not directly contributing to the society. In contrast, those communities which give children the responsibility of taking care of infants often employ the system of letting children participate in adults' social activities, such as economic activities or everyday domestic tasks, by keeping children close to parents or adult groups. She concludes that children are largely shaped by how the community views "childhood" (23), although she also acknowledges the effects of rituals and traditional beliefs. The segregation of children from adult activities indicates that the community views childhood as preparation for life, and this is contrasted with the attitude of viewing children as participants in the community. Thus, child development is greatly influenced by a community's expectation for children, and the expectation is partly formed through everyday social practice.

Identity-with and difference-from can be explored by depicting children who move from one community to another, as in *Mahou no Natsu* (Magical Summer, 2002), by Fujiwara Kazue and Hata Koshiro. In this book, two latchkey children, left alone at home during the summer holidays, are invited to spend their time instead in a seaside town with their maternal grandmother and uncle. The boredom of city life is replaced by everyday rural adventures, and although the two boys quickly make friends, they lack the basic competencies for life in this community: they are physically unfit and lack coordination skills natural to the local children, such as the ability to climb trees. The community, however, is welcoming and embraces them, and they do develop new competencies: an ability to enjoy the natural world, to take a tram alone, to hold a sparkling firework (*senkou-hanabi*) more skillfully, and to catch fish. Their subjectivities shift as they participate in these new surroundings, even though shaped by a constant awareness of *difference-from*, until their stay is truncated by the younger child's fear of difference-from which surfaces in his unconscious as a nightmare: he is not yet ready to move so far beyond the *identity-with* domestic sphere. A subjective transformation is metonymically evident on their bodies, nevertheless, because they are now as tanned as the local children.

Mahou no Natsu is narrated by the older brother, but the illustrations indicate that he has been more adept at moving between social microsystems than his little brother has been. Roberta Berns (drawing on the work of Urie Bronfenbrenner) explains that a microsystem refers to a child's immediate setting, and has three dimensions: "physical space and materials; people in roles and relationships to the child; and activities that people engage in with and/or without each other" (2007, 11). Figure 4.1 demonstrates that the protagonist has become very successful in negotiating the space, roles, and activities of this microsystem, but the pictures also disclose that his brother is much less

Figure 4.1   Mahou no Natsu, page 26.
Source: Reproduced by courtesy of Iwasaki Publishing Company, Ltd. and Hata Koshiro.

successful: he does not wake with enthusiasm, he cannot spit a seed half as far (even from a greater height), and he is still physically inept. The *identity-with* connection between the protagonist's mock despair over his brother's dropped ice cream and the hilarity of one of their companions indicate that the brother is a subject characterized by *difference-from* and is not yet ready for a change of microsystems. Berns also argues that through structures such as microsystems, children and society interact and shape each other. Such intersubjective effects are not inevitable, however, and in this example only, the older child responds to the challenge of the new by having an effect upon it: he is first to wake in the morning and is a winner of small prizes.

Because the microsystems, which consist of family, peers, school, community, and media, are the main agencies which directly interact with children's everyday lives, their influence on developing children is significant, as they inculcate children with the norms, beliefs, and conventions of the society they belong to. Children learn what is desirable behavior in their particular society by observing the behavior of others as a model, as consistently happens in *Mahou no Natsu*, or by receiving positive or negative reinforcement from others in the microsystem. This picture book thus reproduces a relationship between subjectivity and society as envisaged by Berns: children develop as they interact with the society, and the cultural practice of the society they belong to shapes their behavior to a greater or lesser degree (see also Rogoff, 2003 and James et al. 1998).

The two brothers in *Mahou no Natsu* can be understood as contrasting examples of how society shapes children's behavior, and thence their subjectivity, although the underlying principle is the Japanese belief that children cannot become fully independent as long as they can depend on family. Children need to learn how to negotiate with the world at an early stage of life, although a very young child may not at first succeed. To show how representations in picture books reflect the relationship between the developing individual and society, I now turn to the notion of "performativity" as articulated by Judith Butler.

Performativity

Butler, in applying J. L. Austin's account of linguistic performativity to gender theory, argued that gender is determined by repeated acts which reiterate social conventions or the habitual practices of a culture. Such conventions and practices precede the individual who reiterates them and function to shape that individual into a gendered self through performative action:

> [Performativity] consists in a reiteration of norms which precede, constrain, and exceed the performer and in that sense cannot be taken as the fabrication of the performer's "will" or "choice." (Butler, 1993: 234)

In this account, subjectivity is from the outset a state of subjection, although Butler does admit the possibility that subjectivity, as an *effect* that is *produced* or *generated* by social conventions, can be challenged and changed through the accumulation of alternative performative acts because of its constructedness (Butler, 1990: 147). There is thus a space for agency, as later commentators have argued. Kerry Mallan, for example, contends that, "For Butler, agency is located in the way that variations of action, and the possibility of variation in repetition, carry meaning and create identity" (2002, 27). Butler also shows a propensity to rethink the self-other binary along the lines of the *identity-with* and *difference-from* formulation, such that Kathy Dow Magnus argues that, by 2002, Butler has moved away from interpreting the "Other" as a mere danger to subjectivity to a position which assumes that subjective agency requires the support of intersubjective relations (2006, 100).

Children's fiction, as John Stephens argues (2006), highlights how performativity is a social construction. Readers are aware that the characters act out assigned roles in a fictional world and actualize and reproduce social norms familiar in both everyday social interactions and in the conventions of narrative and visual illustration. In Figure 4.1, for example, the protagonist's inner feelings are made ostensibly visible by, respectively, his manic grin, his insouciant posture, and his melodramatic gesture. The represented body here becomes an iconic system, so that the process, whereby a character's subjectivity is constructed through the reiteration of cultural conventions, is thus articulated for readers; although in the actual world, subjects tend to be unconscious of reiterating and being shaped by social practice and ideology. Stephens examines the extreme case of a created machine which enacts humanity as a performative: it takes the role of a character in a narrative, and thus "is constructed in accordance with, and so plays out, recognizable performatives" (Stephens, 2006: 5). This tactic is significant because "it enables a redescription of norms and reinstates possibilities for agency and resistance" (5). Taking this process a step further, I argue that the notion of performativity discloses implicit similarities and differences in the representation of cooperative performances in picture books from two different cultures, Japan and Australia.

Cooperation and Its Representation in Picture Books

The represented body is a site in which subjectivity is imagined, and because this normally occurs in a relationship with an other, it may potentially follow either of two procedures: it may fix the other or subjectivity may be negotiated by and through the other, which is the preferred option in Japanese picture books and depicted therein as a desirable outcome. The third picture in Figure 4.1 enacts a failure of social and personal cooperation, which might enable such a negotiation. Although he is positioned between the two older boys, the distressed youngest child is isolated and unsupported. Michael Argyle suggests that human behavior can be cooperative, competitive, individualistic, or altruistic—the first and last of these are absent from these scenes (1991). If subjectivity emerges from intersubjective relations, then it presupposes that the most felicitous mode of behavior will be cooperation. Argyle offers a working definition of cooperation as, "acting together, in a coordinated way at work, leisure, or in social relationships, in the pursuit of shared goals, the enjoyment of the joint activity, or simply furthering the relationship" (4). Alfie Kohn positions cooperation as the opposite of human competition, and argues that, "Cooperation is an essentially humanizing experience [that] . . . transcends egocentric and objectifying postures, encourages trust, sensitivity, open communication, and, ultimately, prosocial activity" (Kohn, 1990: 93).

At the core of cooperation is the principle that two or more individuals work together and assist one another to achieve a common goal, which may be material or social (Dovidio et al., 2006: 270). Dovidio et al. extend the argument to participants' nonhierarchical relationships in cooperation, in contrast with other types of helping in which the helper might have greater power over the helped: "cooperation represents a *bidirectional* social interaction of supposed 'equals' who understand the benefits of pursuing the best *joint outcomes* for all, and thus coordinate their efforts and actions" (270). For such equal relationships, they emphasize that cooperation tends to generate greater group cohesiveness and more positive interpersonal relations (28).

Such definitions are derived from observation of adult behavior, however, and need to be modified when discussing cooperation represented in picture books, for three main reasons. First, children's range of activity is limited within particular microsystems, such as family, peers, immediate community, and schools. In most cases, children are allowed to act only within the borders set by adults or social institutions, and it is practically difficult to involve more than just two actors to represent a sustained effort or to contribute to the alleviation of a structural problem in society. Nevertheless, as the signifying representation of small-scale actions is transformed into a discursive communication, it may be perceived as metonymic of a greater social issue, which brings me to the second modification. As argued in the introduction to this collection, fictive actions are broadly isomorphic with actions in the actual world of readers, but at the same time, narratives employ various strategies such as narrator's voice, point of view, and character focalization to prompt readers to assume particular preferred subject positions (Stephens, 1992). Information about the represented fictional world is limited to what is essential for plot, and the number of characters, their background, and interpersonal relationships are organized schematically. Thus, actions in narratives are isomorphic with actions in the actual world as a metonymy, rather than as a photographic representation, as cooperative actions familiar in the actual world are transformed into simplified representations. An example of cooperative behavior with collective participants can be narrativized as a story between two friends; an action which helps alleviate an actual social problem can be transformed to problem solving within a microsystem; or a sustained effort of working together can be represented as a one-day story.

The third point is that picture books depict and target inexperienced children and are normally expected to intensively represent the most fundamental social values in a culture. In stories in which children are not accompanied by adults, subjectivity formation is expressed through situations which portray children in a developmental trajectory from the state of solipsism in which one is unable to distinguish self from the other to an intersubjective state in which one acquires the agency to negotiate with others or society. A simple example is *Asae to Chiisai Imouto* (Asae and Her Little Sister, 1982; English translation as *Anna in Charge*, 1988), by Tsutsui Yoriko and Hayashi Akiko, in which Asae (as Anna in the 1988 translation), a preschool child, is left to look after her toddler sister (as Katy in the 1988 translation). While Anna is concentrating on drawing a railway track as a site for play, her sister wanders away and Anna must find her. A sequence of high angle views emphasizes Anna's misplaced attention in acting hierarchically as "helper" rather than "sharer," whereas her search is depicted mostly from a low angle to communicate her feeling of helplessness. The events are a test of Anna's competence at recouping the situation and dealing with her fears for Katy's safety, but importantly no recriminations are expressed. The English text concludes:

> Anna ran towards Katy.
> When Katy spotted her she called Anna's name and waved a sandy hand at her sister.
> Anna gave Katy a big hug.
> "You gave me such a scare," she said. (30–31)

The time frame of the book occupies perhaps less than half an hour, but there is an implication that during that time Anna has grown through her brief encounters with a busy road, an unknown child, and a parent scolding another toddler. Although the final wordless illustration of the hug shows the girls' mother in the distant background arriving to collect them, the point is that Anna has proved her competence and, in doing so, her love for her sister and her own emerging subjective agency have been strengthened.

Hayashi Akiko developed the concept of intersubjective cooperation more fully in *Kon to Aki* (1989; henceforth referred to by its English title, *Amy and Ken Visit Grandma*; 2003). This book reflects a clear assumption that a very young child can become mentally and practically independent and learn to negotiate with the world. How it envisages this process can be contrasted with an Australian picture book about gaining competence, *Henry and Amy* (1998), by Stephen Michael King, a story of cooperation between opposites to make a richer world. *Amy and Ken Visit Grandma* models a close intersubjective relationship through the story of a small girl and a stuffed toy fox that was made by her grandmother and has been her companion since birth. When Ken suffers a split seam on his arm, the two set out to visit Grandma for repairs. Ken elects himself as guide and protector, roles he performs with borderline competence, until they venture into the sand dunes near Grandma's house where Ken is snatched away, mauled, and buried by a passing dog. Now it is Amy's turn to take charge, and she retrieves Ken and piggybacks him to Grandma, where he is repaired and compelled to share a bath with Amy and Grandma. Like folktale foxes in Japanese tradition, Ken is an ambiguous figure that occupies a liminal space between existences: he is a toy, a projection of Amy's imagination which gives her confidence to act, and a sentient being who talks and understands railway procedures and culture. To a large extent, he is an embodiment of Amy's subjectivity—the practical agent, or what Sakai refers to as *shutai* (the *body of enunciation*; 1997, 120)—but his ambiguity also points to a subjectivity that is intensely intersubjective and encompasses the train conductor and Grandma, the discreetly cooperative adults who watch out for Ken and Amy.

Where Ken's ambiguous status serves to resist binary oppositions such as inside/outside, leader/led, and competent/incompetent, *Henry and Amy* pivots on an opposition between Henry's inability to inhabit his world in a competent way and Amy's relentless competence. By reconstructing the opposition as one between imagination and logic, or irrationality and rationality, as embodied by Henry and Amy respectively, and suggesting that a complete human being combines both polarities, King plays with some clichés about Australian attitudes to emotion and feeling. Conventional assumptions about female emotion and male logic are inverted, so that Amy demonstrates the flatness of feeling attributed to Australian males, whereas Henry embodies "female" irrationality. In linking the two children in cooperative play whereby they work together toward a shared goal, share enjoyment in their cooperation, and acquire one another's qualities, *Henry and Amy* projects a notion of subjectivity grounded in individual difference that transcends sociohistorical assumptions about reason, emotion, and subjectivity and deftly mediates *difference-from* and *identity-with*.

Preoccupation with social roles within a family structure can be prominently foregrounded in situations which represent a child experiencing subjective confusion at the birth of younger siblings. Rather than being the object of overt compensatory affection, the older, "displaced" child meets an expectation that she or he will deal with change by developing increased personal competence. Both in Japanese picture books, such as *Chottodake* (A Little Bit; 2007), by Takimura Yuko and Suzuki Nagako, and Australian picture books, such as *Cuthbert's Babies* (2003), by Pamela Allen, or *A Bit of Company* (1991), by Margaret Wild and Wayne Harris, the protagonist is eventually rewarded with the affection desired, but structurally the outcome is arrived at in subtly different ways. In the Australian books, the protagonist must develop mental independence by seeking outside relationships (even when imaginary, as in *Cuthbert's*

Babies), and his increased autonomy and pursuit of a self-oriented goal accords with understandings of Western subjectivity (cf., Lu and Gilmour, 2006: 46). In *Chottodake*, in contrast, Nacchan cultivates "a little bit" of practical independence in such areas as pouring milk, changing into her pajamas, or taking

Figure 4.2   Chottodake (A Little Bit), page 5.
Source: Reproduced by courtesy of Fukuinkan Shoten Publishers, Inc. and Suzuki Nagako.

herself off to play in the park—that is, her actions are based on an unarticulated social pressure that she is expected to act as a big girl, and she begins to accomplish what Japanese parents generally expect of their children. On the other hand, an emphasis on the limited scope of her achievements, together with a constant mental orientation toward her mother and her role as an older sister, reflects the grounding of Japanese subjectivity in awareness of social roles. The delicate complexity of the social bond is evident in an early scene when Nacchan walks with the mother to the shops (see Figure 4.2). Unable to hold her mother's hand, she walks with an expression of assured composure while holding "a little bit" of her mother's dress. The isomorphic reflection of mother and daughter emphasizes on the one hand Nacchan's identity-with positionality in that she models herself on her mother, and on the other the different foci of preoccupation (mother with baby, Nacchan with her own sense of competence). The physical connectedness figures an emotional connectedness that underpins all of the child's small gestures of self-sufficiency.

Chottodake concludes with a strong affirmation of mother–daughter affection when, sleepy after taking herself to the park, Nacchan asks, "Mom, will you hug me 'a little bit'" (2007, 24; my translation). The conversation continues:

"A little bit?" Mom asked.
"Yes, 'a little bit' will do . . ." Nacchan answered, rubbing her sleepy eyes.
"I'd rather hug you more than 'a little bit.' I want to hug you a lot." Mom smiled and went on, "May I hug you a lot?" (26–27; my translation)

Cuthbert's Babies arrives at an analogous conclusion, with Cuthbert and his mother lying on his bed reading a book together in a reprise of the opening page when the mother had hinted that a baby was on the way and Cuthbert immediately rejected the idea. His reaction is a strong contrast to the simple social process that begins Chottodake, whereby the birth of the baby resituates Nacchan as "a big girl." Cuthbert's Babies (like the earlier A Bit of Company) employs comic exaggeration in the story (there are four babies, not one) and in the overstated cartoon images, such that readers can align with Cuthbert's feeling of alienation without particularly empathizing with him, whereas Chottodake promotes intense empathy. This difference of effect is again arguably a reflection of a difference between autonomous/individualistic and socially embedded subjectivities. Nacchan is always discreetly cooperative, whereas Cuthbert rejoins the family unit by suddenly bonding with the babies on the book's penultimate opening.

I conclude this chapter with an extended discussion of the representation of the cooperative nature of friendship and the concomitant negotiation of subjectivity by and through the other in Tomodachi-ya (1998), by Uchida Rintaro and Furiya Nana, and draw some comparisons with another of Stephen King's picture books, Milli, Jack and the Dancing Cat (2003). Like

Chottodake, *Tomodachi-ya* works with several of the main elements identified as key components of cooperation: (1) two or more participants, (2) interdependent and equal relationships, (3) shared goals, (4) coordination of action, and (5) an expectation that the outcome will be a mutual benefit. Components two through five, however, are now initially marked as corrupted or unrealized because of the protagonist's impaired subjectivity and false sense of intersubjective relationships. A Japanese audience is acutely conscious of these failings and will approve the way that *Tomodachi-ya* illustrates personal development through the establishment of intersubjective friendship.

Tomodachi-ya is the story of a fox, named Fox, who wants a friend but is too afraid to pursue friendship because of a fear of rejection. To deal with his problem, Fox starts up a business occupation, "tomodachi-ya," which involves being paid by the hour in return for acting as someone's part-time friend. The folly of such a scheme is disclosed as he experiences a succession of failures. He is first scolded by a quail mother for being too loud and then becomes ill when he works as a bear's friend and eats food unsuitable for foxes. Finally Fox becomes a friend of a wolf. When he asks for payment for playing the role of friend, the wolf gets furious because Fox seeks to turn friendship into money. Fox realizes that he is treated as a real friend by the wolf and happily goes back home with the promise of meeting again the next day.

The book's irony is immediately evident from its title. *Tomodachi* means "friend(s)," and *ya* is an affix marking an occupation, or what one does (it is comparable to the English affix–*er*, as in "singer" or "writer"). Characteristically, *ya* is a colloquial word that imparts an atmosphere of informality to the occupation, or even implies unprofessional-ness. Because "something + ya" is often used by children in role play, this title is recognizable by young children. However *tomodachi-ya* does not exist in the actual world, or even in the Japanese language. But the reader may be confused by this title, because *tomodachi* ("friend") belongs to a formal register and is always related to morality, whereas "ya" is casual and always related to business and money. This confusing title induces readers to perceive the paradox and look for its significance.

Besides its play with a socially valued term in the title, the book often overturns expectations shaped by cultural conventions. A bear, conventionally connoting roughness and masculinity, is depicted in the illustrations as more of a soft male, who wears a floral patterned shirt and decorates his home with flowers, stuffed toys, and a music box, whereas in the text he performs conventional masculinity by calling himself *ore* (a coarse Japanese word only used of themselves by men) and by talking to Fox in an overbearing manner. This gap between the text and the pictures can be interpreted as humor, but also as the deflation of a larger, physically dominant figure. Later, a wolf, which signifies violence in conventional narratives and folktales, is depicted as a gentle, sophisticated character who enjoys wine, cards, and fashionable cars. Those playful tones interrogating the dominant culture have a carnivalesque function, which, as Peter Stallybrass and Allon White explain, depicts a world "of topsy-turvy, of heteroglot exuberance, of ceaseless overrunning and excess where all is mixed, hybrid, ritually degraded and defiled" (1986, 8). Bakhtin finds an analogy between "carnival" as a pop culture which possibly overturns the existing social hierarchy and a narrative strategy which, by employing humor and chaos, interrogates the social hierarchy or the canonization of literature (1984).

Carnival in children's literature, as Stephens shows (1992, 121–57), is playful, expressing opposition to authoritarianism and seriousness, such as parents, teachers, and political and religious institutions. It challenges adult authorities by breaking social norms, with the use of taboo language, overturning of social hierarchy, or making fun of conventional social manners, and so offers "time out" from the habitual constrains of society. An interrogative text often employs a clown or fool for its protagonist which blurs the border between the "ideality" shaped by a dominant ideology and the "reality" of the world. This technique enables readers to be self-conscious in seeing social values from a new point of view, and thus subject positions offered readers discourage simple alignment with the subject position of main characters and offer instead shifting positions among "empathy, delight, superiority, criticism, outrage, revulsion" (124). As a result, this narrative strategy situates the reader "as subject firmly outside the text" (125). Such is the case with *Tomodachi-ya*, where the technique is linked with narrative framing and point of view.

Although the text has an omniscient narrator, it also employs a double structure. An old owl, focalizing only at the beginning and ending, is given a role of observer of the main story in which Fox is focalized. This change of focalization controls readers' subject position. The story ends as follows:

> "Well, well . . ."
> The old owl, who had been listening carefully, nodded.
> It seems that the one in the forest who had most craved company was able to make a friend. (1998, 32; my translation)

This conclusion discloses Fox's true-self which has been hidden by his pretence that he does not need friends. If focalization were always aligned with Fox throughout the story, the last sentence would sound more intrusive because it would work as a decisive comment about Fox's character. By inserting another focalizing character between the narrator and Fox, the narrator's voice is covered by the owl's voice and sounds less intrusive.

Like *Tomodachi-ya*, *Milli, Jack and the Dancing Cat* envisages subjectivity as an issue of identity-with and difference-from and also depicts friendship as transformative, but where *Tomodachi-ya* disparages eccentric difference-from, *Milli, Jack and the Dancing Cat* valorizes it as a higher form of subjectivity. The latter opens with a depiction of Milli as artistic and creative, but isolated within her community. Although she "could take a thing that was

Figure 4.3   Milli, Jack and the Dancing Cat.
Source: Reproduced by courtesy of Allen & Unwin. Copyright©text and illustrations, Stephen Michael King 2003.

nothing . . . and make it . . . a something!," her community had no interest in her talent or its products, but wanted only "ordinary practical, familiar things." They had no time "for anything that was a little different." Where the Japanese text favors identity-with as a source of subjectivity, the Australian favors different-from. Milli's subjectivity is liberated by the arrival of Jack and the Cat, two vagabond minstrels, and together with them, she finds that difference-from can be empowering, even when it is difference-from in different ways. Jack and the Cat eventually move on, enriched by Milli's inventiveness with fantastic musical instruments and colorful new clothes: intersubjectivity is transformative, but it is the individual subjectivity which is transformed. Where Fox in *Tomodahi-ya* is drawn back from outrageousness to identity-with, Milli transforms her shop with strange, impractical sculptures, which even the benighted townspeople stop to gaze at (see Figure 4.3); where Fox will visit Wolf every day, Jack and the Cat, who "still had faraway places to explore" will dance into town whenever they are passing.

Milli's situation in the book's opening is marked by a sense of lack because she is creative. In contrast, Fox's bizarre creativeness comes about because he is lonely. An audience quickly aligns with Milli, initially because inventiveness and the ability to make things is a positive quality. As remarked earlier, audiences are distanced from Fox by narrative framing, but also by his strange appearance and distasteful occupation:

> "Well, here comes 'tomodachi-ya.'
>   Don't you want a friend?
>   Isn't there anybody feeling lonely?

One hundred yen for being a friend for an hour.

Two hundred yen for being a friend for two hours." (1998, 2; my translation)

Fox declares he converts friendship into money, which is normally considered to be an unethical deed or a challenge to social values. This playful use of language and subversion of conventions are the traits of carnivalesque. Also, the unusual clothing affected by Fox indicates that he is given a role of a fool, which is another carnivalesque element. He wears a helmet with an attached flag, itself an old Japanese signboard, on which "tomodachi-ya" is drawn in large characters. A life buoy, goggles, and paper lanterns are not harmonious with each other nor suitable to the situation, and some ornaments sticking out from the helmet are Japanese festival decorations. Most of these obtrusive accoutrements are discarded when Fox has found a true friend in the end, which indicates that he had disguised himself for fear of being vulnerable to the trauma of rejection by others. In his pretence, if he failed to make friends, his temporal, false subjectivity might be damaged, but his true-self behind it would not have been exposed to serious harm. Disguise is his armament for protecting his anthropophobic true-self and for hiding his anxiety about being unaccepted.

According to Stephens, disguise is a common element of carnival and can be a form of "time out" because disguise makes a character take on "a different, temporary role or identity which is put off again at the end of the episode" (1992, 133). Even though he has appeared in disguise since the beginning of the text, Fox's disguise can be interpreted as a form of "time out" despite the fact that he has disguised himself. This is because it is naturally assumed that he does not wear those showy materials when he is alone. His disguise as "tomodachi-ya" might be a "time out" for a quest to overcome his anxiety about making friends, and the quest's accomplishment recalls him to the "reality" where disguise is not needed.

Shifts in reader subject position play an important role in bringing out the significance of this story. At first, implied readers will not align with Fox, because of his imaginary work interrogating social values and his eccentric disguise and because a fox connotes slyness, cunningness, and deceitfulness in Japan. The connotation derives from the Japanese folktale belief that foxes deceive people by taking the form of others (see examples in Tyler, 2002). These narrative strategies evoke negative assumptions about the protagonist and distance readers from him. At this first stage, then, Fox's evident lack of trustworthiness induces readers to reconfirm the fundamental moral that real friends cannot be obtained with money.

Even though Fox appears to be playing on social values at first, his behavior actually respects Japanese social conventions. When he repeats his words of advertisement, he is asked to be quiet by a quail mother and then to speak louder by a bear, and becomes confused by these contrary requests. As an expression of friendliness, the bear serves Fox the bear's favorite sweet meals and encourages Fox to address him in the intimate mode, "Bear," not "Mr. Bear." Fox eats the food, which makes him feel sick, forces himself to smile, and says, "Yes, it's delicious" (1998, 12; my translation). As a result, Fox received two hundred yen and left clutching his aching stomach. At this moment, Fox is entirely subjected to others' intentions, because conforming is the only way he knows to be socially cooperative.

This repetitive conformity might represent Japanese anxiety about self-other relationships. Heine et al. argue that Japanese people, whose culture is shaped by Confucian values, tend to emphasize one's roles within a hierarchy and to live up to the standards associated with these roles, in order to contribute to and secure connection with their relevant groups.

> An acute awareness of information indicating transgressions from the standards of performance associated with their roles aids individuals by highlighting the areas in which they need to make efforts to reduce the perceived discrepancies. Such efforts to more closely approximate the shared standards of performance enable Japanese to affirm their connection with the social unit that maintains this standard. (2001, 435)

Japanese preoccupation to become socially cooperative by contributing to the social unit is explained above. Moreover, Rogoff (drawing upon Lebra) suggests that "Japanese mothers emphasize letting their small children grow up naturally . . . It is commonly believed that, with development, obstreperous conduct will disappear. Through the mother's empathy toward the child and encouragement of the child's empathy toward her own and others' feelings, with time the child brings his or her conduct in line with cultural norms" (2003, 166). Such an emphasis, however, tends to impose a group pressure on individuals that makes people value conformity, with the side effect that Japanese people are conspicuously anxious about other people's evaluations to such a degree that this anxiety can be considered as a national trait.

In the light of this trait, Fox's disguise can be interpreted as a protection from the Japanese anxiety at being evaluated by others, and his repetitive obedience to others as the Japanese tendency of conformity. In other words, Fox, as a fool, self-critically represents performative Japanese interpersonal concerns. Following his experience with Bear, exhaustion is conveyed through his facial expression, stooping posture, shriveled lanterns, withered properties, and a threatening background. The plot suggestion that Fox becomes worn out by interpersonal relationships makes Japanese readers self-conscious about their own performativity of excessively conforming to others. Although readers have not aligned with Fox as a character, reader subject position now vacillates when Fox is perceived to be mentally and physically worn out. When Fox repeats the same words of his advertisement at the beginning of the text, readers might no longer be cautious of Fox's unreliability and are guided to feel sympathy toward him, or even empathy, if they are self-conscious of their own conformity as performativity.

Then Fox is called by a wolf to play cards. The wolf dismantles Fox's armament toward the end, and takes on a significant role in the story. From the first encounter, the wolf calls Fox "Fox," and Fox, without noticing it, throws away his lanterns when he first sees the wolf. Fox, having devoted himself to obeying others, for the first time risks displeasing an other by winning a card game. His helmet thrown away shows that Fox is not in disguise anymore but is completely absorbed in playing. When he asks for money, however, the wolf gets furious and says "MONEY? . . . Are you taking money from a friend? Is that what you think a true friend does?" (1998, 24–25; my translation). The wolf is depicted from a low angle in extreme close-up, and because this is the only opening within the book in which Fox does not appear, readers are positioned to share Fox's point of view. At this moment, readers' entire alignment with Fox is expected.

The ongoing text reveals a conservative moral message in a form of conversation between two protagonists.

> "T . . . True Friend?"
> Fox blinks his eyes.
> "Yes, true friend. I didn't call to such a thing like 'Tomodachi-ya.'"
> In fact, the wolf called to him "Hey, Fox."
> "Then, can I come tomorrow, too?"
> Fox asked as he softly withdrew his hands.
> "The day after tomorrow, too, Fox." (27; my translation)

Readers, having now aligned with Fox, share Fox's pleasure in receiving an unqualified acceptance by others. The flag and festival ornament on Fox's helmet are broken in this scene, which indicates that Fox's quest, or "time out" in disguise, to make a friend is almost fulfilled. The next opening, the climax of Fox's happiness (see Figure 4.4), presents examples of carnivalesque such as the feast and gentle anthropomorphosis of the wolf, with stylish clothes and childish toys like a bat, cap, soccer ball, fancily patterned life buoy, and minicar, which is the wolf's most important treasure (28–29). The meaning and value of the minicar as a token of friendship can be easily recognized by children because they know well how hard it is to give an important toy to others. The two characters are surrounded by a round frame and the dark–light contrast functions as a spotlight. Importance of friendship is reconfirmed with this positive outcome, not in didactic tone, but in a satisfactory atmosphere after accomplishing one's quest.

In the final opening, Fox throws away his disguise, smiling, looking up, and skipping. Previously, large obstacles have hindered Fox's movement from left to right, but now the path that stretches to the horizon before him is free of obstacles, which represents Fox's carefree mind. The words of his advertisement have also changed:

Figure 4.4 Friendship gesture in *Tomodachi-ya*, page 28–29.
Source: Reproduced by courtesy of Kaisei-sha Publishing Company and Furiya Nana.

> Well, don't you want a friend?
>   Isn't there anybody feeling lonely?
>   It's free, all day no matter how long.
>   It's free, all week even if it is every day. (31; my translation)

The plot's moral message emphasizing the importance of friendship is conservative, and its positive ending is conventional as a narrative pattern. But, this carnivalesque story also makes readers self-conscious about Japanese unique interpersonal anxiety and its implications for subjectivity. Fox represents that one cannot have a true friend in pretence and conformity, which is an interrogation of the Japanese performative of being excessively anxious about interpersonal relationships.

Child subjectivity in Australian culture tends to be formed through attempts to act for the pursuit of individuals' goals, in a society where various intentions collide. Children are expected to recognize their own differences from other individuals by contrasting self and other, and are expected to be a cooperative member of a society by acquiring autonomy to make the most of one's individual-ness. This emphasis on individuality can be explained by Lebra's notion of Western self as the opposition of others (2004). On the other hand, Japanese subjectivity tends to be formed in wider society through the child's early joining into social practices. There Japanese children tend to strive for performing more practical roles expected by society and to pursue the assimilation of themselves into society.

Works Cited

Primary Texts

Allen, Pamela. *Cuthbert's Babies*. Camberwell, Australia: Viking, 2003.
Fujiwara, Kazue, and Hata Koshiro . *Mahou no Natsu* (Magical Summer). Tokyo: Iwasaki Publishing, 2002.
Hayashi, Akiko. *Kon to Aki*. Tokyo: Fukuinkan Shoten Publishers, 1989; *Amy and Ken Visit Grandma* (English translation). Tokyo: RIC Publications, 2003.
King, Stephen Michael. *Henry and Amy*. Sydney: Scholastic Press, 1998.
King, Stephen Michael. *Milli, Jack and the Dancing Cat*. Crows Nest, Australia: Allen & Unwin, 2003.
Takimura, Yuko, and Suzuki Nagako (illustrator). *Chottodake* (A Little Bit . . .). Tokyo: Fukuinkan Shoten Publishers, 2007.
Tsutsui, Yoriko, and Akiko Hayashi (illustrator). *Asae to Chiisai Imouto* (Asae and Her Little Sister). Tokyo: Fukuinkan Shoten, 1982; *Anna in Charge* (English translation). London: Penguin, 1988; *Finding Little Sister* (English translation). Tokyo: RIC Publications, 2006.
Tyler, Royall. *Japanese Tales* (1987). New York: Knopf Doubleday Publishing Group, 2002.
Uchida, Rintaro, and Furiya Nana (illustrator). *Tomodachi-ya*. Tokyo: Kaiseisha, 1998.
Wild, Margaret, and Wayne Harris. *A Bit of Company*. Sydney: Ashton Scholastic, 1991.

Secondary Texts

Argyle, Michael. *Cooperation, the Basis of Sociability*. New York: Taylor & Francis, 1991.
Bakhtin, Mikhail. *Rabelais and His World*, translated by Helene Iswolsky. Bloomington: Indiana University Press, 1984.
Berns, Roberta. *Child, Family, School, Community: Socialization and Support*. 7th ed. Belmont, CA: Thomson/Wadsworth, 2007.
Butler, Judith. *Bodies That Matter: On the Discursive Limits of "Sex."* New York: Routledge, 1993.
Butler, Judith. *Gender Trouble: Feminism and the Subversion of Identity*. London: Routledge, 1990.
Butler, Judith. *Kritik der ethischen Gewalt*. Adorno Lectures, 2002. Frankfurt am Main: Institut für Sozialforschung an der Johann Wolfgang Goethe-Universität, 2003.
Dovidio, John F., Jane Allyn Piliavin, David A. Schroeder, and Louis A. Penner. *The Social Psychology of Prosocial Behavior*. New York: Psychology Press, 2006.
Heine, Steven J., Shinobu Kitayama, and Darrin R. Lehman. "Cultural Differences in Self-Evaluation: Japanese Readily Accept Negative Self-Relevant Information," *Journal of Cross-Cultural Psychology* 32 (2001): 434–443.
James, Allison, Chris Jenks, and Alan Prout. *Theorizing Childhood*. Oxford: Polity Press, 1998.

Kohn, Alfie. *The Brighter Side of Human Nature: Altruism and Empathy in Everyday Life*. New York: Basic Books, 1990.

Lebra, Takie Sugiyama. *The Japanese Self in Cultural Logic*. Honolulu: University of Hawaii Press, 2004.

Lu, Luo, and Robin Gilmour. "Individual-Oriented and Socially Oriented Cultural Conceptions of Subjective Well-Being: Conceptual Analysis and Scale Development," *Asian Journal of Social Psychology* 9 (2006): 36–49.

Magnus, Kathy Dow. "The Unaccountable Subject: Judith Butler and the Social Conditions of Intersubjective Agency," *Hypatia* 21.2 (2006): 81–103.

Mallan, Kerry. "Picture Books as Performative Texts: Or How to Do Things with Words and Pictures," *Papers: Explorations into Children's Literature* 12.2 (2002): 26–37.

Rogoff, Barbara. *The Cultural Nature of Human Development*. Oxford: Oxford University Press, 2003.

Sakai, Naoki. *Translation and Subjectivity*. Minneapolis: University of Minnesota Press, 1997.

Stallybrass, Peter, and Allon White. *The Politics and Poetics of Transgression*. Ithaca, NY: Cornell University Press, 1986.

Stephens, John. *Language and Ideology in Children's Fiction*. London: Longman, 1992.

Stephens, John. "Performativity and the Child Who May Not Be a Child," *Papers: Explorations into Children's Literature* 16.1 (2006): 5–13.

Chapter Five
Subjectivity and Culture Consciousness in Chinese Children's Literature

Lifang Li

A historical turning point in perceptions of the character of childhood subjectivity in Chinese children's literature occurred in the early twentieth century with the emergence of a modern children's literature. Because of specific Chinese historical and cultural traditions and the complicated progress of Chinese society during the twentieth century, subjectivities in children's literature, generally represented as aspirations for various kinds of selfhood, involve several levels of complex historical and cultural connotations and are inextricably tied up with ideas about country, nation, society, intellectual concepts of social reform, and children's agency. The subjectivity of children is sometimes more, sometimes less, implicit in a complex of connections which functions as the spiritual core of modern Chinese children's literature. There has been a further gradual development in conceptualizing the subjectivity of children since the early 1980s, but it still has distinctive local cultural characteristics. This chapter outlines the historical processes which have shaped the evolution of subjectivity in the hundred years of modern Chinese children's literature and its main significances. From the time that intellectuals in the beginning of the twentieth century began to envisage a profound connection between social reform and childhood subjectivity, children's literature has been, as Mary Farquhar puts it, "about great dreams of a future China" (1999, 305), about "recreating the nation, with a more egalitarian society and a stronger international position" (306).

"Childhood Imagination" in the Early Twentieth Century

Although people have always attached great importance to children's education in China, in feudal society this was mostly concerned with enculturation into the moral attitudes which were the foundation of Confucian society. Under such weight of tradition, there was no space for the development of an imaginative or aesthetically pleasing children's literature. Beginning in the late nineteenth century, under the influence of contemporary Western views of children, the issue of Chinese children's subjectivity gradually came into being and became highlighted especially around the May Fourth Movement of 1919. Thus elite intellectuals such as Lu Xun (1881–1936) embraced a conception of childhood that attributed it with its own special qualities, and thence a conscious form of modern children's literature began to appear. The idea that childhood and education should be "child-based" and "child-centered" started to influence the advocates of that time.

As the product of the New Culture Movement (Xīn Wénhuà Yùndòng), which flourished from about 1915 to the late 1920s, the concepts of "discovered childhood" (Farquhar, 1999: 13) and "the cultivation of children's literature" were endowed with great value. The two did not exist in isolation, but their specific or symbolic meanings were explored in the wider concepts of individual, humanity, nation, country, and other dimensions. The place of "the child" within the specific history and reality of China was thus imbricated with the values espoused by the Movement, especially recognition of vernacular literature, development of Western scientific method, and democratic and egalitarian values, including a transformation in the status of women and a focus on the future rather than the past. The concepts of a specific "childhood imagination" (and by implication a new form of subjectivity grounded in imagination, creativity, and agency) and a literature to address that imagination were thus embedded within a fertile context.

This particular childhood imagination is initially based on the primary horizons of "human being" and "citizen," and then draws on the physical and mental characteristics of childhood as a period that starts from the beginning of life. It is a way of experiencing existence, which not only is distinct from adult experiences but also plays a key role in the development of a healthy life and a sound personality.

By extension, however, the subjects of the "childhood imagination" are also the intellectuals of Chinese society in which transformation from traditional mode to modern mode is happening, so that in any particular period, the process of imagination and spiritual path must bear a close relationship to the intellectuals' mental states. In a similar way, the romantic conception of childhood (largely derived from European conceptions) in itself happens to reflect the values espoused by intellectuals who at that time fought against social injustice, explored China's possible futures, and fostered new ideals. Therefore, the aesthetic ideal of children's literature, which commonly involved rural settings as part of a romantic return to nature, attracts substantial descriptive attention. The "world of children," for one thing, becomes an independent literary place, which is created by intellectuals to meet children's spiritual needs; for another thing, it is a spiritual home and harbor for the soul of intellectuals who have found themselves in a particular social situation. Carefreeness, as a quality of childhood, can complement and balance the lonely heart of a generation of intellectuals.

In China, "discovered childhood" evolves in parallel with the desire for and advocacy of the building of a modern nation. First, modern children's education plays a crucial part in building a modern China. Second, characteristics of childhood in a new, independent, free national country are enhanced because they partake of those qualities. From the time of the reformer Liang Qichao (1873–1929), writing under the shadow of the late Qing fear that a backward-looking China could disappear as a nation and culture, the concept "Youth" developed a rhetorical function, and then the imaginative schema of "Youthful China" became widespread and deeply rooted in people's minds. The ethos of childhood also acquired an enhanced status—"fresh, hopeful and energetic" life stages are not only an ideal goal of an individual but also a perfect picture of a striving society, nation, and country. The meaning of "childhood imagination" extends into the level of the country and nation's imagination and the development of modern Chinese and China. These two blueprints of imagination therefore coincide perfectly with each other.

It can be seen, then, that from the early twentieth century, the subjectivity of Chinese children's literature has been comprehended in a variety of ways and meanings. These meanings try to resolve problems of different aspects in a period of social transformation, but the core meaning is always "new born." It is a pure existence with a new appearance and a fresh kernel, and its spiritual energy extends to a vast real sphere and a spacious, significant field. It not only marks clearly that it is a reconstruction of the person in one's particular period, the shaping of a new childhood, but also illustrates a kind of newborn courage and striving which nurtures the intellectual's soul. This clear function of aesthetic symbolic significance only occurred in China in its socially, intellectually, and politically tumultuous early twentieth century. Today we can only admire its tremendous spiritual power, broad history, and profound cultural background, because we will never see its like again. Born out of Chinese intellectuals' social thoughts and aesthetic ideals, profoundly describing the historical path of Chinese social transformation, fully showing the features of theory and practice, the early representation of subjectivity in Chinese children's literature becomes a necessary way and a content to understand modern China. Thus grounded in a new subjectivity, "children's literature" as a discipline of modern humanities and social sciences initiates a significant development of modernity in China.

The "Bonds" of Realism

China has been a changing world throughout the twentieth century. The construction of a modern nation has experienced so many setbacks that even nowadays when we look back on history we still feel the pain of the hardships it has endured. From the beginning, in parallel with the progress made in China's history, the twofold conception that books should be, on the one hand, a literary experience that stimulated the mind and imagination of children, and, on the other hand, a means of social change has entailed that literariness has been increasingly replaced by social function. A special case in point is Ye Shengtao's literary fairy tales, which represent a difficult choice confronting writers during the emergence of Chinese children's literature and its early stages of development. In 1923, Ye Shengtao's tale collection *Scarecrow* was published. The first tale in this book, "The Little White Boat," is a model of what its author considered to be authentic children's literature—it is a celebration of the innocence and purity of the romantic child. In a setting which is an idealized pastoral world, two children find a boat in a stream, a boat which will only carry beautiful and pure children. When carried away by a storm, they are returned home by answering three questions which define the subjectivity of the romantic child: birds sing for those who love them, flowers have fragrance because it symbolizes goodness, and the white boat harmonizes with the pure at heart. Insofar as this version of subjectivity envisages a possibility of subjective agency, it lies in empathizing with what is good in the world despite life's vicissitudes. Subsequently, however, Ye Shengtao turned to portray the darkness of reality, and immediately "realism" substituted for the fantastic literary quality of fairy tales, leading to the production of a new mode of writing fairy tale with Chinese characteristics. In a preface to *Scarecrow*, Zheng Zhenduo (1898–1958) wrote: "It is impossible to reproduce the innocence of children and reflect the psychology of children, which is beyond all, especially in the gray clouds of adults" (1962, 103). Zheng's comment is indicative of how Chinese children's literature was to be embroiled in the struggles of Chinese history and Chinese problems, which were to prove barriers to the development of an independent Children's literature.

Since its origins, Chinese children's literature has developed in the context of a tense relationship between childhood imagination and national imagination. In the first place, the production of nationalism constrains the core of childhood imagination, while at the same time the pure new quality of childhood imagination contributes to the flourishing of modern nationality. In the second place, nationalism is deeply rooted in children's literature in that the literature has the capacity to reflect and advocate a magnificent blueprint of the future nation and country by means of the concepts it represents. Hence, a subjectivity with Chinese characteristics unfolds within modern children's literature. In other words, because subjectivity is represented within the frame of practical problems, the Grand Narrative of the nation and country constrains both children and children's literature, with the result that there is a scarcity of diverse subjectivities represented in children's literature. This phenomenon began in the 1920s, developed to be a common "Revolutionary Paradigm" in the 1930s, was reinforced by the founding of the People's

Republic of China in 1949, and reached its highest level in the 1960s when children's literature became a tool of education as a part of socialist ideology. As a result, there were as many restrictions on the development of children's literature as there were for Chinese literature in general at that time.

In the 1950s and 1960s, the mainstream of children's literature was produced within a politically constrained frame and hence largely focused on heroism and education. However, some works of children's literature from the period, which were grounded on folk cultural roots and hence based on folk literature, not only became masterpieces of the time but also represented complex subjectivities. Furthermore, in today's view, these works have been substantially released from the constraints of politics. Two typical works are "Ma Liang's Magic Writing Brush" (1955) by Hong Xuntao and "Wild Grapes" (1956) by Ge Cuilin. Both works describe poor children who lived long ago. "Ma Liang's Magic Writing Brush" tells of a boy who loves painting very much but meets many hardships and finally acquires a magic writing brush that can help the poor. Similarly, "Wild Grapes" tells of a blind girl who, through many hardships, finds wild grapes which have the power to cure herself and other blind people. Expressing both a simple folk emotion and an affinity with common people, these two stories nurture just, kind-hearted, and brave Chinese children who are the descendants of the Emperor Huang, the inheritors of civilization of Hua Xia (China), and the hope and backbone of a rising ancient oriental country. In "Ma Liang's Magic Writing Brush," Hong Xuntao includes a subtle representation of the nature of subjectivity: "on Ma Liang's name card, there are no words but the color yellow. This card recorded that Ma Liang, born on The Loess Plateau, grew up drinking the water of the Yellow River, and is a yellow-skinned Chinese. He is a descendant of Emperor Huang. What Ma Liang has painted is a dragon. He belongs to the dragon family . . . He is the son of the dragon." This plain understanding not only contains a pure ethos of Chinese children's literature but also extends into the writings of later writers, creating countless Chinese Ma Liangs after him.

An illuminating representation of subjectivity in this period, the short story "Little Orange Lamp" (1957), is one of the most widely known stories by Bing Xin (1900–1999), whose writing career spanned seventy-five years and encompassed various conceptions of subjectivity. In her children's series, *Letters to Young Readers* (1926–), Bing Xin assumes a romantic conception of children's subjectivity, but by the late 1950s, her perception is more social realist. Set in the late 1940s, around ten years before its date of publication, "Little Orange Lamp" deals with the heroism of the desperately poor, through an encounter between the story's narrator and a peasant girl aged about nine. While paying a New Year visit to a friend, the narrator is alone in her friend's room when the small girl appears and asks to use a phone in the building. The physical details which describe the child—her thinness, very inadequate clothing, and evidence that she is cold—swiftly evoke a life of penury: "She had a pale thin face and her lips were frozen purple because of the cold. Her hair was cut fairly short, and she was dressed in worn out clothes. She wore no socks, only a pair of straw sandals" (1957, 130). Her mother is in urgent need of a doctor, so the narrator makes the phone call and a few hours later decides to go to the house herself, buying a few oranges along the way. Her stay is brief, but she finds that the mother has been treated, that the child is cooking yam porridge for their New Year's Eve dinner, and that the father has disappeared (it is later disclosed that he has been arrested for pro-communist activities). Twice the child speaks as if to *console* the narrator, in a deft move that underlines how inadequate she herself is, and as the narrator prepares to leave, the child protests that the way is dark and slippery and so ingeniously makes her a lamp out of the peel of the largest orange. The reversed function of the orange demonstrates that the child's capacity for empathy is greater than the adult's (Bing Xin assumed that this greater capacity was a component of child subjectivity), but also that she is very creative despite her straitened circumstances. As the narrator departs, the child's words of farewell and the narrator's reflections on the incident pull together a confidence that such a subjectivity—compounded of "calmness and courage, and . . . optimism," of a highly developed capacity for empathy and creativity—bodes well for the future of China:

> "Dad will soon come back. Then Mum will be well." She drew a circle in the air with her small hand, and then pressed it on mine, and said,
> "Then, we will all be well." Obviously, her "all" included me.
> Holding this ingeniously-made little lamp, I walked slowly up the dark, wet mountain path. In truth, the dim orange light could not reach very far. However, the little girl's calmness and courage, and her optimism, made me feel as though the way in front of me was boundlessly illuminated.

Ideological Production of the Subject

The path was to take a strange turn a few years after Bing Xin's story was written with the onset of the Cultural Revolution in 1965. Very little children's literature was produced in the following decade, and as both Mary Farquhar (1999, 286–287) and Xu Xu (2011, 395) remark, the film *Sparkling Red Star* (1974) exemplifies how the social and educational practices of the era were framed to produce a particular kind of child subject. However, the principle that, as Farquhar puts it, "Children's education as 'revolutionary successors' was to come from experience, not literature" did enable a new version of idyllic rural life to emerge in the stories of Hao Ran (1932–2008). A story such as "Date Orchard" (1962) depicts rural life by means of a deft combination of ideological correctness and simple (almost naïve) realism in language and narrative form. A comparison with "The Little White Boat" and "The Little Orange Lamp" readily shows how subjectivity is now assumed to be produced by ideological interpellation. The opening scenes of "The Little White Boat" and "Date Orchard" afford some obvious contrasts:

> A small stream is a home for all sorts of lovely things. They grow small red flowers, slightly smiling, but sometimes they dance and that is a delight to see. Droplets of pearly dew on green grass, like fairies' clothes, dazzle men's eyes. ("The Little White Boat")

> The dates were ripening. The orchard, stretching for miles around, reminded me of a bride in her wedding clothes smiling bashfully as she waited to be fetched to her husband's home. The interlaced boughs, just beginning to lose their green leaves, were bent under thick clusters of fruit. Under the afternoon sun the dates glowed with color: agate-red, jade-green or a mottled green and russet. The whole orchard was as pretty as a picture. ("Date Orchard")

The language of "White Boat" invites an imaginative response to setting through anthropomorphic metaphor (the flowers "smile" and "dance"), the evocation of "fairies," and a play on perception in the movement between things visually delightful and things that dazzle. It is a setting that is already transcending everydayness. In contrast, "Date Orchard" depicts what will be soon defined as a successful working orchard, which in 1945 fed soldiers resisting the Japanese occupation and today (around 1962) remain "a staple food" (9). Although the effect is quite lyrical, the language resorts to everyday clichés, such as the bashfully smiling bride or "pretty as a picture," and the sense of richness stems from accumulation of realistic detail.

As the narrator continues his story of a return to his uncle's orchard, he is surprised to find himself showered with dates dropped by someone overhead in a tree. His playful assailant is Red Treasure, a girl of sixteen or seventeen, who had been born at the orchard in 1945 and adopted by the narrator's uncle when the girl's mother died soon after while fighting against the Japanese army. The narrator had not seen her since she was ten, when her father had been traced and she moved to the city. Having just completed middle school, Red Treasure had decided not to go to college but instead returned to the orchard and informed Uncle that she had decided to attend "Date Orchard College—to learn from you to be a peasant." Not only is she a dedicated revolutionary, but descriptive language applied to her is highly positive. The narrator's first glimpse of her is in great contrast to the little girl in "The Little Orange Lamp": "Perched there was a girl in black cloth shoes, blue trousers rolled up to her knees and a snowy white blouse, one corner of which had caught on a branch. Her plaits, tied with pink silk bows, were swaying from side to side. . . . She was a girl in her teens with fine arched eyebrows who surveyed me through narrowed eyes, her nose slightly turned up. As she compressed her lips to hold back her laughter, two big dimples appeared in her rosy cheeks glowing with health." She is variously described as cheerful and carefree, laughing, and earnestly studying the art of growing dates. In addition to "increasing our country's food output," Red Treasure has given herself a twofold mission: first, to write down and preserve her illiterate uncle's vast wealth of agrarian knowledge built up over sixty years in the orchard; second, to discover how to make ancient trees bear fruit again. She of course succeeds. In pursuing her ideals, she seems to exhibit considerable agency: she chooses her own future, she is extroverted and emancipated, she negotiates about the future of the old trees in the (now community-owned) orchard with the local brigade leader, she teases her uncle and the narrator, and she discovers that the trees will flourish again if their roots are pruned. Looked at from another angle—the angle of the narrative itself—she is a perfect cadre whose subjectivity reflects and is produced (anachronistically) by Cultural Revolution ideology. Perhaps Hao Ran was the most successful writer during this period, and remained a successful writer subsequently, because of his ability to find value in human activity. Red Treasure is not attributed with the empathic capability of the child in Bing Xin's story, but there is something splendid about her idealism. When his uncle relates how he finally learned that Red Treasure was writing a manual, not just writing because it was something educated people did (and, by implication, was doing something useful rather than intellectual), the narrator imagines a romantic vision of Red Treasure at work:

> The old man beamed as he finished this account. For me, it had conjured up an enchanting scene: A summer night, hazy moonlight, with not a breath of wind to stir the trees, the silence unbroken by voices or the shrill of insects. A girl, bent over a small table, was writing intently under an oil lamp. From time to time she paused, frowning thoughtfully, then took up her pen again. Beads of sweat from her heart-shaped face dripped on her hand as she transcribed the experience the old man had amassed in sixty years of hard work, transmuted by her own ardent enthusiasm.

Diversification and Development of Subjectivity in the New Period

When the Cultural Revolution was over at the end of 1976, Chinese society had been totally transformed. At the beginning of a new historical era, people with an optimistic attitude tended to refer to the circumstances of society by names such as "a Crucial Turning Point," "New Era" and "New Age." Since then, the concept "new age," which is usually used in politics, has spread widely in the literary field. In October 1979, at the Fourth National Writers' and Artists' Congress, representatives strongly expressed their desire to achieve "literature and art democracy." With reference to the sensitive issues of directing and controlling literature and art, the conference affirmed that the ruling party's guidance on literature and art does not mean issuing orders or requiring literature and art to serve temporary, specific, direct political purpose, but allowing literature and art to develop on the basis of their own aesthetic principles without interference and thus to create better conditions for culture workers to build a more thriving culture business. Moreover, the conference reiterated the effective implementation of the guidelines, "Let a hundred flowers bloom, let a hundred schools of thought contend" which was first promulgated in 1956 and has not been implemented effectively. Since then, Chinese contemporary literature has entered a new era.

Children's literature since the 1980s, having been released from political and ideological constraints, has developed a renewed interest in subjectivity from two perspectives—that of children, and that of literariness. The academic area of literature at that time also realized that children's literature should not be constrained as a tool of children's education but should have its own unique ethos and literary qualities. As a tool for representing the life of children and satisfying children's mental demands, childness must be its spiritual core. Radical change was evident in 1982 with the release of "PiPi Lu," a new character in fairy tales, and the public image of its extrovert maker Zheng Yuanjie. Zheng's unruly imagination, the unconstrained style of fairy tale logic, and the magnificent farce-like aesthetic features strongly challenge traditional modes of education. The wild imagination and the bustling atmosphere also overturn the pedantry of the traditional educational fairy tale, leading to a long-desired sense of playfulness. PiPi Lu, as an enlightening figure, showed the way to a new aesthetic school in Chinese children's literature, which later became known as "the bustling school of fairy tales." This style of children's literature respects the specific subjectivities of children and represents a real implementation of the idea of a "child-centered" children's literature. Its carnivalesque and iconoclastic qualities constitute a rebellion against the constraints placed upon children's subjectivity by some long-standing educational assumptions and practices. Because of his iconoclasm, Zheng Yuanjie has long occupied an eminent position in China.

In light of the return of literariness as a criterion of value and a rejection of the assumption that children's literature is primarily a tool of education, Chinese children's literature began to explore new directions. At the same time as "the bustling school" was developing in the 1980s, "the lyrical school of fairy tales," which expresses literary emotion, also arose. These contemporaneous schools constituted two spectacular views of Chinese children's literature in the 1980s. The lyrical school, from its language to its artistic conception, stressed literariness and strove for aesthetic beauty. However, its deep focus on literariness meant that it appealed to a minority taste and gained only a small readership, for which it was criticized at that time. Even so, the establishment of a lyrical mode of writing exerted a far-reaching impact on the development of Chinese children's literature.

Over the thirty years since the attention of children's literature turned back to the concepts of childness and aesthetic quality, representations of subjectivity in the literature have continued to change and reflect developments in

Chinese society, in which reform and opening up have predominated, and thus subjectivity has become endowed with several highly influential, marked features of this period.

As stated above, the "bustling school of fairy tales" of the 1980s, represented by Zheng Yuanjie, laid primary emphasis on the potential of literature to entertain, and turned its back on the educational function. It has been hugely influential, as illustrated by PiPi Lu's millions of readers. In the 1990s, Qin Wenjun also explored the use of humor in depicting a modern teenage subjectivity in *Schoolboy Jia Li* (1993), which has since sold over a million copies. Speaking at an IBBY conference in 2006, Qin Wenjun detailed what she perceived as the key qualities of children's literature and in doing so defined the context in which contemporary Chinese children's literature represents subjectivity. These qualities are: perception of an aesthetic dimension; a sense of belonging; a capacity for introspection; an awareness of the consequences of an action; imagination; and awareness of "secrets and pleasures" specific to childhood. Based on her understanding of the reality of Chinese children's lives, Qin has made an important contribution to defending and protecting the value of both "Children" and "literature." For the development status of the local children's literature, Qin has a very comprehensive observation and deep reflection. She thus goes further than rejecting the 1970s production of subjectivity through dogmatic education, and her original path has placed the literature on a solid foundation.

In the first decade of the twenty-first century, the series *Ma Xiaotiao*, written by Yang Hongying, depicts children in their early years of school as their experiences begin to shape their subjectivities. Their central character, naughty Ma Xiaotiao, is a comic figure in his misperceptions of his day-to-day world (for example, he can't work out how his mother always knows about his mischief). In short, simple stories such as "Best Friends," Yang depicts the individuality of "Mo" (as he is renamed in the English translation) as he pursues his desires and profoundly reflects the problems of Chinese education. In "Best Friends," Mo's class teacher allocates his archenemy, Man Man, to be his desk-mate, because Ms. Qin knows Man Man will always reveal Mo's mischief-making. When Man Man makes a snide comment about her beautiful friend Lily—"Lily was so full of herself that she didn't notice what anyone else was doing"—Mo decides Lily would be a perfect desk-mate as she wouldn't notice his mischief. Mo's desire to change his desk-mate becomes a problem, and he can't understand why none of his friends will help him (one wants to be his desk-mate, whereas another suggests a different girl, presumably because he knows she likes Mo; finally, Lily's present desk-mate, Penguin, refuses to change, despite a small bribe, because he likes sitting with Lily). Readers engage imaginatively with the story, often using their own experience to interpret the characters' motives, but the crux of the problem lies in the Chinese education system and the nature of the authority and control adults wield over children, which still prevails today. Mo is a unique child.

Yang Hongying reveals the complex relationships between children under this system of education through Mo. It is a delicate, subtle, and amusing story, and it should come as no surprise that since the publication of the first *Ma Xiaotiao* book in 2003, sales figures for the twenty books in the series have passed twenty-two million.

Zheng Yuanjie, Qin Wenjun, and Yang Hongying epitomize the three pivotal stages in the development of the outlook on Chinese children over the last thirty years, with one climax in every decade. At the same time, the characters in their works, especially PiPi Lu, Jia Li, and Ma Xiaotiao, also signify unfolding aspects of the conception of children's subjectivity which have become central to the "phenomenon of Chinese children's literature." It has been a long road for Chinese contemporary society to reach its current understanding of children because of the long history of China's feudal society, the many vicissitudes of modern history, and restrictions on the reformation and transformation of the Chinese education system and ideas about education. If contemporary children's authors can truly respect children and be willing to break through the constraints of the traditional mode of education, to establish a new modern outlook on children's education, to discover and interpret the characteristics of children's lives, to accentuate the communication between adults and children, to create works according to the real life of children, they will have an unexpected impact on Chinese society. Chinese children's literature can evolve and maintain a natural healthy development only if people change their outlooks on children.

A major impediment is that the publication of children's books is affected significantly by economic imperatives and commercialism. This may be because China has a large population of children and the sales of children's books have become a huge cake which can entice many people to seek to profit from it. Consequently, those highly influential writers become the touchstones of publishers' ambition, and hence their works attract numerous imitators. It has thus come about that a large number of works about school life, naughty children, and humorous aspects of children's lives have been published without too much consideration for their impact, and the industry has therefore produced a considerable number of shoddy books. This situation has in turn resulted in a negative impact on society and consequently condemnation of the excellent writers who are thought to be responsible for it. So in the rapid economic advance of China in this new century, the emancipation of children's literature meets an unprecedented challenge. The concepts of respecting children and emancipation of children are more likely to be replaced by intentions to please children and make profits, a tendency that Qin Wenjun noted in her 2006 IBBY address. This mixed marketplace condition badly needs researchers to discriminate between the dross and the excellent. In recent years, the children's literature community has been appealing to the public to reject superficiality in the writings of Chinese children's literature, to develop a more sophisticated understanding of the game, to avoid taboo topics as a basis for humor, and to avoid rude jokes as a cheap means to attract readers. Such deviations have the potential to destroy the literary vitality of Chinese children's literature. What I wish to emphasize here is that the irreversible trend of the emancipation of children's subjectivity must not be diverted by processes that come about because the market takes advantage of characterization and story lines which trivialize subjectivity. The Chinese children's literature community—writers, scholars, and publishers—need to engage with the current complicated situation, stick to their literary values, and strive for a children's literature which continues to foster the emancipation of children's subjectivity.

In addition to attributing children with dynamic subjective characteristics, Chinese children's literature has also expanded in the aspects of caring for children and reaching the child's inner heart. Especially in works with young adult themes, these works particularly reflect the confusion of maturing children in Chinese history and reality. In addition to the works discussed above, there are many works which focus on a young girl's spiritual growth. Since the mid to late 1990s, there has been a great interest in exploring the potential of fantastic literature for expressing children's subjectivity, although the genre has not yet developed very far.

Once writers are released from political constraints, they are able to delve deeply into the background of national history and social development to consider the value of children's literature on a broader cultural and aesthetic horizon. When Chinese children's literature returned to the path of normal development in the 1980s, children's author and professor of Chinese Literature, Cao Wenxuan argued that children's literature authors shape China's future national character, and thus have a far-reaching impact. Positioning children's literature within a national view, Cao freed himself from the constraints of narrow ideology and developed the proposition that the tradition of Chinese literature not only concerns itself with nation, country, and social values, but also, based on the current situation, aspires to use literature to foster and improve Chinese children's national character under the background of the new times. This concern for value endows children's literature with a great historical mission: the proposition that there must be a close relationship between children and nation, which was raised in the early twentieth century when Chinese children's literature first came into being, has returned as a regular development and construction. Child subjectivity is positioned as an aspect of culture consciousness, specifically Chinese tastes, aesthetic conception, and constructions of reality.

Since the advent of "new times," Cao Wenxuan has been not only an advocate for the concept of children's literature but also an excellent representative of authors. Persisting in his outlook of "pursuing eternity" featured in his works on history, tradition, and folklore, he has described the memorable days of childhood and the hardships that people experienced. He also paid close attention to the weak, drew a picture of love of the oriental nation, and highlighted the graceful elements in Chinese personality. Cao Wenxuan's work demonstrates that Chinese children's literature dealing with national themes has begun to go deeper than the surface.

Concepts of transhistorical social and personal values are also evident in fairy tale, which always occupies an important position in the representation of subjectivity in Chinese children's literature. This status is perhaps also connected to the literariness of the fairy tale's style and its affiliation with aesthetic qualities in Chinese culture and the philosophizing habits of the Chinese mentality. Fairy tale is a mode of writing popular with writers who uphold independent literary tastes and aesthetics. Over the past thirty years, the lyrical fairy tales have grown to be an influential style, especially as practiced by Jin Bo and Bing Bo. For example, Jin Bo's fairy tales combine an exquisite poetic quality with a far-reaching conception. Thus in *Blue Snowflakes*, he depicts an astonishing, pure world, in which a completely blue snowflake appears in the sky and shines out in its blueness before a blind grandmother, Mei. By this means, the blue flower fairy, named "Lanlan," manages to enable Mei, who is blind and alone, to live happily for the rest of her life. In a parallel strand, the boy Zhizhi's hospitality toward his neighbors not only moves human beings but also affects the heart of nature itself. *Blue Snowflakes* is a song of harmony between man and nature, in which the subjectivity of the children and of beautiful nature become mingled. Many female writers also excel in the fairy tale mode, which they use to great advantage to explore the subjectivities of girls through focus on material conditions, female emotion, and gender positionality.

An important area in which contemporary children's literature needs to be concerned is the impact on children's lives of great changes in the social reality of modern China. Many works focus on the issues of children's living conditions and their mental problems, such as the issues of left-behind children,[1] children from single parent homes, and general spiritual anxiety. These issues are also pertinent to education and family, especially during the present transformation period of China's education system, when some reform policies cannot be put into practice effectively, and a great number of teachers need to be trained. Instead of trying to develop a child-centered approach to education, these teachers do much harm to the children. This situation leaves a kind of "emptiness" in the mental world of many children and places them in implicit danger. In fact, creative work in this field always faces a kind of barrier because works of great social influence have not yet been created. This may be because the writers of Chinese children's literature lack critical consciousness.

In parallel with, and contributing to, the desire for ongoing educational reform, authors, including children's writers, have interrogated 1960s politics through the form of historical fiction and memoir. In children's literature, excellent narratives about historical children's experiences of social politics in the 1960s emerged by the end of the 1980s. The representative writer is

Chang Xingang, who, born in 1957, draws on his own actual experiences for his writing about recent childhood histories. In *The Waste Grassland of Youth* (1989), winner of the second national children's literature of China Writers Association prize in 1993, Chang strives to realize a kind of original emotion of adolescence and to represent the whole "world of history experience." He depicts the path of spiritual construction of an adolescent in a particular period—a selfhood constructed in place of a lost individual childhood subjectivity that has been suppressed by real life and by loneliness and desolation, which is highlighted by the meeting of vibrant youth and desolate land in North China:

> I'm waving my pale thin arms in my narrow bitter young spirit . . . I'll just live like this. But I did not get rid of the ever-following shadows. I often heard a voice while in loneliness. I'm always stunned by the sad sound played by great human purity. (1989, 224)

In *The Waste Grassland of Youth*, the center and basic background of the history are evil and dark, the root cause of alienation of the young man's subjectivity. The means by which the protagonist overcomes his alienation is his youthful passion and the power of memory to recall and come to terms with the pain of his youth. This powerful force is eventually dredged from the cry of the soul. In mapping the evolution of a young man's spirit, Chang Xingang is able to make a comment on the concept of national historical destiny.

The work *Ground-glass City* (2004) endeavors to highlight historical truth by tracing the metamorphosis of modern history. The past has a seeming transparency and depth of substance, as if it were a frosted glass city, but its invisible fabric is held together by fragile and illusory "glass" rather than by a solid architectural structure. People who enter into it will become lost, as the play of surfaces induces them to lose the capacity for memory. Once inhabitants of this city have learned to conform and obey, they become a lost people. As in the scenario of *The Waste Grassland of Youth*, Chang's protagonist in this novel is a resistant teenager, and it is he who makes this unreal city disappear.

The Children under the Chimney (2010) recounts 1960s childhood memories but breaks away from the trap of the historical narrative and works instead with the highly symbolic historical implications of key images, especially the central image of a tall chimney from which attached loudspeakers broadcast propagandistic information about current social events. The children who encircle the chimney are vital, strong, and bored by the long winter in the North of China, and their vitality and restlessness act as a force of resistance against control from the center and the adult figures motivated by political considerations. The children's resistance constitutes a reemergence of will and agency in opposition to those who shape events, so that the function of childhood memory in the novel is to explore the past and its representation in a discourse that achieves deep social criticism. For a long time, people have neglected the capability of children's literature to embody forms of subjective agency that oppose the so-called center and powerful which may strive to stifle individual subjectivity. *The Children under the Chimney* demonstrates this capability.

Chang Xingang's historical writing about childhood, presented from the viewpoint of children, has a broad interpretive scope. By attributing authority to children, he creates possibilities for children to know and reexamine society and history and provide a new perspective for the course of history. This is of irreplaceable value for enriching the significance of contemporary Chinese children's literature.

From an overall view, Chinese children's literature with over 100 years' history grows with the development of Chinese society. The generation of forms of subjectivity in different times and social factors variously reflects Chinese traditional ethics, literature values, and the oriental aesthetic spirit. Between traditional and modern, Chinese children's literature is always finding a breakthrough and makes great efforts to approach culture and literature consciousness, and is exploring a more natural way of writing. Surely, all of this is based on the promotion of the whole Chinese civilization.

Notes

1. The left-behind children in China have been a prominent social problem in recent years. With China's rapid social, economic, and political development, a growing number of young farmers rush into the cities as migrant workers, leaving their children in the countryside and their well-being to the care of relatives. This special group of young people is known as the left-behind children. It is difficult to guarantee their physical and mental health. The problems they are confronting are lack of comfort, health care, and compulsory education, which may easily lead to deviation from their cognition and self-value and abnormal personality and psychology, some children may even commit crimes. According to data that investigated a sample of 1 percent of the population in 2005, the number of left-behind children is calculated to be fifty-eight million.

Works Cited

Primary texts

[Bing Xin] 冰心：《小桔灯》（ "Little Orange Lamp"　　1957年1月31日。
[Bing Xin. "The Little Orange Lamp." Translated by Gong Shifen in *Renditions* 32 (1989): 92–107, 130–132. http://www.cuhk.edu.hk/rct/toc/toc_b32.html]
[Chang Xingang] 常新港：《青春的荒草地》（*The Waste Grassland of Youth*），新蕾出版社，1989年。
[Chang Xingang. *The Waste Grassland of Youth*. Beijing: China Children's Press & Publication Group, 2010.]
[Chang Xingang] 常新港：《毛玻璃城》（*Ground-glass City*），中国少年儿童出版社，2004年。

[Chang Xingang] 常新港：《烟囱下的孩子》（*The Children under the Chimney*），二十一世纪出版社，2010年。

[Ge Cuilin] 葛翠琳：《野葡萄》（"Wild Grapes" 1956年第2期。

[Hao Ran] 浩然：《红枣林》（"Date Orchard" 1962年。

[Hao Ran, "Date Orchard." Translated by Marsha Wagner in *Chinese Literature* 4 (1974): 36–48.]

[Hong Xuntao] 洪汛涛：《神笔马良》（"Ma Liang's Magic Writing Brush" 1955年第3期。

[*Ma Liang and His Magic Brush*. Adapted by Han Xing. Beijing: Foreign Languages Press, 1980.]

[Jin Bo] 金波：《蓝雪花》（*Blue Snowflakes*），浙江少年儿童出版社，2009年12月。

[Qin Wenjun] 秦文君：《男生贾里》（*Schoolboy Jia Li*），少年儿童出版社，1993年。

[Yang Hongying] 杨红樱：《淘气包马小跳》系列20本 （*Naughty Boy Ma Xiaotiao*），接力出版社，2003年7月-2009年1月。

[Yang Hongying. *Mo's Mischief (5)—Best Friends*. London: HarperCollins, 2011.]

[Ye Shengtao] 叶圣陶：《稻草人》（*Scarecrow*），上海商务印书馆，1923年。

[Zheng Yuanjie] 郑渊洁：《皮皮鲁外传》（"PiPi Lu" 1982年第4期。

Secondary Texts

Farquhar, Mary Ann. *Children's Literature in China. From Lu Xun to Mao Zedong*. New York: East Gate, 1999.

Qin Wenjun. "Children's Literature: The Light That Illuminates the World," presented at the IBBY Conference. September 21, 2006. http://www.ibby.org/index.php?id=689. Accessed March 5, 2012.

Xu Xu. "'Chairman Mao's Child': *Sparkling Red Star* and the Construction of Children in the Chinese Cultural Revolution," *Children's Literature Association Quarterly* 36.4 (2011): 381–409.

Zheng Zhenduo. The Preface of Scarecrow. Selected Essays of Children's Literature (1913–1949). Shanghai: Juvenile and Children's Publishing House, 1962.

Chapter Six

"How Can I Be the Protagonist of My Own Life?"

Intimations of Hope for Teen Subjectivities in Korean Fiction and Film

Sung-Ae Lee

In East Asian cultures, . . . the self-in-relationship-with-others is believed to be the locus of thought, action, and motivation. The symbolic boundary between the self and other such selves is blurred and constantly negotiated through social interaction. Personal selves are quite important; yet, they are constructed in accordance with the fundamental assumption about the interdependence of the selves involved.

Uchida, Norasakkunkit, and Kitayama (2004)

In conversations which compare and contrast ideas of subjectivity in East and West, it is common to adduce an antithesis between a script grounded in independence and autonomy, which defines the Western self and the connectedness and interdependence of self with others which grounds subjectivity scripts in East Asian (and other non-Western) countries (Uchida et al., 2004: 224). Although the antithesis can be overstated, the differences do reflect local beliefs and ideologies, and, above all, narrative representations in which the Western teen characters, shaped by assumptions about personal growth and development, are constructed under the fundamental assumption that each self is independent and separate from other selves, whereas the development of Korean teen characters (my focus in this chapter) is predicated upon a complex, social interaction. The complexity is encapsulated in a moment that occurs late in the film *Sunny* (2011), when Im Na-Mi reflects back on her life and comprehends something she lost when she became an adult:

> I lived as a mother and a wife for such a long time. Na-Mi as a human being was only a distant memory. Now I've remembered I am at least a protagonist of my own life, with a history.[1]

The issue here, I suggest, is that interpellation of the self into social practice is nuanced in subtly different ways in Korean fiction and film. It is of course common for a Western wife and mother to feel that she is no longer the protagonist of her own life, but the difference lies in the way the experience is contextualized and what is meant by one's own humanity. For Na-Mi, finding herself entails engaging more fully with group interdependencies, offering support to rediscovered friends, and becoming a more effective and affectionate wife and mother. In envisaging such a differently nuanced subjectivity, *Sunny* continues a process at work in the creative arts over the preceding decade, and which at the start of that decade Cho Hae-Joang identified as a need "to acknowledge the differentiation of society and build a new system upon a foundation of differentiated subjects" (2000, 66).

Social relations are equally important in West and East, and people everywhere are created by, constrained by, and responsive to their various interpersonal contexts (see Markus and Kitayama, 1991: 228), so how are traits unique or specific to Korea to be pinned down? As Na-Mi attempts to bring together the girl gang of her high school days (which called itself *Sunny*) for a reunion with Choon-Hwa, their leader, who is dying of cancer, the film explores the possibility for the self to be an agentic center of thought and action. This chapter will explore how teenage characters are depicted in the struggle to be the protagonists of their lives and have a future to look forward to in two novels—Kim Hye-Jung's *Hiking Girls* (2008) and Yang Ho-Moon's *Here Come the Losers!* (2008)—and two films—*Sunny* (2011) and *Once Upon a Time in High School* (2004).[2] Some brief comparisons will also be made with a number of thematically related films, such as *A Light Sleep* (2008) and *Bleak Night* (2011). *Hiking Girls* and *Sunny* deal with the circumstances of girls, whereas *Here Come the Losers!* and *Once Upon a Time in High School* deal with boys.[3] All of these texts depict characters who, engaged in a directionless present and unable to look forward to an adulthood that promises to be any different (only worse), are faced with a profound inability to make sense of their identities. *Sunny* uses its temporal shifting to thematize this situation, when Choon-Hwa mails out a DVD in which her old friends, as schoolgirls, speak to themselves from an imagined successful future—their vision is a harsh contrast with the reality. As the DVD exemplifies, characters strive to find meaning within group interdependence, but the social formation which privileges the group also ensures that they become outsiders pushed to the social periphery. The negative outcome is foreshadowed in Choon-Hwa's declaration that in her imagined future, she is proud to have survived in a harsh, male-dominated society.

Herein lies a paradox for the representation of subjectivity in Korean narrative. On the one hand, pervasive social ideology valorizes the self-in-relationship-with-others; on the other hand, society puts barriers in the way of this normative goal of connecting to others and renders it unachievable. Further, however, society does not enable independence as an alternative cultural goal, whereby an individual's behavior "is organized and made meaningful primarily by reference to one's own internal repertoire of thoughts, feelings, and actions, rather than by reference to the thoughts, feelings, and actions of others" (Markus and Kitayama, 1991: 226). Characters whose behavior is modeled on this alternative principle are invariably depicted as failed human beings who by the end of the film are abjected, have disappeared, or have died. The paradox not only has been something of a commonplace in Korean fiction and film since the early 1990s but also, from an imagological perspective, has been used to demonstrate a national characterization which depicts Korea as an endemically dystopian society. Hence the schematic nature of narrative representations must be taken into account in analysis of how subjectivity is represented in text or discourse.

Imagology has a particular interest in the dynamics between those scripts which characterize the Other (here, images and behaviors of adults, bullies, and those more or less clever or talented or beautiful) and those which characterize the self (especially a capacity for responsibility, creativity, other-regardingness, and altruism). Subjectivity takes shape in a discursive environment and is produced by literary, filmic, and discursive conventions, which may in turn model social realities or cultural desiderata. Imagology is thus concerned with the typology of characterizations and attributes, with their currency and with their rhetorical deployment. *Once Upon a Time in High School*, for example, which is set in 1978 when the military dictatorship was at its most powerful and just a year before the dictator, Park Chung-Hee, was assassinated, reframes a practice of aggression and violence by building an intertextual relationship with the martial arts films of Bruce Lee. The high school in Maljuk Street is characterized by a constant battle for dominance among the boys, a situation structured by a militaristic enforcement of hierarchy, and by verbal and physical (sometimes sexual) abuse by teachers and seniors. The Confucian principle that someone older has natural dominance, such as adults over children, or "seniors" over "juniors," generates a leader/subaltern structure that is nothing more than physical and psychological bullying. The school also sustains a regime of punishment that is tantamount to torture, entailing severe abuses of human rights. Consequently, there is a regime of violence among the boys, and there is no counter model because those in authority themselves consistently employ physical and psychological violence. Even the school principal is depicted striking one of the teachers in view of the students. The school thus functions as a microcosm of modern South Korean society, as it has been described by Cho Hae-Joang:

> Modernization through popular mobilization not only reduced the personal dimension of daily life, but also produced a totalitarian culture in which people were trained through discipline and surveillance, leaving no room for the emergence of civil society. It is a society in which it is dangerous for an individual to think or act from different subject positions other than that of one's national or familial identity. (2000, 60)

For the gentle, introverted protagonist, Hyun-Soo, who has internalized the principle of interdependent social relationships and aspires to a different kind of subject position, the school environment foreshadows a future for him as "a surplus man," as his father puts it: a person lacking skills or qualifications (specifically a degree) and hence with no place in Korean society. Pushed to the brink of suicide by abjection and unrequited love, Hyun-Soo suddenly sees a way forward and begins to train his body according to *Jeet Kune Do*, the principles of his martial arts hero Bruce Lee. If the interdependent society has ceased to function, then the way forward may be to dismantle it to put things right, as the martial arts hero does. Hyun-Soo thus focuses his attention on overcoming the school's supreme bully, Jong-Hoon, and his four accomplices. The process of training that elevates both body and mind above the corruptions of Korean society—its violence, power struggles, corrupt business practices, enforced obsequiousness—aligns *Once Upon a Time in High School* with the martial arts film tradition that has spread from Hong Kong and China to East and Southeast Asia and beyond. A montage (Figure 6.1) that embeds a scene in which a teacher beats students in the classroom within the sequence in which Hyun-Soo trains by reading Bruce Lee's manual expresses an ideological relationship with the tradition. As Ma Ning defines it:

> The martial arts genre (*wuxia*) has throughout its history typically addressed questions such as what constitutes just use of violence and who can be called a hero? Usual semantic/syntactic structures contain binary oppositions such as nature/culture, virtuocracy/despotism and order/disorder embodied in different types of narratives, such as a chivalric figure learning martial arts from a master in order to kill a despot, avenging one's victimized family, resolving rivalries and contests among different groups or completing some quest essential to the survival and prosperity of a given community. (2011, 171)

In terms of the story, Hyun-Soo's single-handed victory over the five villains in a desperate showdown on the school roof presages little practical change for the school, but provokes an intensified flow of audience empathy toward him and invokes change symbolically. Having learned from (his study of)

Bruce Lee how to overthrow the despot, and having avenged his friend, Woo-Shik (even though he knows that Woo-Shik is self-regarding and overtly resists interdependent relationships), Hyun-Soo walks out of the school with a measure of subjective agency. His reward is reconciliation and a more equal relationship with his taciturn father, and attendance at an adult education institution where students are motivated and attentive, and learning is shared and cooperative. The ironies in his victory over the bullies are twofold: first, as he walks away from the school for the last time and shouts "Fuck all schools in the Republic of Korea" at the teaching staff, the slogan "Promoting Restoration Education" is seen blazoned across the front of the school. However, the

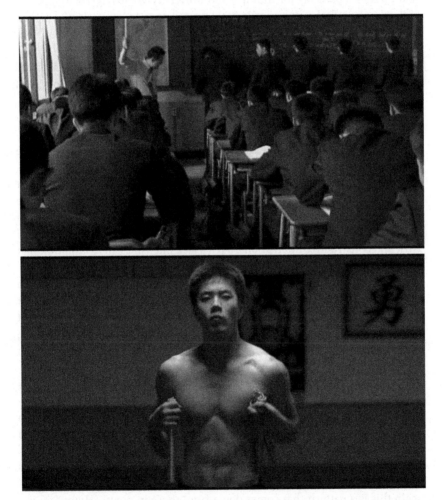

Figure 6.1 Abjection and Agency: The martial arts practitioner prepares himself to resist the regime of tyranny (note the map of Korea as background to teacher violence in the top picture).
Source: Once Upon a Time in High School.

school's militaristic structure has offered nothing but conformity to govern-ment ideology and rote learning. Second, a scene set in the hospital where the injured students lie illustrates how in this society perpetrators can be refig-ured as victims: as Hyun-Soo's father kneels to beg forgiveness, the mother of one of the students complains that Hyun-Soo is merely a gangster who has injured "my precious son"—one of the real gangsters. Hyun-Soo's father apol-ogizes for educating his son wrongly and begs for reconciliation, but it seems evident he is playing the necessary game to collude in injustice because there is no chance that the school will be investigated. An audience can deduce this from what follows: instead of beating Hyun-Soo, as is his habit, he points out that there is a pathway for him to go to university without graduating from high school, and asks, rhetorically, "Did Bruce Lee go to university?" There is, of course, a joke here for Bruce Lee fans, who would know he graduated from the University of Washington in 1964.

Once Upon a Time in High School intimates that, even in a culture depicted as self-regarding and abusive, the self-in-relationship-with-others model of subjectivity is still possible. On the other hand, the barriers to this possibility are also well exemplified in the film. The construction of subjectivity depends on intersubjective relationships, regardless of whether subjectivity is inde-pendent or interdependent. In a society where other-regardingness (or simple altruism) is depicted as an exception, communities consist of abject subjects. When one of the teachers makes the apparently high-minded assertion that attaining a good moral character is more important than high marks, he is easily recognized as a hypocrite. The lack of ethical practices within the school, both among teachers and students, precludes possibilities for mutual trust and constructive interactions. Such a lack intensifies an assumption that peer relationships are grounded on mutual obligation rather than on inter-subjective processes such as mutual responsibility or altruism. This malaise is even more sharply represented in the bully character, Gi-Tae, in *Bleak Night* (2011): as the film moves rapidly back and forth among scenes set at different points on its timeline, it follows Gi-Tae's father's attempt to learn why Gi-Tae committed suicide. Although he will never find the answer to his question, an audience will construct some version of a failure of the self-in-relationship-with-others model of subjectivity, and this will be emotionally complex as audiences at different times empathize with this alienated and abject charac-ter and are repelled by his unpredictable and often cruel behavior. Although he demands that his friends accept his excesses, and even collude in his acts of bullying, he gives nothing in return.

The martial arts theme in *Once Upon a Time in High School* foregrounds an assumption that violence may be the first option in problem solving, and again this is a pattern that comes down from those in power. Hyun-Soo is a transferring student, but within minutes of arriving for his first day at school, he is brutally beaten with a baseball bat for failing to wear correct uniform (his collar had been taken from him on the bus by a senior). In recent fiction and film, the Korean society represented contends that young Korean people have long had to deal with violence as part of their daily lives, and the recurrent figure of the school bully usually functions as a metonym for the history of violence within Korean political processes, especially the Gwangju Massacre of 1980 and the turbulent June Democracy Movement of 1987, which led to crucial democratic reform of the political structure, and hence justified violent protest against the bullies wielding power. Again, the allusions to Bruce Lee's films add nuances to this theme. As Chiao Hsiung-Ping points out, with reference to the original reception of the films in Hong Kong, "Lee's films are virtually products of people's insecurity and paranoia. The majority of the audience longs for a means to clean up the world of rampant crime and injustice" (1981, 34). *Sunny*, a delightful and subtle film which disregards temporal linearity, anachronistically uses the tragicomic struggle for authority between the "Sunny" gang and their rivals, "Girls' Generation,"[4] as an analogy for the June Democracy Movement of the following year (1987). The implication is that although these personal, social, and political events have receded into the past, they shape the present just as the girlhood of the main characters is a specter that haunts their adult lives. In the novel *Here Come the Losers!*, violent demonstrations against the country's rulers are seen as necessary for democracy: "Our country [Korea] regards demonstrations as bad, but they are the people's last option for self protection and direct expression of opinions. Freedom of decision, of assembly, and of demonstration is the essence of democracy" (Yang, 2008: 157). Violence thus begets violence. If, as fiction and film for and about teenagers suggest, a school is a microcosm of a society, then violence is rife in Korean society, and an effect of evoking the 1970s and 1980s is to affirm that contemporary society has not changed. Classrooms are constant sites of teacher violence—both physical and mental/verbal. Such violence is not only depicted as inflicted upon boys, as in *Once Upon a Time in High School* and *Here Come the Losers!*, but also seen as prevalent in girls' schools, where male teachers physically assault female students and student bullies beat and rob chosen victims (*Sunny* depicts this as still rife in 2011).

The propensity for violence to be gendered impacts strongly upon the representation of teenage girls, who are normatively depicted as subject to a persistent gender hierarchy. Because within Confucian and patriarchal tradition males presume superiority, it is assumed that women are available to be exploited. Schoolgirls in particular are deemed to be available sex objects by teachers (as in the *Whispering Corridors* group [1998–2009]), by adult males more generally (as depicted in Kim Ki Duk's confrontational *Samaritan Girl* (2004), in which schoolgirl complicity in underage sex leads to moral collapse and death), and by schoolboys (as in *Once Upon a Time in High School*, in which the circulation of pornography particularly degrading of women—depictions of women having sex with animals are especially sought after—shapes boys' attitudes). These attitudes lead to an assumption that sex is the only point of a relationship and that girls themselves have no other desires. In every case, girls are depicted as complicit in their exploitation because social formations position them as already abjected. Indeed, the principal female character in *Once Upon a Time in High School*, Kang Eun-Joo, is shown to be so interpellated by gender conventions that she cannot envisage a relationship in which she is not abjected. Male–female relations are a key situation in which the self-in-relationship-with-others model is shown to be impossible. Hyun-Soo is strongly attracted to Eun-Joo but expresses his attraction as respectful adoration from a distance. He is depicted as a Korean version of "the new man"—gentle and other-regarding, unlike his peers. At one point when Eun-Joo asks him how he and Woo-Shik can be friends, because their attitudes are so different, she remarks that she feels more comfortable with Hyun-Soo than with her female friends. Perhaps this is a problem for Hyun-Soo at that historical period: a girl doesn't understand how to relate to a "new man," and Eun-Joo destroys the possibility of a relationship by running away with Woo-Shik, who is dominating and contemptuous of women. This love triangle affords a crucial realization of subject-constitution, in that each character is oriented differently to the self-in-relationship-with-others model: for Hyun-Soo, it is the ground of subjectivity; for Woo-Shik, it is a possibility he glimpses when he considers the well-being of others, but it is a mark of weakness and to no extent might include females; and for Eun-Joo, abjection is the normal female state, despite her intelligence and beauty.

A final element which has a strong negative impact on the production of agentic subjectivity is the absence of an effective socioeconomic safety net for families or individuals in need of support, who belong to an underclass, or whose changing circumstances consign them to poverty, homelessness, and other abjected states (cf., Cho, 2000: 64). Children and young people are especially susceptible when one or both parents die, become unemployed, or simply disappear, and the children find themselves abandoned to an uncertain future as "surplus" people. This motif has been widely deployed in recent films—such as *Sunny, Bleak Night, A Light Sleep* (2008), *Cherry Tomatoes* (2007), *Treeless Mountain* (2008), among others—and in TV dramas, where it may function as a catalyst for a rags-to-riches story, as in, for example, *Cinderella's Sister* (2010). One of the characters in *Sunny*, Yoo Bok-Hee, who is initially presented as a pretty and vivacious girl, left school with an inadequate education because of the financial disaster of her mother's hairdressing salon, and, after a divorce, lives as an alcoholic and prostitute and has entrusted her daughter to a "facility." The fantasy of *Sunny* provides a safety net in the reconstituted female network, when Choon-Hwa at her death provides a legacy that gives Bok-Hee rehabilitation, a home and a secure small business, and hence a happy life. The point of this moment in the film is not only to critique a society in which a vastly uneven distribution of wealth creates an abjected underclass but also to illustrate how the model of the self-in-relationship-with-others has failed in this dystopian society.

The possibility of failure and its consequences hangs heavily over young Korean people. They embark upon their high school years within a heavily social constructivist framework, and hence there seems to be little scope for subjective agency. What constitutes selfhood is subjected to pathways determined by notions of a successful school career—that is, a career that leads to subsequent admission to a prestigious university. To achieve this goal, students must set aside their own desires and sacrifice their lives—and especially the final year of high school. Implicit in this process is a social system that assumes—and creates—systems of elites and underclasses through competition and comparison. Korean juvenile fiction of the twenty-first century (in general a recent phenomenon) turns its attention toward young people from these underclasses, those who are militated against and marginalized by a society that oscillates between a modernized individualism and a persistent sense of hierarchy. In examining how young people are pushed to the social periphery, and their concomitant sense of hopelessness, the fiction and film challenge current directions in Korean society. Social systems change over time, as South Korea has experienced over the past half century, and such change entails changes in the type of human subject thereby produced, but also suggests that the direction of change is not inevitable.

Both *Hiking Girls* and *Here Come the Losers!* represent characters who move in from the periphery by means of self-in-relationship-with-others social experiences that enable them to reground their identities. The two principal characters of *Hiking Girls* are guilty of petty crimes (not to mention the social crime of failing at school), and the narrating character, Eun-Sung, has been guilty of bullying. Her companion, Bo-Ra, in contrast, has been an abject victim of bullying. These girls are offered a choice between a juvenile detention center or taking part in a pilot program for resocialization of delinquent juveniles: they are to walk 1200 kilometers through the Gobi Desert along the old Silk Road. The girls are still not expected to be integrated within the mainstream of Korean society, however—their fate as surplus people has already been decided. Similarly, the four boys in *Here Come the Losers!* are already precluded from the mainstream because they attend an industrial high school in provincial Choon Chun, where they are ostensibly in their final year. Afflicted with the malaise of hopelessness, they hang around PC (computer game) rooms, pool tables, department stores, and cinemas in the city and only go to school to get a free lunch when they run out of pocket money.

In *Hiking Girls*, the characters find a sense of direction as their journey becomes metaphoric. In *Here Come the Losers!*, the boys find a social place for themselves when they agree to work in a summer job in a remote village. There they become more aware of aspects of their society's history and of how powerful elites create underclass communities, and their participation in resistance transforms them from aimless, thoughtless half humans to nascent humans who are conscious of social justice, of the need for altruism, and most of all of what they want to do in the future. Both novels suggest that agency, albeit limited, can be actively sought and can function as the beginning of a refashioning of both self and society.

Coincidentally, both novels were published in the same year as the Korean translation of Louis Sachar's *Holes* (2008; original English edition, 1998), with which they have several themes in common. All use the premise that a close experience of a harsh environment will transform and enrich the subjectivities of wayward or maladjusted young people, but in particular, all three depict the transformation as a makeover, of both the body and subjectivity, which leads to transformed perceptions of self and social relationships. There is also a contrast with *Holes*, however, which throws further light on how Korean texts represent the interpellation of the self into social practice. Friendless, overweight, and victimized by bullies, at the beginning of *Holes*, Stanley Yelnats is convicted of a crime he did not commit and sentenced to eighteen months of detention in a camp in the desert. Stanley is thus utterly abjected. At the camp, detainees are compelled to dig a hole five feet deep and five feet across every day. Contrary to the camp's purposes, Stanley makes friends and develops both a strong, healthy body and a capacity for other-regardingness. At the close, the narrator alludes to Stanley's weight loss but dismisses it as a superficial change and continues, "the reader probably cares more about the change in Stanley's character and self-confidence. But those changes are subtle and hard to measure. There is no simple answer" (2008, 230). Subjectivity, then, is elusive and hard to define, but is evident in character teleology. Kimberley Reynolds observes that central to Stanley's makeover are "lack of focus on self and increased alertness to the needs of those around him," behavioral traits which set him apart from subject positions associated with hard-bodied masculinity and align him rather with "a more general, gender-neutral prescription for coming to terms with self-identity" (2002, 107). Other-regardingness, however, is subtly different from self-in-relationship-with-others, in that some notion of the self as autonomous and self-actualizing is the locus of action rather than an intersubjective blending.

In contrast, self-in-relationship-with-others is what needs to be internalized by the characters of *Hiking Girls* and *Here Come the Losers!* Unlike Stanley, *Hiking Girls'* Eun-Sung and Bo-Ra are guilty of minor offenses, although it is clear that their behavior is socially produced. Eun-Sung beat up a classmate and the victim's more powerful parents refused a reconciliation agreement with her mother; and Bo-Ra was caught stealing, which was her outlet for the stress caused by her victimization by the school bully. The two girls walk side by side for seventy days, along the Silk Road, from Urumqi to Dunhuang, and they quickly grow up during their time on the hot desert road as they experience various adventures and reflect upon their past, future, and family. The narrator/focalizer Eun-Sung was born to a single mother, with whom she does not get along, and from her outsider position questions the norms of society: what constitutes an ideal family?; what is happiness? Such questions are prompted by the way people envisage social norms and therefore presume that she is unhappy and somehow emotionally damaged because she does not have a father and lives with a single mother. Eun-Sung sees things differently:

> I've never been unhappy because I didn't have a Father. It was only other people who decided that I was unhappy.
> "There's no father? A wretched thing, Tut, tut."
> "Her mother is a single mom? Gosh, this family has so many problems. How difficult it is to live without a Father!"
> People decided freely that I was unhappy without asking me. (Kim, 2008: 214–215, my translation)

Eun-Sung's situation is a precise example of the paradox that society itself blocks its ideal of the self-in-relationship-with-others. If the ideal presupposes a fluid personhood, social structures themselves need to be fluid rather than hammered into rigid patterns. The pivot of the problem here is adherence to a Confucian, patrifocal script for the family. Patrifocality, as defined by Mukhopadhyay and Seymour, is a kinship and family structure that may take various forms but always implies the subordination of individual goals and interests to the welfare of the larger family; patrilineal inheritance; patrilocal descent and residence; gender differentiated family roles; family control of marriage arrangements; and an ideology of appropriate female behavior emphasizing chastity, obedience, domesticity, and adaptability (1994, 3–4). The extent to which such a script prevails in contemporary Korean society is evidenced by thematized interrogation of it across a wide range of creative genres. It is particularly evident in *Sunny*, in which each of the seven adult women exemplifies a different version of the patrifocal script, with the implication that the only one who has been "the protagonist of her own life" is Choon-Hwa, and she has achieved this by divorce and remaining childless. Na-Mi, for example, has an amiable relationship with her husband, but from the beginning of the film, she is clearly positioned as subordinate: she is shown as first to wake and get up, and the camera lingers on her fluffy slippers, and when her husband leaves on a business trip, he hands her a generous amount of spending money in an envelope. The patrifocal script emerges in diverse ways in other narratives, as with the wicked queens who betray their husbands in historical dramas (in, for example, *Jumong* [2006–2007], the most watched of Korean TV drama series). It may also be double-edged, as in *King of Baking, Kim Tak-Goo* (2010), in which the wife who schemes against her husband is finally abandoned in her expensive house, where she walks up and down uttering absurdities at the brink of insanity, whereas the two half brothers who have vied for control of the family business surprisingly collude to hand it to their highly competent sister. *King of Baking* thus offers a more fluid representation, whereby patrifocality is understood in relation to ethical behavior.

The inflexible application of patrifocal assumptions condemns Eun-Sung to abjection despite anything she does: she has no possibility of subjective agency, and indeed every time she makes trouble, her behavior is attributed to her lack of a father. *Hiking Girls* generalizes the failure of the social ideal still further by defining how the imposition of social patterns prevents self-in-relationship-with-others because it does not envisage that the self will have input into the social field. Eun-Sung comes to such a conclusion as she muses about the question of what constitutes a good/ideal life for individuals, in contrast to the script for a model teenage life envisaged by Korean society:

> "There are so many standards in the world. Standards such as you have to study diligently, just like so-and-so,[5] and then become as rich as so-and-so. Why should we follow such standards? It's better to live just like me. Why should we always compare ourselves with people around us and then get anxious if we find ourselves lacking? It's nonsense."
>
> Bo-Ra kicked a roadside rock.
>
> "Well, isn't it like a sample answer?" ...
>
> A sample answer is a credible answer prepared beforehand. There's always a sample answer to a subjective descriptive problem, and you get higher marks if you write an answer close to the sample answer.
>
> "Because it's not easy to live, just follow the sample answer. It's easy to follow the answer already set down. And it makes sense to do that."
>
> "But sample answers are only samples, not real answers. Sample answers are fake."
>
> "That's right!" Bo-Ra shouted.
>
> Sample answers pretend to be the exact answers, pretend to be genuine. My answers are certainly right, but teachers flatly say they are wrong because they are not like the sample answers. And then if they find out the answers are written by unreliable Lee Eun-Sung, the mark is unconditionally halved. (Kim, 2008: 225–226, my translation)

In contrast to Eun-Sung's rebellious and often violent behavior, Bo-Ra has spent her life following the patrifocal script and this has entailed an equivalent abjection:

> Women should be quiet and obedient, so I always lived quietly; and students should study hard, so all I did was study. I never did anything I wanted to do. I did things because my parents told me to and the teacher told me to. It's the same story that brought me here. My mom told me that I should go here, heaven knows where she found out about it, because this way I didn't have to go to a children's detention center. That's why I came. And I have been walking according to the rules. (212, my translation)

Like Stanley and Hector in *Holes*, Eun-Sung and Bo-Ra climb a mountain. What this action signifies in each case further illuminates the contrast between the autonomous-self script and the self-in-relationship-with-others script. Tapping (albeit somewhat comically) into a genre embracing the wilderness survival narrative and robinsonade, *Holes* depicts the two boys struggling up Big Thumb. Stanley has to carry Hector up the final stretch, where he finds a field of wild onions moistened by water seeping from a spring. The boys dig a hole to capture water and stay there for a couple of weeks, living on onions and water. As Lenz argues, the struggle against an extreme landscape raises questions about what it means to be human, about the meaning of life more generally, and about what constitutes human happiness, and survival can be an assurance that it is possible to build a new life (1986, 24). After a few days on the mountain, Stanley feels transformed:

> Two nights later, Stanley lay awake staring up at the star-filled sky. He was too happy to fall asleep. . . .
> It occurred to him that he couldn't remember the last time he felt happiness. It wasn't just being sent to Camp Green Lake that had made his life miserable. Before that he'd been unhappy at school, where he had no friends, and bullies like Derrick Dunne picked on him. No one liked him, and the truth was, he didn't especially like himself.
> He liked himself now. (186)

Stanley's transformation stems from the assumption that the core of subjective agency is self-awareness. In contrast, Eun-Sung's experience of a very different kind of mountain landscape shows her that subjectivity begins with fluid personhood, which she finds imaged in the landscape. The mountain the girls climb is Mingsha Shan (鳴沙山, literally 'Echoing Sand Mountain'), a sand dune famous for the thunderous sound of the wind moving the sand about. The view from the summit includes Crescent Lake, an oasis that has existed for two millennia, because as sand falls toward the lake it is caught by the wind and blown away across the mountain. The oasis thus symbolizes a symbiosis of water, wind, and sand. Eun-Sung's thoughts, however, are more caught up with the ever-changing contours of the dune:

> The wind on Mingsha Shan does not blow in one direction. So the contour and shape of Mingsha Shan change every day according to how the wind blows . . . there is nothing that does not change in the world. . . . my grandmother said she would always be with me, but she left me. Will I change gradually too? Maybe I am changing now. (Kim, 2008: 269, my translation)

Hiking Girls does not narrate what happens to the girls after their 1200 kilometer trek has reached its end, but by emphasizing the innate metaphoricity of such journeys and relating Eun-Sung's reflections on her life journey, it suggests that they will now move forward and strive for the intersubjectivity they have been lacking. Eun-Sung concludes: "It doesn't matter if what I believe is a mirage. An oasis will appear one day if I keep walking. An oasis is bound to be hidden in a desert. . . . From tomorrow, a new hiking will begin" (282).

To move forward, the girls will need to work out how to become adults, but in both *Hiking Girls* and *Here Come the Losers!*, adults and the worlds of adults are depicted negatively. The narrator of the latter, Son Jae-Woong, is bewildered by the same script for a model teenage life that baffles Eun-Sung and deprives teenagers of agency. He is assured that the only pathway is study, and reflects that if this were truly possible for him, then his mother's nagging, the indifference of teachers, and the dark shadow which lies over the future will all disappear (Yang, 2008: 28). The objective of study, however, is put into conflict with the self-in-relationship-with-others script, and the vision of a dog-eat-dog society projected by teachers is simply a version of the Korean dystopia. The typical teacher's warning, according to Jae-Woong, follows this script: "You're soon going to become an adult . . . I'm worried about you. Worried. Like it or not, you're about to enter the world. You don't know how dreadful the world is. If you're not focused, you'll soon become prey for others. No wonder your mother is worried" (26). Success in life is then measured by gaining entrance to a good university (regardless of major personal interest or adaptability), and both the novels and films thematize this requirement as a pressure upon subjectivity. University graduates are deemed higher than high school graduates regardless of type of employment, even though many individuals would perform far better in practical schools. Bo-Ra (*Hiking Girls*) would like to become a graphic artist, but her mother always tears up anything she draws; Na-Mi (*Sunny*) has the same talent, but is never able to develop it (her parents have invested heavily in the *good university* script). Social prejudices and discrimination toward graduates from industrial high schools are well represented in *Here Come the Losers!*, where the four boys are deemed to be future "surplus men" in society only because they attend industrial/vocational high school instead of normal high school where students prepare for university entrance. They have internalized their abjection, and because they see life as purposeless, they often think about committing suicide:

> What's the use of living like this? Even if we become adults, will things change? Hey, friend, should we just kill ourselves?
>
> Whew, you're right! Ah, I've been really wanting to kill myself recently too.
>
> A vague anxiety makes itself felt. I graduate next year. (Yang, 2008: 33, my translation)

Suicide as a response to social abjection and pressure to perform in a patrifocal dystopia has been a recurrent motif in Korean teen films since it emerged in the *Whispering Corridors* series (1998–2009), especially in *Memento Mori* (1999) and *A Blood Pledge* (2009). Indeed in *Memento Mori*, the students share a belief that a school is closed down after seven students have committed suicide. Alternatives to suicide, which perform a similar thematic function, are disappearance or drug addiction.

A particularly delicately nuanced representation of the struggle to survive in the dystopia is the film *A Light Sleep* (2008), in which the protagonist, sixteen-year-old Yul-Lin, who lost both parents two years before the beginning of the film, devotes herself to constructing the semblance of a normal life for herself and her much younger sister, Da-Rin. Often on the edge of exhaustion, Yul-Lin suffers from chronic insomnia and has become addicted to sleeping pills. The depiction of her attempt to maintain an appearance of normality and withstand the pressures applied to a young adult has significant implications for subjectivity. If subjectivity is developed from intersubjective family, peer group, and social network relationships, what happens to a teenage girl who is suddenly orphaned and has a preschool sister to care for? Thematically, much of the film pivots on a paradox of responsibility and agency, focused especially through Yul-Lin's relationship with Da-Rin: she feeds her, gets her to preschool, and shows her love, but these actions also diminish Yul-Lin's own agency. Yul-Lin is caught between her obvious love for her little sister and her desire to retain some elements of a teenage life: she can't go to parties or go on dates with groups, and her closest female friend (Soo-Jin), who is quite solipsistic by comparison and resents Joo-Go's attention to Yul-Lin, behaves petulantly in response to Yul-Lin's evasiveness about joining in. The self-in-relationship-with-others script cannot be instantiated because, as the opening sequence titled "Protective Color" makes clear, she conceals her impoverished orphan state from her peers and the precariousness of her everyday existence from the adult world by ensuring that she and Da-Rin are neat and well-presented and by lying to adults. She only seems to fit in—for example, she has the technological accessories usual in her peer group, but they are superseded models; she shoplifts to acquire small nonessentials. In one classroom scene, the teacher (with his back to the class) threatens to punish all girls who are texting (it is the entire class)—affluent, unfocused, these girls have no experience to compare with Yul-Lin's (who is texting Soo-Jin to refuse a party invitation). When Yul-Lin meets with a social worker responsible for her case, the counselor is friendly but asks only bland, routine questions to which Yul-Lin easily gives lying answers.

The film works by obliquity and suggestion—e.g., the possibility that Yul-Lin is selling her body to raise the money to support herself and her sister is only hinted at: a predatory older male, Mr. Kim, one of the people with some responsibility for the girls, proposes that she just sleep with him (a proposal Yul-Lin rejects); she sometimes leaves her little sister alone (for example, leaves her in KFC), but the film doesn't follow where she goes; she is reluctant to maintain a relationship with the boy (Joo-Go) who likes her and discretely empathizes with her situation. Joo-Go, however, is positioned outside Korean patrifocality and embodies an ideal version of masculinity—caring, discrete, not dominating. A fantasy sequence near the end of the film segues from photographs of Yul-Lin as a small child with her parents to her seventeenth birthday, still in the future, which she shares with Joo-Go and which implies that she has finally entered the self-in-relationship-with-others script. In reaching such a closure, *A Light Sleep* coincides with all of the texts discussed in this chapter. It may not be a social fact in Korea that subjectivities are shaped in this way, but it is a social formation strongly advocated in fiction and film. To conclude this chapter, I now return to *Sunny*, a film which both strongly intervenes in representations of subjectivity and was a huge box office success.

The narrative about a group of high school friends and their future lives as women twenty-five years later sensitively explores the possibilities of subjective agency in South Korea. Writing in 1995, Cho Hae-Joang commented that, "Unlike middle-class housewives in most industrial societies, Korean women have little interest in charitable work or community welfare programs. . . . They invest their time solely in immediate familial interests" (1995, 141–165). This is still the behavior of women represented in film and television in the first decade of the twenty-first century, but now in the context of the increasing disintegration of the idea of the family as a consequence of the rapid modernization of the last quarter of the twentieth century. As I remarked earlier, *Sunny* uses its intersecting narrative paths to valorize the self-in-relationship-with-others script. As its temporal line slides back and forth between 1986 and 2011, it develops contrasts between the girls' optimism about their future and the diminished lives of the adults. Geum-Ok, for example, boisterous and playfully violent as a girl, with aspirations to be a writer, is virtually enslaved by her husband and mother-in-law and lacks even the agency to pause to drink coffee when her old friends track her down and visit. Lacking resources of her own and unable to go out, she asks Na-Mi to take Choon-Hwa a small gift of money. It's a painful, embarrassing scene, rendered even more so when Na-Mi draws on her husband's monetary gift to add respectability to Geum-Ok's offering. In a parallel scene, Na-Mi and Jang-Mi visit Bok-Hee in the bar where she works as a prostitute, but now, to fend off Bok-Hee's employer, Na-Mi uses her husband's money to buy food and drink—and, with playful irony, pay for the time Bok-Hee would spend with a client. In these ways, the present time story begins to feel its way toward finding an equivalence with the way the girls cared for and enjoyed each other, regardless of difference. In fragmenting the story of seven women at two points in time when their lives intersect, the film deconstructs the classical bildungsroman narration of a coherent subject and replaces it with interstices and incoherencies, with micronarratives that have thematic impact but little or no closure.

I conclude with a brief account of two episodes which, building on the temporal slipping of the narrative, contrast different ways of representing the self-in-relationship-with-others script. The first example develops a gentle emotional closure to an incident in Na-Mi's life. As a girl, she had a crush on an insouciant, handsome young man named Han Joon-Ho, and secretly made a conte sketch of him and had it framed. When she attempted to give it to him as a present, she found him kissing Soo-Ji and felt heartbroken. As an adult, she uses the detective hired to locate the members of Sunny to find Joon-Ho as well and makes a trip to his town to meet him. He does not recognize her, and she doesn't reveal herself, but simply hands him the sketch in its wrapping, saying, "I can at last give this to you," and leaves. He is no longer the romantic figure of her girlhood but a nondescript middle-aged man. As she walks home through an autumnal evening on a path scattered with fallen gingko leaves, she is depicted moving from right to left across the screen, and as the mode shifts into magical realism, her direction becomes a movement into the past, as she meets her young self, disconsolate after her dream has been crushed. In the film's most drastic departure from realism, the older Na-Mi wordlessly comforts her younger self (Figure 6.2), in a move that declares that many of the film's images are to be interpreted metaphorically. This is an emotionally moving scene, even as the medium distant view, the slightly elevated angle, and the canting of what was previously a level surface maintain the magical realist framing. Subjectivity is formed over time and through relationships, and as sorrow transforms into nostalgic regret, the self reforms and finds sources of comfort. The resolution of such small personal griefs is part of the process whereby the self-in-relationship-with-others comes into being.

In quite a different vein, *Sunny* incorporates many carnivalesque elements. This mode first appears when two rival groups of girls confront each other and engage in a *flyting*, or ritual exchange of insults, to borrow a term from medieval Scots poetry.[6] The carnivalesque reaches its acme when Na-Mi discovers that Ye-Bin, her daughter, is being bullied at school. Na-Mi (wearing Ye-Bin's school uniform), Jin-Hee, Choon-Hwa, and Jang-Mi ambush the

Figure 6.2   Na-Mi comforts her younger self.
Source: Sunny.

bullies and thrash them, as they had dealt with bullies twenty-five years ago. Subsequently arrested by some bemused police officers, the four women are traveling in a police car when the radio plays the version of the song "Sunny" as performed by the 1970s–1980s Europop group *Boney M.*[7] As the women one by one begin to reproduce the hand movements they had practiced long ago, the scene cuts to a sequence when the young Sunny members dance to the same song. This scene is later reprised by the women as adults at Choon-Hwa's second funeral ceremony, attended only by the members of Sunny, when the final clause of Choon-Hwa's will specifies that the group should perform one more time, there and then, in her honor. Is it proper to dance at a funeral? Is it proper for a solicitor in the same time and place to read aloud a will written throughout in the girls' foul language? Across the film's time span, the carnivalesque signifies a possibility of agency, of resistance to interpellation into a social practice that demands conformity to state ideology, ritualized learning, and diminished lives within patrifocality. Its subversive quality is encapsulated in a comical remark made by Jang-Mi as she reflects on the assault on the schoolgirl bullies: "Designer handbags are awesome. They can split open a skull with one blow." Choon-Hwa's will is the culmination of the film's carnivalesque impulse, as it envisages a new Korean society and subjectivity grounded in the self-in-relationship-with-others script. Its discourse is comically disruptive, but its content is judicious and compassionate. Most of the money is left to charity. To her wealthy friends, she leaves nothing; to Na-Mi, she bequeaths leadership of Sunny and hence a responsibility to sustain the group's newly regained intersubjectivity; to Jin-Hee, she leaves the statement, "You're rich, bitch!" and a coda that makes her Na-Mi's deputy. And for Jang-Mi, Geum-Ok, and Bok-Hee, she builds a safety net appropriate to the situation of each to enable her to feel self-worth.

The novels and films discussed in this chapter concur in the view that the construction of subjectivity depends on intersubjective relationships, and seek a balance between representations of subjectivity according to the independent or interdependent model. To be the protagonist of one's own life—to fashion a self as an agentic center of thought and action—is seen as possible within the self-in-relationship-with-others ideology of subjectivity, but society is depicted as failing its own implicit ideal by limiting possible subject positions to what is assumed to be permissible national or familial identity. Hence the interdependent model can only be recuperated by behavior that effectively transgresses it through the espousal of a more independent subject position, as is the case in all of the texts discussed. These novels and films also concur in representing Korean society as a dystopia (the situation depicted in the 2008 novels effectively reproduces the historical situations shown in the films), and by focusing attention on the processes that prevent actualization of self-in-relationship-with-others, they depict a social reality, and they model more desirable ways of being. That these works are symptomatic of a dominant theme in contemporary fiction and film points both to an awareness that there is a problem and to the urgency of the desire for social change.

Notes

1. The original reads:

   나 꽤오랫동안 엄마, 집사람으로 살았거든. 인간 임나미 아득한 기억 저편이었는데 나도 역사가 있는 적어도 내인생의 주인공이 더라고.

2. The title is more literally, *The History of Cruelty in Maljuk Street* (말죽거리 잔혹사).

3. Because of South Korea's still prevalent Confucian heritage, schools are mostly single-sex.

4. The name of the girl gang is another example of the film's many cheeky, creative anachronisms. *Girls' Generation* (소녀시대) is a nine-member South Korean pop girl group formed in 2007 and an international success by 2011. The leader of Sunny's rival gang mentions that the name is not very sophisticated, and so she wanted to change to "Fin.K.L" (핑클): this refers to another Korean pop girl group, active during 1998–2002, and one of the most popular girl groups in Korean pop history.

5. In *Here Come the Losers!*, the social network pressure referred to here is more closely specified as: "Mom's Friend's Son/Daughter" (엄친아, 엄친딸).

6. One of the box office appeals of *Sunny* is the virulence of taboo language in the conversation of women and girls. Even when the women have become adults, profanity and abuse are part of everyday speech: they commonly refer to one another as "bitch" and eventually it becomes an affectionate and intimate term. The Korean word "년 *nyun*" literally means 'bitch,' but is usually combined with demonstratives in vocatives (e.g., "야이년들아," 'hey, you bitches'); it is always offensive when addressing a stranger, so Geum-Ok takes umbrage when Choon-Hwa's lawyer so addresses them when repeating the words from Choon-Hwa's will. Unfortunately, subtitles cannot capture the flavor of the film's taboo language or its exploitation of dialect. Young Na-Mi, for example, has transferred from Bulgyo, Jolla Province, and when she loses self-control, her determination to speak the standard dialect of Seoul is swept aside by her heavy Jolla Province dialect. There are particularly funny moments when she imitates the foul language of her provincial grandmother, whose dementia has removed all social barriers. Na-Mi utterly routs Sunny's rival gang, *Girls' Generation*, by imitating her grandmother, to the extent that Jin-Hee, "the queen of foul language," wants to take lessons.

7. This is a plausible coincidence, as *Boney M* was both popular in South Korea in the 1980s and is still played as classic pop in the present day.

Works Cited

Chiao, Hsiung-Ping. "Bruce Lee: His Influence on the Evolution of the Kung Fu Genre," *Journal of Popular Film and Television* 9.1 (1981): 30–42.

Cho, Hae-Joang. "Children in the Examination War in South Korea: A Cultural Analysis." In *Children and the Politics of Culture*, edited by Sharon Stephens. Princeton: Princeton University Press, 1995.

———. "'You Are Entrapped in an Imaginary Well': The Formation of Subjectivity within Compressed Development—A Feminist Critique of Modernity and Korean Culture," *Inter-Asia Cultural Studies* 1.1 (2000): 49–69.

Kim, Hye-Jung. *Hiking Girls* (하이킹 걸즈). Seoul: Biryongso (비룡소), 2008.

Lenz, Millicent. "The Experience of Time and the Concept of Happiness in Michel Tournier's *Friday and Robinson: Life on Speranza Island*," *Children's Literature Association Quarterly* 11.1 (1986): 24–29.

Markus, Hazel Rose, and Shinobu Kitayama. "Culture and the Self: Implications for Cognition, Emotion, and Motivation," *Psychological Review* 98.2 (1991): 224–253.

Mukhopadhyay, Carol Chapnick, and Susan Seymour, eds. *Women, Education and Family Structure in India*. Boulder, CO: Westview Press, 1994.

Ning, Ma. "Rules of the Forbidden Game: Violence in Contemporary Chinese Cinema," *New Cinemas* 8.3 (2011): 169–177.

Reynolds, Kimberley. "Come Lads and Ladettes: Gendering Bodies and Gendering Behaviors." In *Ways of Being Male: Representing Masculinities in Children's Literature and Film*, edited by John Stephens. New York: Routledge, 2002.

Sachar, Louis. *Holes*. New York: Farrar, Straus and Giroux, 1998. Korean translation by Kim Yeong Seon. Houston: Changbi/Tsai Fong Books, 2008.

Uchida, Yukiko, Vinai Norasakkunkit, and Shinobu Kitayama. "Cultural Constructions of Happiness: Theory and Empirical Evidence," *Journal of Happiness Studies* 5 (2004): 223–239.

Yang, Ho-Moon. *Here Come the Losers!* (꼴찌들이 떴다!). Seoul: Biryongso (비룡소), 2008.

Films and Dramas

Bleak Night (파수꾼). Dir. Yoon Sung-Hyun. Korea: Filament, 2011. Film.

A Blood Pledge (여고괴담 5: 동반자살, *Yeogo goedam 5: Dongban jasal*). Dir. Lee Jong-Yong. Korea: Lotte Entertainment, 2009. Film.

Jumong (주몽). Dir. Lee Joo-Hwan and Kim Geun-Hong. Korea: MBC, 2007. Television.

King of Baking, Kim Tak-Goo (제빵왕 김탁구). Dir. Lee Joon-Sub. Korea: KBS, 2010. Television.

A Light Sleep (가벼운 잠). Dir. Lim Sung-Chan. Korea: Kino-Eye, 2008. Film.

Memento Mori (여고괴담 2, *Yeogo goedam* 2). Dir. Kim Tae-Yong and Min Gyoo-Dong. Korea: Cinema Service, 1999. Film.

Once Upon a Time in High School (말죽거리 잔혹사). Dir. Yoo Ha. Korea: CJ Entertainment, 2004. Film.

Samaritan Girl (사마리아). Dir. Kim Ki-Duk. Korea: Cineclick Asia, 2004. Film.

Sunny (써니). Dir. Kang Hyung-Chul. Korea: CJ Entertainment, 2011. Film.

Whispering Corridors (여고괴담, *Yeogo goedam*). Dir. Park Gi-Hyung. Korea: Cinema Service, 1998. Film.

Chapter Seven
Contingent Subjectivity and Masculinity in Japanese Film for Young People

Christie Barber

A range of terms has been used to describe the Japanese sense of self: "socially defined," "contextualized," "embedded," "contingent" (Lebra, 2007: 127); "situational" (Bachnik and Quinn, cited in Clammer, 2003: 24); and "interdependent" (Markus and Kitayama, 1991: 227). What all of these terms focus on is the central idea that subjectivity in Japanese terms is constructed and expressed dependent upon context and relationships (between the self and others). Subjectivity can shift depending upon context, and the ability to shift effectively between and within contexts, achieved through sensitivity to others and self-discipline, is seen as the realization of mature subjectivity (Bachnik, 1986: 68–69). Key to this shifting is individual agency: the self must determine what degree of informality or spontaneity is acceptable, or what degree of politeness, formality, or distance is required for the specific social interaction (Bachnik, 1992: 24; Kondo, 1987: 263; Markus and Kitayama, 1991: 228).

In this chapter, I will explore the idea that subjectivities are constructed and expressed in varied ways, relative to context and/or relationships, referring as my examples to two Japanese films from 2001, *Go* and *Blue Spring* (青い春; *Aoi Haru*). I will consider in particular the depiction of gender (in this case masculine), given its inextricable link to the development of subjectivity, and suggest that the gender identities of the central characters are also constructed as contingent upon varied situations and relationships. These relational masculinities serve to both reinforce and challenge the dominant model of masculinity. Although both films share the same central theme (the experiences of male students nearing the end of their high school education), they also offer contrasting portrayals of subjectivities (and masculinities), and this contrast will also be an underlying theme of my discussion. *Go* offers a positive portrayal of male subjectivity, as the central character learns to manage the challenges of his existence, developing meaningful subjective agency despite his position outside the dominant model of Japanese masculinity. *Blue Spring*, in contrast, presents male subjectivities that are disconnected from the broader world, and thus remain almost frozen in immaturity, lacking self-awareness and responsibility. The male characters portrayed in *Blue Spring* may also fall outside the dominant model, but the isolation and hopelessness of their condition conveys a pessimistic message.

Identity can be imposed upon a subject by community assumptions about who belongs and who can be deemed peripheral. *Go* tells the story of Sugihara (or Lee Jong-Ho, his Korean name), a high school student in Tokyo whose parents are North Korean. The film begins with a quotation from *Romeo and Juliet*: "What's in a name? That which we call a rose by any other name would smell as sweet." Sugihara's voice-over also soon reveals that this will be a love story, and the film does indeed center on his relationship with a female Japanese student, Sakurai Tsubaki. However, it is clear from the opening scene of the film that we are also being told about Sugihara's experiences as *Zainichi Kankokujin*, a Korean permanent resident in Japan:[1] Sugihara stands surrounded, on a school basketball court, by fellow students who verbally (with the insult, *Zainichi*) and physically attack him. Sugihara was born in Japan and speaks Japanese fluently, but until his final year of junior high school, is educated in Korean at a *minzoku gakkō* (literally, national school; a school for North Korean students) and is thus bilingual.

As the *Romeo and Juliet* epigraph signals, the love story has an inherent barrier of difference. Sugihara's relationship with Tsubaki begins once he leaves the North Korean school to attend a Japanese high school (the scene of the discrimination described above). This decision was not a simple one, however; Sugihara's Korean peers belittle him, and one of his Korean teachers labels him a "traitor to his nation" and physically abuses him in the classroom. Before moving to the Japanese school, Sugihara, in the company of his Korean friends Wonsu and Tawake, was rebellious and wayward: in the second passage of the film, Sugihara, as part of a challenge given by his senior Tawake, fearlessly outruns an oncoming subway train from a standing start on tracks. After Sugihara has been captured by police, his parents arrive to collect him, but before they return home, his father, a former professional boxer, brutally beats him, as the police and Sugihara's mother watch, unable to intervene. Returning home after this beating, Sugihara's father makes the decision to travel to Hawaii with his wife, using this as the premise to unexpectedly and unnecessarily change his citizenship to South Korean, a decision that means that Sugihara can also change his citizenship. Upon making his decision, Sugihara's father says to Sugihara, "What'll you do? . . . You can easily change your nationality . . . See the world. Choose for yourself" (*Dō surunda?... Kokuseki nanka kantan ni kaeru zo... Hiroi sekai wo miro. Soshite jibun de kimero).* Given the ability to choose his nationality by his father (and as such, the option to leave the *minzoku gakkō* and attend a Japanese school), Sugihara says, "I felt like I was treated as a human for the first time" (*Boku wa hajimete ningen to shite atsukawareta yō na ki ga shita*). He soon changes his nationality to South Korean, gives up "smoking and fighting" (*tabako mo kenka mo yamete*), and enters the Japanese high school.

Sugihara's relationship with his father is a representation of subjectivity defined within and through the other. Takie Sugiyama Lebra writes, "the Japanese person not only acts in response to but also *perceives* him/herself as contingent upon a given social nexus" (2007: 127). The actions performed by Sugihara's father, and his father's actions within their relationship, allow Sugihara to perceive of his self for the first time. The use of the passive verb *atsukawareta* (was being treated) by Sugihara makes it clear that this development of subjectivity is an interdependent process; in turn, the treatment he receives enables him to actively determine the course of his future.

Sugihara's Korean ethnicity immediately positions him as subordinated other within the Japanese social order, and to some extent this determines (and constrains) the social roles and relationships he can have. Through his delinquency, Sugihara actively reinforces this othering. With the understanding that his son will experience discrimination because of his ethnicity, Sugihara's father has taught him to box from a young age. In flashback, we learn Sugihara's father's vital lesson, delivered partly as a warning and partly as a challenge:

> The circle you make with your fist is roughly the size of you as a human. Do you understand what I am saying, boy? If you stay in that circle, and don't go beyond the reach of your own arms, you will get through life unharmed ... But as for boxing: you need to break through the circle with your fist, and take something in from the outside ...
>
> There are lots of tough people on the outside, and they will come into your circle. Hurts to hit and hurts to get hit. Still wanna box? You know it is safer inside the circle.
>
> *Omae no kobushi ga hiita en no ōkisa ga, daitai omae to iu ningen no ōkisa da. Itteru koto ga wakaru ka? Bōya.*
>
> *Sono en no mannaka ni isuwatte, te no todoku han-i no mono ni dake nobashiterya, omae wa kizutsukazu ni ikite ikeru ... Bokushingu to wa nanzoya? Sono en wo, onore no kobushi de tsukiyabutte, soto kara nani ka wo ubaitotte kuru kōi da.*
>
> *Soto ni wa tsuyoi yatsu ga ippai iru zo. Soitsu ga omae no en no naka ni hairikondekuru. Nagurarerya itē shi, naguru no mo itai tte koto da. Sore de mo yaru no ka? En no naka ni iru hō ga anzen da yo.*

Sugihara's father delineates the form of Sugihara's subjectivity here. There is a boundary Sugihara controls, but it is fluid; Sugihara's self is also necessarily connected to others. Sugihara's father's message—expressed through the contrast he sets up with the terms "staying inside the circle" and "breaking through"—is that by breaking through the "circle" and taking from the outside, Sugihara will develop meaningful subjectivity. Sugihara needs the outside, regardless of how painful that interaction may be, to develop into a capable human being. Sugihara's father is also teaching him what he believes are the necessary skills to ensure that development of subjectivity is directed through Sugihara's own agency.

Sugihara's relationship with his father also demonstrates the way in which hierarchy functions contingently. Robert Smith describes the ordering of relations between self and other as "hierarchy in action" (quoted in Bachnik, 1986: 71); Lebra labels it "double hierarchy," asserting that self-other exchange is a bidirectional process, where both parties have power conditioned by their position (2004, 17). Sugihara's father beats him brutally twice in the film; first at the police station and second after Sugihara berates his father, who is drunkenly reminiscing with stories of his childhood in North Korea after hearing that his younger brother has died. Sugihara tells his father that he is stuck in the past, part of a generation of complainers that never change. After they fight, Sugihara's father concedes that his generation's time has passed, and the time has come to be more open-minded. This admission is reinforcement of Sugihara's decision to change schools and thus take more control of and responsibility for his future. Sugihara's father also recognizes the knowledge he receives from his son; his son, although lower in the social hierarchy, has the ability to influence him, demonstrating the way in which their relations are bidirectional.

Lebra uses the term "embedded" to describe the way in which the Japanese self is enmeshed in the social order (2007: 127). In Sugihara's case, his understanding of his connection to the past, and his actions in the present, demonstrate the embedded nature of his subjectivity and the way in which that subjectivity is negotiated *within* and *against* a range of social, political, and cultural conditions. For example, at the birthday party of a friend, Sugihara blocks out the noise of dance music and the other guests by listening to a tape of *rakugo*, traditional Japanese comic storytelling. Further, when he meets Tsubaki's family over dinner, he asks Tsubaki's father if he knows the correct meaning of the name of their country, Japan (*Nihon*); when Tsubaki's father makes a guess, Sugihara comments that it is unusual how many Japanese do not know the correct meaning and origins of this word *Nihon*. And, in conversation with his closest friend, Jong-Il, and a waitress at a restaurant, Sugihara explains that the origins of the Japanese race are in such places as China and Korea[2]—in other words, even though they may be labeled differently now (that is, Korean or Japanese), they share the same roots. Sugihara's interest in *rakugo*, as well as his knowledge of the name and origins of Japan, shows us that he is connected to a past; he is embedded within a history. This serves to demonstrate a subjectivity that, despite having fluid and uncertain boundaries, and shifting relative to situation, is not destabilized or rootless.

The camera in *Go* works to highlight the interdependent nature of Sugihara's subjectivity. Sugihara's voice-over narration connects us closely with his perspective of events, but the key scenes of the film are usually shot as views of Sugihara with whomever it is he is interacting, with each character occupying roughly equal shares of the frame. For example, when Sugihara and Tsubaki go to a hotel to spend the night together for the first time, Sugihara feels it necessary, before they take this step in their relationship, to tell her that he was born in Japan but has South Korean (and previously) North Korean citizenship. Her reaction is one of fear and disgust; she says her father told her that the blood of Chinese and Koreans is "dirty" (*chi ga kitanai*), and she is scared of sleeping with him (*Watashi no karada ni Sugihara ga haittek-uru no ga kowai*). This scene does feature some shot-countershot sequences, but in the pivotal point of the scene, the use of perspective and light guides our interpretation of the interaction: Sugihara stands on the left of the screen, beside the bed, his face and torso lit by white light entering from a nearby window; Tsubaki, on the right of the screen, is seated on the bed, hunched under the covers, unlit and hidden under her loose dark hair falling over her body (see Figure 7.1).

Another way in which the film explores the idea of contingent subjectivity is its focus on *how* characters relate to each other and the world, rather than *what* those characters are labeled. Jane M. Bachnik writes that although in Japanese and Western conceptions of the self the poles of self and other are shared, the way in which those poles are viewed is different. Bachnik states that in viewing "social life" the West focuses on the poles of self and other— that is, the individual and society, objectified and viewed as dichotomous— whereas the Japanese focus on "the relationships *between* the poles" (1986: 61),

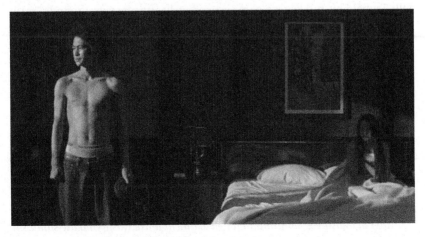

Figure 7.1   *Go*: Sugihara and Tsubaki.

on "the relation of self to society" (68). Bachnik neatly describes this Japanese perspective as a focus on the *how* instead of a focus on the *what*.

As mentioned earlier, the film opens with Shakespeare's "What's in a name?," and this connects directly with Sugihara's commentary in the first scene of the film:

> I am a born in Japan . . . I am a born in Japan, so-called Korean Japanese. I don't think I am any different to a Japanese person, but they call me *Zainichi!*
>
> *Boku wa Nihon de umareta . . . Boku wa Nihon de umareta, iwayuru Korian Japaniizu. Ma, boku wa Nihonjin to amari kawaranai to omotteirun dakedo, yatsura wa kō yobu . . . Zainichi!*

This somewhat clunky translation is deliberately rendered as such to indicate the way in which the *how* (the action [born] and the location [in Japan]), not the *what*, is brought to our attention in this scene. Sugihara is Korean Japanese, but an important aspect of the relationship he has with society is the fact that he was born in Japan. In fact, *Boku wa Nihon de umareta* is a complete sentence, meaning, 'I was born in Japan.' This is repeated by Sugihara, giving emphasis, and it is only when he adds the final phrase that we learn that this sentence is in fact a modifying clause, explaining what kind of *what* he is.

When Sugihara asks Tsubaki her name, she initially only gives him her surname because she says she does not like her first name, so he does the same. In fact, throughout the film, we never learn Sugihara's first name in Japanese, only his full Korean name. When Sugihara tells Tsubaki his Korean name at the hotel, she tells him her full name for the first time: Sakurai Tsubaki. She says she was afraid to tell him as she believes her name, because it refers to two key floral emblems of Japan (*sakura*, cherry blossoms, and *tsubaki*, camellia), "sounds really Japanese" (*mecha mecha Nihonjin mitai*).[3] When Sugihara tells Tsubaki his full Korean name immediately after, he says it sounds "really foreign" (*mecha mecha gaikokujin mitai*), so he was scared to tell her. Here both characters express fear or discomfort because of the labels describing *what* they are; until this point their relationship with each other had defined how they interacted, but Sugihara's label as *gaikokujin* (foreigner) changes the dynamic. Then, walking home after leaving Tsubaki at the hotel, Sugihara meets a police officer, and they fall into conversation, where Sugihara says:

> There are times when I seriously wish my skin was green. That way I would not forget that I am Korean Japanese, and the people who think I'm scary would stay away from the start.
>
> *Ore jibun no hada no iro ga midori-iro dattara ii nonitte honki de omou toki arimasu yo. Soshitara jibun ga Zainichi datte wasurenakute sumu shi, kowaitte iu yatsu wa hana kara chikayotte konai shi.*

The policeman responds with:

> There are times when I wish my policeman's uniform wasn't so cool. Maybe a sailor suit,[4] or a leotard. That way no one would ask me for directions . . . Regardless of what your nationality is, they will come. Because you are a good person.

> *Ore mo omawari-san no seifuku ga motto dasakattara ii no ni na, to omou koto aru yo. Sērā fuku to ka, reotādo to ka, na. Soshitara dare mo ore ni michi kiitari shinai jan . . . Nanijin daro to, yotte kuru yatsu wa yotte kuru daro. Omae ii yatsu dakara sa.*

These scenes highlight that Sugihara connects to others within and through relationships in ways that are perceived as appropriate; his social relationships are made solid not by *what* he is labeled but by *how* he effectively interacts with others. When labels are attributed or exposed, these relationships are affected, limiting his subjective agency.

In the final scene of the film, Sugihara and Tsubaki reunite after six months apart. His first question to her, shouted aggressively, is, "What nationality am I? What am I?" (*Ore wa nanijin da? Ore wa nanimon da yo?*) When she replies that he is "*Zainichi* Korean" (*Zainichi Kankokujin*), he tells her that calling him that is like saying he is a stranger planning to leave his country. He refuses to accept labels that he believes are given to him by Japanese who are scared and ignorant. He shouts, "I am not *Zainichi*, or an alien. I am me." (*Ore wa Zainichi de mo eirian demo neen da yo. Ore wa ore nan da yo*). Tsubaki replies, "I don't care what nationality you are" (*Mō Sugihara ga nanijin datte kamawanai*). Sugihara raises his fist so it is level with Tsubaki's face, replaying the scene where his father taught him about breaking through the circle, even repeating the line, "Outside the circle there are lots of scary guys. Have to break through" (*En no soto ni tegowai yatsu ga ippai iru. Buchiyabure, sonna mon*). He grabs Tsubaki with his outstretched arm and brings her toward him, and they warmly embrace. Here, Sugihara actively constitutes who he is, *through* his relationship with Tsubaki, regardless of *what* he is labeled.

This analysis of the use of labels in the film brings us to further exploration of the way in which the Japanese language—specifically referential terms, such as personal pronouns—expresses the notion of contingent subjectivity. Both Lebra and Kondo highlight how referential terms change, contingent upon the relationship between the speaker and the addressee and the context (Lebra, 2004: 33; Kondo, 1987: 243, 1990: 29). For example, the term for "I" changes depending on gender, kinship, the relative age and status of the participants, and a range of factors determined by context (such as the content of the dialogue, where the dialogue is taking place, or the degree of familiarity between the participants). The range of terms available illustrates that the boundaries of self and other are always shifting because different social relationships or roles require different definitions of self.

The night they start their relationship, when Sugihara speaks to Tsubaki, he uses the male pronoun *boku* for "I"; to this, Tsubaki comments that it "does not suit him" (*Bokutte iu no, niawanai yo*)—her perception of him (appearance, age, and so on) and interaction with him has led her to suggest a shift in the term of reference. Sugihara's Korean friends call him *kurupā* (stupid); on the rare occasion that he does address him, his father calls him "boy" (or a derogatory term of some sort); and his Japanese friends, as well as Tsubaki, all address him by his surname, Sugihara (which is not unusual in Japanese, even between close friends), using variants such as "Sugi-chan" (the suffix ~*chan* indicates intimacy between speaker and listener). The surname Sugihara situates him within a family, but Sugihara is a Japanese name taken by Sugihara's father to replace his Korean surname, Lee (a practice followed by some Korean residents in Japan). The absence of Sugihara's first name in Japanese in the film's dialogue may imply that Sugihara's subjectivity is hidden, but this is not the case. Instead, the boundaries of Sugihara's subjectivity are constantly shifting, dependent on with whom he is interacting: the self and other are defined *within* and *by* situations and the participants in those situations, through the wide range of terms used to address him.

Given the role of power relations in the formation of subjectivity, and that this film focuses on the experiences of a male lead character, it is pertinent to specifically address the way in which masculinity is presented in the film. An obvious place to start that discussion is to examine the film's violence. As already mentioned, the most brutal scenes of violence are those between Sugihara and his father, wherein Sugihara's father repeatedly and easily (through his expertise as a professional boxer) asserts his dominance over his son. As mentioned earlier, Sugihara is also beaten by his male homeroom teacher at the North Korean school, who is furious that Sugihara will enter a Japanese school. The violent behaviors used against Sugihara are claims of masculinity within these marginalized masculinities, indicating and reinforcing the hierarchy that exists between them (Connell, 2000: 10, 2005: 80–83).

However, as discussed earlier, Sugihara's father also sees boxing as a way for his son to develop as a human being. Dorinne Kondo comments that, "When the full energy of the *kokoro* (heart/mind) is thrown into a task, one can withstand the greatest difficulties. Thus undergoing hardship and surviving it were keys to a *sunao na kokoro* (a gentle sensitive heart that accepts things as they are)[5] and to a happy life . . . In Japanese society generally, hardship is considered one pathway to mature selfhood. . . . Without undergoing suffering, one was condemned to remain childlike" (1987, 264). Hardship from Sugihara's father's perspective is learning to box, then hitting and getting hit, but obtaining this skill will enable Sugihara's development. This development is realized (without violence) in the final scene of the film when Sugihara reaches "outside the circle" and draws Tsubaki to him, thus confronting and then embracing the outside. In saying this, for the most part, Sugihara uses violence to defend himself against other males. Starting with a crazed physical outburst in response to the *Zainichi* taunt on the basketball court in the opening scene of the film, Sugihara spends the early part of his time at the Japanese school participating in fights with other males, who upon hearing of his outburst, arrive at his classroom to challenge him. Due to his boxing skills and intellect, Sugihara defeats all of them. Even from his marginalized position, Sugihara uses violence to assert his dominance over other males.

A pivotal event in the film is the murder of Sugihara's friend, the man he "most respects" (*Ore ga mottomo risupekuto suru otoko*), Jong-Il, who is studious, reserved, and sometimes socially awkward. But, it is Jong-Il who helps a Korean girl who becomes distressed when a male Japanese student tries to talk to her on a crowded subway platform. Jong-Il and the Japanese male scuffle, and Jong-Il is stabbed in the throat and bleeds to death in the arms of the Korean girl while strangers on the platform refuse to give aid. At Jong-Il's funeral, Wonsu demands that Sugihara join them the next day to take revenge on the student who murdered Jong-Il. Sugihara refuses, out of respect for Jong-Il, and accuses Wonsu of simply wanting to perpetrate violence. The significance of this refusal is twofold: first, it demonstrates Sugihara's attainment of some degree of maturity and contrasts with his earlier delinquent behavior in concert with Wonsu and Tawake. In a discussion of research on motorcycle gangs in Japan, Futoshi Taga notes that delinquent behavior among young men who are not committed to work or study is "one of the socially available means to providing masculine identity" (2003: 151). Sugihara, at the North Korean school, describes his life as, "these days of no future" (*Nō fyūchā no mainichi*), and it seems he finds a sense of masculine identity in his delinquency. However, in changing his nationality and shifting to a Japanese school, he takes responsibility for his future, and in so doing, is crafting a new masculine identity. Second, it demonstrates Sugihara's ability, on this occasion, to control the fighting skills he could easily use in revenge. It is clear that Sugihara is at this point in control of whom he brings in to, and whom he keeps out of, his circle.

At the start of the film, highly conscious of his otherness (not simply his ethnicity but also his social position at the North Korean school: the other students call him *kurupā*, "stupid"), Sugihara assumes that the options available to him in the future are limited:

Japanese, at any rate, probably mix into society. But as for my future . . . Since the North Korean school opened I've been called the school idiot, so perhaps something like this? (Scene cuts to a group photograph of a *yakuza* family, with Sugihara scowling from the back row; he is envisioning a future job as a *yakuza* thug.)

Even if, starting from now, I study, go to university and get a job, I'll have to do something like this . . ." (Scene cuts to a suited Sugihara, working as a salaryman, sliding down a city street, robotically handing over his business card and bowing ingratiatingly.)

Or I could work myself almost to death and become a lawyer or a doctor . . . but my nickname is stupid so . . . That's probably impossible.

Nihonjin wa izure shakai ni mazatte iku darō. Demo boku no mirai wa . . . Minzoku gakkō kaikō irai no baka to yobareta boku dakara, konna kanji ka? Ima kara benkyō shite daigaku haitte shūshoku shite mo, konna mon da. Shinu hodo doryoku shite, bengoshi ka isha ni naru ka . . . Ma, adana ga kurupā da shi . . . Muri desho.

When Jong-Il asks Sugihara if he will go to university, Sugihara says he is still considering it, but he is certain that he will not work. His reason for this is that he can never become company director:

From the beginning your greatest hope is taken away, and for your whole life you are trapped in the organization, unable to fulfill your goals. What a nightmare!

Saikou no nozomi wa hajime kara tatarete, soshiki no naka de isshō kaikorosareru. Akumu jan!

This indicates a rejection by Sugihara of the model of Japanese hegemonic masculinity. Here, hegemonic masculinity refers to the "dominant" and "most honored and desired" form of masculinity (Connell, 2000: 10–11, 2005: 77). The form of masculinity usually described as hegemonic in contemporary Japan is the middle-class, heterosexual, white-collar "salaryman," or corporate/office worker (Roberson and Suzuki, 2003: 6–8; Dasgupta, 2000: 192–193, 2003: 118, 2005: 168–169; Ishii-Kuntz, 2003: 199). This model emerged during the Meiji period (1868–1912), when the state required men to work to achieve rapid industrialization and modernization of the Japanese nation after a long period of almost complete national isolation, and for women to bear and raise children. Salaryman masculinity became firmly dominant after World War II, and the state-led recovery and success of the postwar period again required men to work in corporations and further reinforced the gender division of labor. The idealized male as worker becomes the provider for his family, and a term often used to refer to the salaryman husband/father as provider here is *daikokubashira* (literally, central pillar [of a house]) (Roberson and Suzuki, 2003: 6–8; Dasgupta, 2003: 120–123). Thus hegemonic masculinity, given the assumed responsibilities toward family, is an inherently social role. Without a family and without assuming the responsibility for supporting that family, men cannot reach the masculine ideal. Indeed Romit Dasgupta uses the term "*shakaijin* (literally, social person; a full member of society) masculinity" to express the social responsibility attached to men as providers (Dasgupta, 2005: 169). Ishii-Kuntz, when discussing the centrality of work in the life of the salaryman, notes the physical and psychological strength needed as a corporate employee and also highlights the competitive nature of the corporate environment. Masculinity, then, "is equated with competence and control over self and others" (2003: 199). The construction and expression of masculinity, therefore, is contingent upon relationships with others.

From the 1990s, when Japan's economy fell into recession after the bursting of the economic bubble, the salaryman model of hegemonic masculinity became destabilized. This is because the recession threatened the very foundations of hegemony: work. Increasing unemployment and less secure employment conditions meant that men's livelihoods, and therefore their dominant position as providers—and as such, as men—was undermined. A number of other factors have also weakened the salaryman model of masculinity: greater female participation in the workforce; increasing dissatisfaction with the idea that life is work; increasing participation by men in home and family responsibilities; changes to sex discrimination and child care leave laws, as well as government campaigns to encourage men's involvement in child care (Dasgupta, 2000: 199, 2003: 130–131, 2005: 180; Ishii-Kuntz, 2003: 199–201; Roberson and Suzuki, 2003: 9–11; Taga, 2003: 138–140, 2005: 155–157). However, despite these changes, the model of salaryman as provider maintains its hegemony, and men are still expected to aspire to the hegemonic form of masculinity (Dasgupta, 2003: 131, 2005: 180; Ito, 2005: 150; Mathews, 2003: 122; Roberson and Suzuki, 2003: 8; Taga, 2005: 161–162).

Bearing this in mind and returning to *Go*, we can explore the basis of Sugihara's rejection of the hegemonic masculinity model. The construction of Sugihara's masculinity is affected by his position as other, due to his ethnicity and his socioeconomic status (although they are not poor, Sugihara's father's income would not be especially high: he runs exchange counters for *pachinko*, a form of gambling at which punters exchange their winnings for various prizes) (Connell, 2005: 75; Roberson, 2003: 129). As depicted in his visioning of his future career, Sugihara sees future employment opportunities relative to his status: without education, he envisages a career in a criminal gang; and even with university education, he sees himself humiliated as a salaryman, unable to achieve his goals. Sugihara is expressing his desire to have a meaningful existence within Japanese society, while simultaneously protesting against the social structure that marginalizes him. Importantly, inspired by the advice of Jong-Il, Sugihara chooses, after the death of his friend, to apply himself to his studies and go to university. In one sense, this decision reconciles Sugihara with the dominant model, as it guides him toward the idealized life course of the salaryman; in another, however, he offers a challenge to the dominant configuration, as he remains marked as other by his ethnicity, and therefore offers viewers an alternative model of masculinity. His masculine subjectivity is what Kondo calls "a mobile site of contradiction and disunity, a node where various discourses intersect in particular ways" (1990: 47); it is a negotiated subjectivity, which offers to viewers the possibility of constructing different forms of agency (Stephens, 2002: xi). The way in which Sugihara recognizes and manages the social conditions and requirements of his existence demonstrate his attainment of self-awareness and maturity. As Markus and Kitayama comment, the attainment of mature subjectivity is demonstrated by the ability to behave appropriately relative to situation, but this

> does not result in a merging of self and other, nor does it imply that one must always be in the company of others to function effectively, or that people do not have a sense of themselves as agents who are the origin of their own actions. On the contrary, it takes a high degree of self-control and agency to effectively adjust oneself to various interpersonal contingencies. (1991: 228)

Sugihara accepts his otherness as a condition of the Japanese social order, but recognizes his agency in constructing his selfhood and others' perceptions and treatment of him.

Thus despite its depiction of the hardships faced by Korean residents in Japan, Go is generally positive in its portrayal both of male subjectivities and of a future where alternative forms of subjective agency are not only possible but also meaningful. Blue Spring, in contrast, offers a more pessimistic take on Japanese subjectivities, with its fundamentally bleak portrayal of male subjectivities.

Blue Spring is the story of a group of male students in Tokyo in their final year of high school, with particular focus on two members of that group, Kujō and Aoki. It is clear from the opening scenes that the students spend little time learning at this school. They wander in and out of lessons taught by disengaged teachers, to practice guitar or draw pictures in filthy, empty classrooms, smoke in graffiti covered stairwells, or entertain themselves on the roof of the main school building. The start of the film depicts the process for determining a new leader of the aforementioned group: those willing to challenge for the role must stand on the ledge of the roof, outside the railing meant to prevent them from falling, then let go of the railing and clap as many times as possible, before dropping to his haunches then quickly rising to grasp the railing again. The student who can clap the most times without falling becomes the leader (banchō); the student who earns this title is Kujō. Graffiti is spray-painted in the corridor to mark the school as "Kujō's territory" (Kujō no shima).

It is soon apparent that Kujō is a reluctant leader. He describes his new responsibility as "a pain" (mendokusai), but he is also an effective leader, as he is capable of indifferently and fearlessly using violence against those who threaten him. Kujō's new role is more meaningful to his closest friend, Aoki, whom he has known since childhood. Aoki is outgoing and boisterous, a strong contrast to the reserved, quiet, serious Kujō. Aoki constantly seeks Kujō's approval and reassurance, and is eager to praise Kujō; Kujō, while rebuffing Aoki's at times exaggerated admiration, is also fond of Aoki, expressing this by addressing him as, "Aoki-chan." Indeed, Kujō tells another student that Aoki is his only friend and a "good guy" (*ii yatsu*).

The relationship between Kujō and Aoki is, in Japanese film, a quite common representation of the contingent nature of subjectivity. Aoki's sense of self is determined by his position within the narrow social order in which he exists: that of the group led by Kujō. Aoki frequently pressures Kujō to uphold the hierarchy of the group by asserting his dominance as leader. Aoki's insistence on the maintenance of order reflects a desire for stability and connection in this insular world, in which the participants wander aimlessly and are constantly under the threat of losing their privilege. The way in which Aoki relies on Kujō's approval and reassurance (at least initially) indicates that Kujō plays an important part in defining Aoki's selfhood. Their interdependent relationship is illustrated when Kujō consoles Aoki, after Aoki has been bullied by three second-year students. They are on the roof of the school together, and Kujō is cutting Aoki's hair (an arrangement that Aoki regrets, as Kujō botches it). Aoki complains that his luck has been awful lately, and Kujō responds:

> "It's definitely a problem with your character."
> "Is my personality that bad?"
> "It's better than mine."
> "Than you? That is a low standard [to compare to]."
> "You're more of an adult than me."
> "Like I said, it's a low standard [to compare to]."

> *Kitto jinkaku no mondai da yo.*
> *E? Sonna seikaku warui, ore?*
> *Ore yori wa ii yo.*
> *Ore yoritte . . . reberu hikui yo.*
> *Ore yori wa otona da yo.*
> *Dakara reberu hikuitte iu no.*

This dialogue indicates a process of comparison (expressed in Japanese through the repeated phrase *yori wa*, used by Kujō), through which their subjectivities are defined. Aoki's playful comment that the standard of comparison is low indicates both his affection for Kujō, as well as his awareness of the narrowness of the social order within which they interact.

Kujō, like Aoki, seeks connections with others to define his subjectivity. In his case, his aim seems to be to find answers that tell him who he is and give him direction and focus. He even tells a teacher at the school, "People who know what they want scare me" (*Jibun ga hoshii mono wo shitteiru yatsu wa, kowai desu*). This aim to fill in some kind of emptiness is reflected in his often blank facial expressions and the cold, unfeeling way in which he usually converses with others. Kujō asks Aoki about his plans for the future:

"Aoki, what will you do after graduating? Work? University?"

"University is impossible for us."

"Impossible, you think?"

"Well we're missing class right now."

"Right. Yeah, probably impossible."

"What will you do Kujō?"

"Well, I don't know."

"You don't know? We're talking about *you*!"

"*That* I know. But I just don't know."

"OK, I've got it. Do you want to go work together on a tuna fishing boat?"

Aoki-chan dō suru no, sotsugyō shitara? Shūshoku? Shingaku?
Oretachi, shingaku wa muri da yo.
Muri ka na.
Datte sa, ima jugyō chū jan.
Sō ka. Muri ka mo.
Kujō wa dō suru no?
Sa, shiranai.
Shiranaitte omae. Jibun no koto daro.
Sore wa shitteiru. Kedo wakaranai na.
Ja wakatta. Issho ni maguro gyosen demo notte, kasegu?

Kujō asks the same questions to another student, Yukio ("What will you do after graduating? Work? University?"), to which Yukio responds that he will join a team of superheroes. The repetition of the same questions, even down to the intonation of the phrases, gives the impression that Kujō plans to repeatedly survey respondents for knowledge that he cannot generate for himself. Unlike Sugihara in *Go*, Kujō shows limited self-awareness and limited desire to take control of, and responsibility for, his future.

Kujō's inability to connect with his social situation, and with others (aside from Aoki), highlights another way in which the social world and characters of *Blue Spring* differ from those of *Go*. In their insular social world, which exists only within the school, the students appear to be disconnected from broader society. They also seem disconnected from any form of history, in the sense that we learn very little of their connections to family, or the past. This isolated social world constrains its members, so the choices available to them are suffocating and self-perpetuating. It is not surprising that Kujō is unable to clearly define his subjectivity in relation to his context. This is in clear contrast to Sugihara, whose father tells him to "see the world and decide for yourself," and in the final scene of *Go*, Sugihara reaches out of his circle to broaden his relationships with others. Conversely, Kujō has no wider world to learn from, and he remains afraid and unwilling to explore what is outside his social world and to expand his social relationships.

Earlier analysis of *Go* discussed the idea that mature subjectivity is achieved through appropriate behavior according to context. As Bachnik writes, "the ability to shift successfully from spontaneous to disciplined behavior, through identification of a particular situation along an 'inner' or 'outer' axis, is a crucial social skill for Japanese, and a paramount requirement to function as an adult" (1992: 7). If we relate this idea to *Blue Spring*, we can again appreciate a strong contrast in the depictions of the main characters of each film. As shown previously, Sugihara in *Go* realizes some degree of mature subjectivity during the film, but in *Blue Spring*, we might consider the characters as remaining in childhood, lacking responsibility for, and control over, their actions. This is first implied through the title of the film: *aoi haru* (青い春; literally, 'blue spring') is clearly connected to youth, for the same Chinese characters are used in the word *seishun* (青春), "youth" or "adolescence." Further, at the site of the clapping "game" on the roof is graffiti of the children's song, "If you're happy and you know it clap your hands" (*Shiawase nara te wo tatakō*). The use of this song to accompany their life-threatening behavior highlights not only the unreal, immature understanding they have of their situation, but also the extent to which their situation is disconnected from the wider social environment. Their framing as children is also depicted through another student, Yukio, who stabs a fellow student, Ōta, to death in a toilet cubicle, then calmly washes his hands of blood and walks into the corridor to smoke and practice his guitar. In a scene following the stabbing, a voice-over recounts an interview between Yukio and a career adviser. She asks him, "Yukio, when you grow up, what do you want to be?" (*Yukio-kun wa, otona ni nattara, nani ni naritai no?*) The question is repeated: "When you grow up . . . when you grow up, what do you want to be? When you grow up . . ." (*Otona ni nattara . . . Otona ni nattara, nani ni naritai no? Otona ni nattara . . .*). The sentence remains unfinished, implying that Yukio has not yet become an adult and therefore will not (or cannot) do anything. At the same time, a photo recalls Yukio as a child. As he squats, looking directly at the camera, he could be any innocent child, with a future as yet undecided. Yukio is soon arrested, and as he is taken away, he cries and screams uncontrollably, begging to be released. This infantile Yukio is the antithesis of the young man smoking in the corridor, ignorant of the consequences of his actions. Once Yukio must take responsibility for his actions in the wider, real social world, his positioning as a child from the school social world becomes clear.

As the movie progresses, Kujō, on more than one occasion, does not meet Aoki's expectations of him as leader. Aoki is much more willing than Kujō to use violence to threaten or punish others, and this immediately destabilizes Aoki. When Kujō's leadership is challenged by another student, Leo (a second-year student), and Kujō easily defeats him in the clapping "game," it is Aoki who brutally beats Leo as Kujō stands aside, uninterested. When Aoki questions Kujō's reluctance to punish Leo, Kujō tells Aoki to stop relying on him for everything and to handle the second-year students himself (*Nandemo*

kandemo ore ni tayoru na, Aoki. Ninenbō no chōkyō kurai temē de shiro).
The next day, Aoki tries repeatedly to apologize to Kujō, but Kujō unfeelingly ignores him. When interaction is severed in this way, Aoki panics: he viciously beats another student in the school corridor, and the next day, Aoki arrives at school with a new haircut (the underside shaven, the top slicked back), thus ridding himself of the appearance given to him by Kujō's botched haircut. Aoki begins a campaign of violence against other students and teachers, asserting his dominance against Kujō; indeed, despite Kujō's disconnection from Aoki, Aoki still defines himself in relation to Kujō. The rift in their relationship results in a confrontation in the school corridor, and again their interdependent subjectivities are conveyed in this scene (see Figure 7.2). They walk toward each other from opposite ends of the corridor, until the tip of Kujō's unlit cigarette meets Aoki's, which he uses to light his own.

They proceed to alternately blow smoke into each other's faces without speaking, until the cigarettes drop from their mouths, and the physical violence begins. Holding each other by the hair, so that even their physical positioning and movement reflects and is controlled by the grasp of the other, they begin exchanging punches, and Aoki begins,

"Who the hell do you think you are?"
　"Stop talking shit!"
　"Who put you in charge?"
　"What are you talking about?"
　"Die!"
　"Leave if you don't like it here!"
　"I love it here, you asshole!"
　"Then stay 'til you die!"
　"I'll make it hell on earth!"

Figure 7.2　Aoi Haru: Confrontation between Aoki and Kujō.

"You couldn't manage it!"
"I'll do something you can't!"

Omē wa, nani sama da yo?
  Chōshi notterun janē yo!
  Sonnani yaritē no ka?
  Nan da yo?
  Shine!
  Koko ga iya nara kurun janē yo.
  Daisuki nan da yo, kuso yarō.
  Ja shinu made yo.
  Jigoku ni shite yaru yo.
  Omae ni wa muri da yo.
  Omē ni dekinē koto shite yaru yo.

Aoki's desire for control and domination seems to be an expression of his wish for some sense of order and safety, something which Aoki has until this point tried to find in his relationship with Kujō. At the end of this exchange, Aoki makes his final claim to dominance: he will do something that Kujō cannot do, which turns out to be obtaining the highest score in the clapping game. Aoki goes to the roof of the school, singing, "If you're happy and you know it, clap your hands," and spends the night staring at the school gate. The next morning, as Kujō walks through the gate, Aoki is standing on the roof ledge, outside the railing, counting his claps. Kujō understands Aoki's aim immediately and desperately begins running, and as he rushes out the door to the roof, we see that Aoki has spray-painted his name and "thirteen times" on the door. As Kujō reaches the roof ledge, Aoki is already falling to his death, counting to thirteen.

This central interdependent relationship of *Blue Spring* sits in contrast to the mutually beneficial relationship between Sugihara and his father. Aoki achieves his dominance over Kujō, but at the cost of his life. Moreover, Aoki's violent and self-destructive reaction to the disruption in his relationship with Kujō may be a representation of the wider circumstances that the film is engaging with: the frustration, instability, and hopelessness experienced by young men when they are unable to determine how they fit in relation to the (real) Japanese social order.

The masculinities of *Blue Spring* provide another important site of comparison with *Go*. As in *Go*, violence plays a key role in the relationships between men in *Blue Spring*. Violence is used to dominate other males and assert authority, but unlike *Go*, the characters show limited ability to control their physical impulses or the desire to use violence to achieve personal ends. Indeed the meaninglessness and brutality of the violence in the film conveys not only the immaturity of the characters in *Blue Spring*, but also the way in which the relationships between men are often dysfunctional, a product of, and response to, the insular social world within which they exist.

Kujō, like Sugihara (but to a greater extent), deliberately excludes himself from others. Kujō also shares with Sugihara (although this refers to Sugihara only at the start of *Go*) a limited vision of the future, constrained by his circumstances: Kujō acknowledges that it is unlikely that he will be able to go to university due to his poor performance at school. Kujō actively refuses to follow any established order, seemingly wandering within an environment that he cannot assimilate to; this otherness sets him outside the dominant model of masculinity. Unlike *Go*, however, this challenge to hegemony is not overall a positive portrayal; it reflects a sense of hopelessness and aimlessness that pervades the film. This comes across as a criticism of the social order of Japan and its inability to accommodate those who do not fit the norm.

The contingent construction and expression of subjectivities is represented in different ways in *Go* and *Blue Spring*. Intersecting with the development of subjectivity is the field of gender, and the masculinities presented in these films show the ways in which gender identity is also constructed relative to context. *Go* leaves the audience with a positive expression of the possible alternative forms of agency that may come from challenges to the hegemonic form; *Blue Spring*, despite its pessimistic underlying message, is equally meaningful in its function as criticism of the inability of Japanese society to accommodate nonnormative masculinities.

Notes

1. Korean permanent residents in Japan are a minority group who, despite their long-term membership of and participation in Japanese society, have experienced various forms of discrimination (see Weiner and Chapman, 2009). Their situation, especially in socioeconomic terms, is improving, however (see Kim, 2011).

2. It is worth noting that Sugihara has missed (or is not stating) that the origins of the modern Japanese race lie in the merging of two prehistoric human groups in Japan: the Jōmon people, descendants of migrants to the Japanese archipelago from Southeast or Northeast Asia (conjecture on their origins continues) and migrants from Northeast Asia (today's Korea and northern China), who arrived during the Yayoi period (300 BCE–300 CE) (Hanihara, 1991: 24; Hanihara and Ishida, 2009: 311–312; Temple et al., 2008: 164–165).

3. Sakurai Tsubaki, as a name, can be further unpacked: *sakura* bloom in spring and *tsubaki* bloom in winter; this expression of the changing seasons also stresses Japaneseness. *Tsubaki*, although a key floral emblem in Japan, came from China, and the combination of these two particular flowers in her name may be an expression of her ability to accept, later in the film, Sugihara's "foreign" heritage.

4. A "sailor suit" is a type of school uniform for girls.

5. This translation is based on the explanation of this phrase in Kondo's work.

Works Cited

Primary Texts

Aoi Haru (Blue Spring). Dir. Toyoda Toshiaki. Tokyo: Aoi Haru Seisaku Iinkai, 2001. Film.
Go. Dir. Yukisada Isao. Tokyo: Tōei, 2001. Film.

Secondary Texts

Bachnik, Jane M. "Time, Space and Person in Japanese Relationships." In *Interpreting Japanese Society: Anthropological Approaches*, edited by Joy Hendry and Jonathan Webber. Oxford: JASO, 1986.

Bachnik, Jane M. "The Two Faces of Self and Society in Japan," *Ethos* 20.1 (1992): 3–32.

Clammer, John. "Europe in Asia's Imaginary: Disciplinary Knowledge and the (Mis) representation of Cultures." In *Europe and the Asia-Pacific: Culture, Identity and Representations of Region*, edited by Stephanie Lawson. London: Routledge Curzon, 2003.

Connell, R. W. *Masculinities*. 2nd ed. Berkeley: University of California Press, 2005.

Connell, R. W. *The Men and the Boys*. Cambridge: Polity, 2000.

Dasgupta, Romit. "Creating Corporate Warriors: The 'Salaryman' and Masculinity in Japan." In *Asian Masculinities: The Meaning and Practice of Manhood in China and Japan*, edited by Kam Louie and Morris Low. London: Routledge Curzon, 2003.

Dasgupta, Romit. "Performing Masculinity? The 'Salaryman' at Work and Play," *Japanese Studies* 20.3 (2000): 189–200.

Dasgupta, Romit. "Salarymen Doing Straight: Heterosexual Men and the Dynamics of Gender Conformity." In *Genders, Transgenders and Sexualities in Japan*, edited by Romit Dasgupta and Mark McClelland. London: Routledge, 2005.

Hanihara, Kazuo. "Dual Structure Model for the Population History of the Japanese," *Japan Review* 2 (1991): 1–33.

Hanihara, Tsunehiko, and Hajime Ishida. "Regional Difference in Craniofacial Diversity and the Population History of Jomon Japan," *American Journal of Physical Anthropology* 139.3 (2009): 311–322.

Ishii-Kuntz, Masako. "Balancing Fatherhood and Work: Emergence of Diverse Masculinities in Contemporary Japan." In *Men and Masculinities in Contemporary Japan: Dislocating the Salaryman Doxa*, edited by James E. Roberson and Nobue Suzuki. London: Routledge, 2003.

Ito, Kimio. "An Introduction to Men's Studies." In *Genders, Transgenders and Sexualities in Japan*, edited by Romit Dasgupta and Mark McClelland. London: Routledge, 2005.

Kim, Bumsoo. "Changes in the Socioeconomic Position of Zainichi Koreans: A Historical Overview," *Social Science Japan Journal* 14.2 (2011): 233–245.

Kondo, Dorinne K. *Crafting Selves: Power, Gender, and Discourse of Identity in a Japanese Workplace*. Chicago, IL: University of Chicago Press, 1990.

Kondo, Dorinne K. "Creating an Ideal Self: Theories of Selfhood and Pedagogy at a Japanese Ethics Retreat," *Ethos* 15.3 (1987): 241–272.

Lebra, Takie. *Identity, Gender, and Status in Japan*. 2 vols. Kent: Global Oriental, 2007.

Lebra, Takie Sugiyama. *The Japanese Self in Cultural Logic*. Honolulu: University of Hawaii Press, 2004.

Markus, Hazel Rose, and Shinobu Kitayama. "Culture and the Self: Implications for Cognition, Emotion, and Motivation," *Psychological Review* 98.2 (1991): 224–253.

Mathews, Gordon. "Can a 'Real' Man Live for his Family? *Ikigai* and Masculinity in Today's Japan." In *Men and Masculinities in Contemporary Japan: Dislocating the Salaryman Doxa*, edited by James E. Roberson and Nobue Suzuki. London: Routledge, 2003.

Roberson, James E. "Japanese Working Class Masculinities: Marginalized Complicity." In *Men and Masculinities in Contemporary Japan: Dislocating the Salaryman Doxa*, edited by James E. Roberson and Nobue Suzuki. London: Routledge, 2003.

Roberson, James E., and Nobue Suzuki. "Introduction." In *Men and Masculinities in Contemporary Japan: Dislocating the Salaryman Doxa*, edited by James E. Roberson and Nobue Suzuki. London: Routledge, 2003.

Stephens, John, ed. *Ways of Being Male: Representing Masculinities in Children's Literature and Film*. New York: Routledge, 2002.

Taga, Futoshi. "Rethinking Japanese Masculinities: Recent Research Trends." In *Genders, Transgenders and Sexualities in Japan*, edited by Romit Dasgupta and Mark McClelland. London: Routledge, 2005.

Taga, Futoshi. "Rethinking Male Socialisation: Life Histories of Japanese Male Youth." In *Asian Masculinities: The Meaning and Practice of Manhood in China and Japan*, edited by Kam Louie and Morris Low. London: Routledge Curzon, 2003.

Temple, Daniel H., Benjamin M. Auerbach, Masato Nakatsukasa, Paul W. Sciulli, and Clark Spencer Larsen. "Variation in Limb Proportions between Jomon Foragers and Yayoi Agriculturalists from Prehistoric Japan," *American Journal of Physical Anthropology* 137.2 (2008): 164–174.

Weiner, Michael, and David Chapman. "Zainichi Koreans in History and Memory." In *Japan's Minorities: The Illusion of Homogeneity*. 2nd ed., edited by Michael Weiner. Oxford: Routledge, 2009.

Chapter Eight
Strong Is Beautiful
A *Thai-Thai* Happiness

Salinee Antarasena

Introduction

> Individuals frequently account for events and experiences in their lives in terms of their relative store of merit . . . One's moral actions are aimed at altering this balance in a favorable direction, moving one further along the path to the ultimate religious goal. (Kirsch, 1977: 246)

The traditional concept of the *karmic law*, obviously or covertly, still holds sway in Thai society, and as an often implicit ideology can shape the representations and understanding of subjectivity in texts—whether fiction or film—which address youth audiences. This chapter explores the correlation between karmic law, degree of power or dominance, social status, and degree of well-being or life satisfaction, and thence the consequent implications for the representation of subjectivity.

In the study, a total of ten films have been analyzed—namely, *The Sign, Anan, Little Prince, Baby Mind, Cool Bangkok, Hua-Naa, Peun-Yark, Dek-Long, Remote Control,* and *Taxi, the Hero*—all filmed during 2005 and 2006 by award-winning directors for an independent cinema campaign launched by the "Child Media Program" (transliteration: sor-sor-yor) under the Thai Health Promotion Foundation (ThaiHealth). One may argue that it is all too convenient to elucidate the correlations drawn only from the films in this collection as at least twice the number of films were produced for youth audiences during this period; however, if only these films were presented to the public as representative of appropriate-for-children films affirmed by ThaiHealth, these films encompass the whole population.

Social Structure and Prestige: The Superior and the Subordinate

> Hierarchy in Thailand is based on a variety of overlapping vertical axes, wherein, for example, royalty are considered superordinate to common-ers, religious specialists have superiority over laity, urban dwellers are thought more advanced than rural folks, seniors take precedence over juniors, and males are normatively superior to females. (Cook and Jack-son, 1999: 9)

An examination of the organization of hierarchical social structure discloses that the prominence of Buddhism and the theory of Karma as its long-entrenched legacy certainly play a significant part. As Kirsch remarks, "Popular belief affirms what sophisticated doctrine teaches: the merit balances of some are better or more favorable than those of others. Both sophisticated doctrine and popular belief sanction the notion that there are intrinsic inequalities among humans with respect to their moral status" (1977, 246). Jackson also makes similar observation with regard to the functioning of Thai social structure as a whole in accordance with the consequences of karmic acts which "originally denoted an ethical and psychological theory which related a person's present sta-tus of well-being or suffering to the moral or immoral quality of his or her past actions," and which "equated seniority in the social order with well-being and past morality, and correspondingly related a low social order with present suf-fering and immorality in previous lives" (1989, 41). Puntarikawat in his obser-vation of Thai social order agrees with this theory claiming that such temporal order was originally systematized by the principle of a multilevel merit system, which leads to an unsurprising explanation of how and why individuals differ from one another in terms of desirable degree of dominance and well-being (2002). Further, the governing principle also systematizes the traditional meta-physical cosmology or the three worlds of Buddhist cosmology—that is, heaven, hell, and earth: the first two are populated by a diverse range of supernatural entities according to their respective levels of merit or demerit (Kirsch, 1977; Jackson, 1989; Puntarikawat, 2002; Amnuay-ngerntra, 2007). In other words, this scale of all beings characterizes and concretizes karmic actions and their due effects in the form of a corresponding order and degree of dominance in the hierarchical system. The principle also has it that there are various levels of well-being or life satisfaction ranging from the lowest of those placed below the human realm (the underclass) to the highest possessed by very exalted beings, or what we might regard as gods, at the top.

The following analysis investigates such hierarchical structure when mul-tiple causation is present—that is, (1) the principle of karmic law which posits the specified order of beings in the hierarchical system; (2) the principle of karmic law which also connects the specified order via the law-determined degree of power; and (3) the degree of life satisfaction, as independent vari-able, which determines also the specified order (see Figure 8.1).

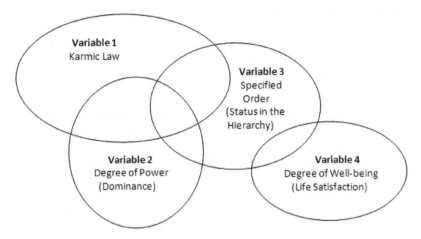

Figure 8.1 Multiple causation of social status.

As indicated in Figure 8.1, an individual's designated position in the hierarchy consists of three variables: the karmic law, the degree of dominance, and the degree of well-being. The causal relationship between these variables is illustrated in Figure 8.2.

The equation which describes this causal process of individual designated order (as illustrated in Figure 8.1 and 8.2) is:

$$V_3 = b_1V_1 + b_2V_2 + b_4V_4 + \varepsilon$$
$$V_2 = b_1V_1 + \varepsilon$$

To put it simply, the equation above measures (and forecasts) the degree of possible variability of the three variables affecting social status in the hierarchy, namely the karmic law, the degree of power, and the degree of well-being;

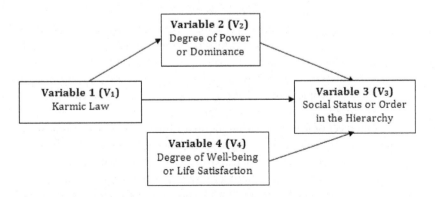

Figure 8.2 Multi-causal relationships of social status.

and to guard against the objection that it can be too rigid to assume only three variables as a good fit and deny all other unknown (but possible) variables, the residual error (ε) placed at the end indicates any possibility that has been left out at the time of calculation.

As stated in the equation, the karmic law, the degree of dominance, and the degree of well-being all play an influential role in determining the place of the individual in the order and consequently, as in the films, determine the relationships with other characters that share or differ in matters of socio-economic condition. While fictionalizing a challenge familiar in the world of children, each of the selected films follows this multicausal process, with karmic law and degree of life satisfaction wholly independent of each other, and degree of power being in part caused by karmic law. Given that the specified order here is assigned to an individual in the present life (inborn characteristic), the status remains static, and in this respect, all of the films share one thing in common: a persistence of zero social mobility.

Phi: The Lowest Social Stratum

A genre which problematizes subjectivity in both Asian and Western traditions is the ghost film. The Thai film industry has a thriving horror genre in which the monster to be feared is a ghost (*Phi*), which also serves as a metaphor for a mental or psychological source of fear. By taking the form of a ghost, an individual undergoes deprivation of subject status and becomes acutely abjected. As in other parts of Southeast Asia (where there is a ready market for Thai ghost films), ghosts may be understood as symptoms of trauma, especially because, as Rosalind C. Morris argues, they mark the site of "an inassimilable (because premature) event, one whose untimeliness robs it of the structure of causality within which it could be more properly interpreted" (2008, 236). Although human life expectancy is uncertain and many causes of death are not simplistically explicable, a concurring statement about premature death can also be found in *Abhidhamma*, in which it is explained that sentient beings are destined to go on living as long as their life span and karmic forces permit and that physical death may be due to four causes: expiry of life span, cessation of karmic forces, combination of the first two, and last, in line with Morris's explanation, untimely death (*Uppachedaka*). In Thai culture, a *phi*, which ordinary people readily comprehend as a sentient form that has morphed into existence from an unnatural or untimely death, is either a metaphor or a literal object of fear. In developing their films for the series, both Aditya Assarat (*The Sigh*) and Sanipong Suttiphan (*Anan*) play with the ghost genre and in particular its paradoxes of causality. An early segment of *The Sigh*, for example, exploits an over-the-shoulder shot to position viewers to experience and explore the wrecked remains of a site along with the lead character. The film, whose title is an echo of an American thriller film *Signs*, opens with a typical ghost story setting—a vacant and abandoned factory with broken windows, dilapidated roof, and cracked, damaged walls—and a teenage protagonist playing the role of a paranormal investigator, as he desperately tries to prove the existence of a disembodied voice phenomenon in the factory. The film technique then builds its suspense gradually while adroitly constructing the protagonist's fear by means of a "claimed-to-exist" voice—hissing, whistling. The camera then pans around to detail every corner of the remains of the factory: that it was formerly a major site for film production suggests an ironic metafictive purpose, for this perfect site for the reappearance of the dead is actually haunted by stories and representations. It is fitting, then, that the noises the character hears are only inside his own head.

Anan treats the concept of the underclass of abjected ghosts more metaphorically. The existence of *Phis* is immediately suggested by the film's title, which implies a continuous series and movements of birth and rebirth of all sentient forms of life and also by its opening, a time subsequent to a horrific accident in which the mother of the main character, a boy named Ton, has died. The film then creates a nostalgic atmosphere when it depicts an empty room where Ton, after a chase scene involving ominous *Phis*, finds the spirit of his father sitting on a chair reminiscing about his happiest moment before the accident and truly shutting himself away from the world. This room resembles the ICU room where Ton's father lies in a coma.

In their narrative trajectories, both films appear as an affirmation of Thai belief that different sentient forms occur in a cycle over time and that the realms of ghost and human forms exist below and on the surface of the earth, respectively. On the other hand, however, the films reflect an ideological assumption that once the karmic law is triggered it is inexorable and immutable in its working; thus, just as the different sentient forms can metaphorically represent this implacable law of compensation, so too mobility between different realms or social strata is not possible. A good example of this zero mobility between humans and their lower status counterparts can be seen in the epilogue of *The Sigh*, when it is disclosed that the mysterious sound heard solely by the lead character, which implies that he is endowed with a paranormal ability to make contact with *Phis*, is no more than a common symptom of Tinnitus. In this scene, when the astonished character confronts the truth, Assarat seems to be posing a question to the audience: "Is every paranormal phenomenon nothing more than a coincidence?" A parallel question is presented in *Kalama Sutta*, a key Buddhist text that exhorts the believer not to believe in anything without a sound, logical, reasoned argument. This kick in the film's surprise ending leaves viewers with a paradox: the existence of ghosts is not strongly denied, but the film argues that mobility between earthly existence and the realm of the afterlife is not just unlikely but completely impossible.

This contradiction in attitudes is reaffirmed in *Anan*, in that the film employs the concept of an afterlife-like realm which is the setting for a rescue mission launched by children to save Ton's father. The climax of the action affirms a strong belief in the existence of ancestral spirits when it transpires that Ton's imaginary friends who participated in the mission are in fact his deceased ancestors and recently deceased mother. Nevertheless, the film has its own twist at the end when Ton, asleep on a bench in the hospital corridor, is woken by his aunt and to a thought-provoking question: "Was it all just a dream?" The narrative combination of feeling responsible for his father and finding spiritual support from his forebears also premises a particular concept of subjective agency as grounded in absolute subjectivity—individual action is enmeshed in a sense of community unbounded by time, and individualistic action is only an illusion.

The contradiction of this classic Thai premise regarding the existence of the underclass and the denial of the possibility of their upward mobility may sound illogical, but an explanation lies in the definition of an alternative term for *Phi*: *Viyana*. Unlike the colloquial term *Phi*, *Viyana*, which also means 'spirit,' is mentioned in Buddhist teaching (*Abhidhamma*) as covering a broader context, which is how the human mind perceives and the capacity of perception to influence how the world is seen. This renders plausible the previous argument—how *Phi* or the spirits of the deceased can exist although they cannot be made visible. Viyana makes the formless formed, in the minds of the characters and the viewers. Without taking on a concrete form, the existing spirit is thus formed and shaped in accordance with the desire of the mind's owner: *Phi* in *The Sigh* and the spirits in *Anan*. The assumption of Viyana also justifies the usage of asynchronous and contrapuntal sound in *The Sigh*, which precedes the film sequence; neither the lead character nor the viewers is shown any clue as to where the mysterious sound originates—but because of the scary scenarios, their minds are tempted to believe that the spirit is visible and the sound can't be anything but a sign which precedes the appearance of a *Phi*.

The Viyana assumption is also applied to rationalize a small incident in the final scene of *Anan*, when the film shows that immediately after the children save the spirit of Ton's father from the underclass realm and Ton is suddenly woken by his aunt, Ton's father opens his eyes, and the ICU heart monitor quickly shows that his heart has started to beat once again at a normal rate. This miraculous recovery from a comatose state is too coincidental to deny the existence of Ton's quest with his imaginary friends in the other realm, even though none of it was visible in this world.

The Poor: The Underclass on the Surface of the Earth

As argued earlier, subjectivity is both shaped and constrained by the assumption that status in the hierarchy is static, so that subsequent karmic actions, with good intentions or bad, will not change the sentient form one is possessed of in life (specified order as inborn characteristic), as clearly seen by leaving the existence of *Phi* in question (visible proofs are withheld). *The Sigh* and *Anan* preclude any possibility that the borders between realms might be permeable: no single shot concretely confirms that any character—neither human nor the underclass *Phi*—is able to move up or down from the realm they inhabit. Nevertheless, as the law of causation has it that every act has a reaction, the second group of films in this collection—*The Little Prince, Cool Bangkok,* and *Baby Mind*—poses the question of whether there is compensation for subsequent acts such as merit-making: that is, whether or not the due effects of merit-making can possibly have profound implications as a future force within karmic causation.

The same concept of zero mobility is again present in shaping the subjectivity of the principal characters of Tossaporn Mongkol's *The Little Prince,* in which neither increased social status nor abundant well-being (for example, material improvement in life) are given to these characters as rewards. The story revolves around the life of a rural boy, Saen-dee, and the choice he is forced to make at the end. Although his name means "kindhearted," he feels an acute lack of agency because fate decides everything for him: a father who died an untimely death, a mother who never stays with him, and an old grandmother who can only pack him a lunchbox with wild and garden vegetables. Saen-dee always dreams of reversing his pitiful fate by acquiring the better fortune of a classmate who belongs to a very rich family. However, instead of envisaging that Saen-dee and anyone else in his family could change their lives, the story ends when Saen-dee learns the lesson that he is a rich boy already, rich in being kindhearted to his rich classmate by sharing his vegetables with him and by ceasing his persistent jealousy—both actions which could be considered (primarily by himself and his mother) as merit accumulated from virtuous acts. The film ends with Saen-dee still leading a life which is materially poor—and so do his mother and grandmother.

Significantly, social inequality is presented through Saen-dee's perspective and thereby his limited and constrained subjectivity is defined. If, as George Butte argues, subjectivity is a dialogue between intentionality grounded in bodily experience and gesture, on the one hand, and "a mirroring of other bodies, gestures, experiences and discourses" (2004, 5), on the other, Saen-dee's refusal to accept his form of sentient life in the earthly realm (illustrated by his persistent jealousy of the rich in the beginning of the story) is thwarted because mirroring of others is restricted by zero mobility. The jealousy makes him see that people such as himself and his family work hard but other people are better off, and the lives of those people are more fulfilling and healthier than the lives of the hardworking. Although self-doubt continues to trouble him through his perception that such inequality violates the principle of karmic compensation, whereby the good deserve to be rewarded, the film does not examine further the question of fairness, or develop any situation in which he strives to or succeeds in moving to a higher societal level, but forecloses such possibilities by making frequent shifts between Saen-dee's waking life and an imaginary world.

In the imaginary world, Saen-dee interacts with his mother, and to affect this the film draws on a film convention of musical interludes (the only film in the collection to do so). The mother, out of nowhere, dances and sings *Likay* (a traditional theater performance employing speech, singing, dance, lavish glittering costumes, along with a classical Thai orchestra), and through her song for Saen-dee redefines the concept of "merit." As her song reveals, *merit* is a broad term not only denoting the material comforts and worldly happiness with which Saen-dee is concerned but also extending to cover a peaceful life and favorable character that is socially accepted. Thus the reward of merits, in accordance with the law of compensation, if not a matter of material abundance, is a matter of best practice toward other human beings, which explains an incident at the end of the film when Saen-dee's classmate is kinder and more compassionate to him.

The imaginary sequences also affirm the desirability of Saen-dee's final decision to follow his mother's advice and develop a perfect harmony with his richer fellow through the use of clothing choice, the *Likay* costume. This traditional clothing is always presented when the film silences the voice and inner thoughts of Saen-dee and at the same time amplifies his mother's voice (attempting to consolidate the rejection of flexible social mobility throughout the story) urging him to behave himself by warding off jealousy and all other evil thoughts directed at his richer fellow. On a subtler level, this choice of clothing can also signify that conformity to zero social mobility is inculcated across generations when the Likay costume is first donned by the mother to perform, and then in the epilogue of the film, Saen-dee subsequently learns to dress in Likay costume and dance and sing Likay just like his mother. This abstract concept of obedience is also made concrete at one point when Saen-dee is dancing Likay, dressed in a mix of his school uniform and Likay costume, while the background is occupied by a half-built Thai Buddha image. Saen-dee's mother reminds him that half finished Buddha images are respected by people, and people prostrate themselves before those images, just as they do before completed statues. The implication is that satisfaction with ascribed status is desirable.

If given material wealth is a measure of designated position in the hierarchy in the earthly realm, the relationships of Ton and other characters in *Anan* are also explicable because the primacy is given to the subjective right of his richest aunt. In order to maintain her financial prowess in relation to everyone in the family, including Ton's other aunts, and to ensure her collective well-being, this aunt relentlessly refuses to give adequate assistance, either to Ton or his father in the coma.

The same willingness to conform to designated position in the hierarchy can also be seen in two other films, *Cool Bangkok* and *Baby Mind*. In *Cool Bangkok*, Lek Manont expresses this concept through the colors of black and white. He tells the story of an imaginary Bangkok and its neighboring lands, delineating the border of each by means of a sharp contrast between the two colors. Bangkok (urbanized areas and buildings) is set against a pure white background, whereas areas surrounding Bangkok (rural areas and wetlands) are characterized by black color, traditionally reflecting an ominous undertone. So, later in the film, Manont introduces a fisherman from the black area as an antagonist of the story by showing the rural intruder sneaking into the white Bangkok, as a thief.

The use of colors to illustrate how this imaginary society distributes resources among its citizens is especially important, not only because it emphasizes the status differences between the rich and the poor but also because it gives support to the dominance of the rich. *Cool Bangkok* clearly displays both differences through the pursuit of the well-being of the poor who feel inadequate and associate themselves with low levels of well-being, and by means of the white and black contrasts which virtually create social orders of urban and rural dwellers.

As noted earlier by Cook and Jackson, and in line with the principle of karmic causation in Figure 8.1, this hierarchical order depicts the rural fisherman as penniless and impoverished, much like Saen-dee and his family in *The Little Prince*, as the fisherman fails to catch fish in a contaminated black river, the only river found outside the white Bangkok. As if developing a counterargument, the film then stresses the anxiety of the fisherman when he sees that the clean and plentiful resources (such as the fish farms) are reserved exclusively for the inhabitants of the white city. The importance of the river for the wetland in which he lives can hardly be exaggerated as it is, for him, the only river which ever gave him access to clean water fit to drink and a source of food. Scratching his head in bewilderment, the fisherman is troubled that his fellow citizens do not allow him a fair share of well-being—a fair share of resources needed just to survive.

A similar fate is also assigned to the other principal character, a rural migrant working as a servant in the white city. Here, he guards the property of the rich, of whom the farm owner is both his employer and the owner of clean water supplies. Even after showing diligence and faithfulness to protect the farm from the thief, this migrant is not rewarded for his virtue with upward mobility. The film ends when the farm owner, still maintaining primacy even after repeated incidents of fish stealing, can successfully ward off the rural intruder himself and keep his farm safe, and also dispel his faithful servant's dream of a rich city life and banish him back to the black area. It is thus assumed that people born into a low socioeconomic status are deprived of the basic necessities of life and also are apt to have little control over their status as they are predestined to live as the underclass of their richer fellows.

In line with this assumption, *Cool Bangkok* does not grant success to the fisherman's mission to "Rob the rich to feed the poor," nor does it allow either of the rural characters to improve their status by other means. Instead, the film projects that in order to break this endless cycle of poverty endured by the inhabitants of the black area, the hungry poor must move onto paths of self-reliance. Such resolution is made possible by the sympathy and generosity of the rich: when the owner of the fish farm decides to release some clean water from his farm to flow outside and into the dirty river, the river then becomes clearer so the black area inhabitants can now catch fish. Hence, now able to feed themselves and stay in their land, they give up the desire to infiltrate the white land of the rich. Again this concept affirms the explanation of the incident found at the end of *The Little Prince* when the story is resolved after the rich are kinder and more compassionate to the poor and the poor no longer experience jealousy or a desire to revolt against the rich.

The concept of conformity toward individual zero social mobility while accepting the dominance of a certain group, power, or material wealth also underlies *Baby Mind*, in which the concept is played out through the lives of three beggars in a city. The perception of karmic law nonetheless seems to be challenged in the film's opening scene when a homeless boy succeeds in pretending to amputate one of his healthy arms and his dog's leg to attract sympathy—and money—from people passing by. Unlike the poor in other films who seem to acquire accumulation of merits such as Saen-dee or the faithful servant in *Cool Bangkok*, this film opens by introducing the life of the poor marked by a negative trait—deceit. If merit-making cannot reasonably imply a consequent possibility of upward mobility in the life one is living, then a question posed by the opening of *Baby Mind* is whether the opposite of merit-making can effect change. This is a trick question, for not everyone will consider all deceit a negative trait.

In answer to the question—"In what circumstances can deceit not be marked as negative?"—some may argue that the act of deceit here can be explained by two separate Buddhist teachings: first, sympathy and generosity (*Metta*) which promote the well-being of less fortunate others is a common practice through which Buddhists accumulate merit; and second, neither of the beggars has stolen the money of these kindhearted people (the Second Precept says, "abstain from taking what is not given," but the money has been 'given' to them). In accordance with this explanation, the film withholds judgment on the deceitful actions of the fake lame beggars and allows both to enjoy spending some of the money as its rightful owners. This period does not last long, however, before a third character, a Dachshund, steals all their money; thus in the end, the rich still constitute a closed group, and the film does not allow any characters upward mobility. All beggars remain in the lower division of the human realm—the same division as the thief in *Cool Bangkok*. This restrained intrahierarchy mobility indicates that insofar as the assigned order in the hierarchy is concerned, the compensation of subsequent acts, whether considered merits or demerits, provides no mobility particularly when upward mobility is based on monetary grounds.

The Weak: The Underclass in a Wider Context

The films discussed so far demonstrate that the karmic law of causation in relation to an individual's status in society, degree of dominance, and well-being acts to interpellate and bind subjects. The final group of films—*Hua-naa, Peun-Yak, Dek-Long, Remote Control,* and *Taxi, the Hero*—do not include overt underclass characters that express their material needs and strive for material possessions. These films depict instead a struggle between social equals to assert dominance through physical strength.

Hua-Naa (literally, "the leader") is a comedic fantasy about the struggle for dominance among children marooned in an imaginary town, where they have developed a dense social hierarchy which is a reflection of adult society in the everyday real world. Its structure thus has much in common with (especially) film versions of *Lord of the Flies.* The fabular quality of the film is emphasized by its use of a third-person omniscient narrator whose voice-over not only conveys the events of the story but also comments on the actions and thoughts of the principal character, Ohm, and follows those of other characters in certain episodes. At the beginning of the story, Ohm is the leader of the dominant clan (the King Kong clan) and is trying to overcome other clans attempting to intrude upon his territory. After his many victories, smaller boys grow fearful and inevitably allow Ohm to take over their spaces, while Ohm, in order to assert his position as leader, immerses himself in the ferocious bullying of the weak(er). He temporarily enjoys his higher status and total power as it endows him with privileges and respect from smaller boys. The film's tension increases when Ohm is dethroned and has to flee from his clan and live in complete solitude on a desert island, as Robinson Crusoe. This phase of the film offers some amusing moments, for example when he gazes at his sandals and comes to realize that being a person of highest status is already a form of miserable solitude, and the struggle to be alone at the top entails an endless cycle of fighting. When he returns to the town, he turns for companionship to every leader of the clans he previously defeated and conveys the key message that they should live in a structure of peaceful intersubjectivity, not hierarchy and dominance. As a result, he is soon restored to a position in which he is everyone's equal. The film, however, does not end here. Ohm eventually meets with the leader of the Panda clan, a sadistic, cruel older boy who defeated everyone in Ohm's clan while he was away and who beats and bullies him like a weak and helpless animal. In the end, Ohm loses everything he has gained at the beginning of the film and during his rise to power, and thus shares a similar fate with the principal characters of the two previous categories. The film concludes with a view of Ohm's bruised and battered face from the last fight as he realizes that the quest for absolute power is a road without an end.

Some temporary flexibility within the realm achieved through physical domination in the earlier episodes which can challenge the allegation of zero social mobility is again present in *Peun-Yark* whose title suggests a double entendre—literally either "unlikely to make friends" or "a true friend." The film simply has two schoolboys, each of whom continually devises some kind of trick, however annoying to other classmates and their teacher, to defeat one another. One evening after a day of constant conflict between the two boys, they are made to stay back and clean their classroom together as a fitting punishment for their fighting and annoying behavior. By working together, they discover that cooperation is preferable to conflict, but the turn also delivers the message that physical domination cannot lift one beyond one's class.

In *Taxi, the Hero*, the physical domination of the strong over the weak is displayed in a comedy about a taxi driver who, as the title suggests, dreams of fighting crime like Superman, but who finally becomes another example of zero mobility. As in many films featuring the superhero, the taxi driver disguises himself as an ordinary man, which in reality he is, and hides his full name. His mind becomes fully preoccupied with code-breaking and violent, explosive eruptions in all the major areas of Bangkok when he picks up a Thai-Muslim passenger whom he mistakenly identifies as a bomber. By speculating that the passenger's handbag is actually an explosive device, the terror of firearms and of the threat of terrorism aired on the radio overwhelms him, and the driver becomes fearful. This fear is clearly shown by the driver's willingness to agree to the passenger's wish to be taken on a tour of Bangkok. Near the end of the film, after fantasizing that he has a super intellect that can solve the details of the planned explosions, the driver reveals his big decision (to himself) to dedicate his life to protect the safety of the public and thus to fight with the passenger. Because it is all a misunderstanding, however, there is no superhero here and his dream of becoming a superhero to save the nation can never be fulfilled.

In the last two films, *Dek-Long* and *Remote Control*, the concept of the weak is extended to the cross-dressing, or *Katheoy*—the term which denotes a person (a man or a woman) who "exhibits behaviors that are not considered appropriate to their sex" (Barea, 2012: 191). The comedy-drama story *Dek-Long* (literally, "lost-way-home child") follows the life of a *Katheoy* named Jiggi who has a muscular, heavy body and who appears in the beginning of the film with a very short skirt, sleek knee-high boots, and heavy makeup, and hence becomes an object of public ridicule. The other principle character, Bamee, a cheeky girl whom Jiggi accidentally bumps into in a crowded market, also keeps jeering at Jiggi by calling her "auntie" and *Katheoy*, throughout the very long hitchhiking journey they undertake together. During their journey, when Jiggi suddenly falls for a good-looking man, he soon afterward steals all her money and beats her while making an escape to avoid capture. As the film ends, Jiggi's position in the hierarchy is still immutable.

The same perception of *Katheoy* is also employed in *Remote Control*, a film developed as an analogue for an Aesop fable, "The Frogs Who Desired a King." By following the basic pattern of the fable, the film presents a *Katheoy* as the least favorable choice of a boy who considers his mother abject because of her ugly appearance and who uses a magical remote control newly invented by his father to force her to undergo two metamorphoses: first from an ugly woman to a beauty and then from a beauty to a *Katheoy*. Embarrassed by and regretful for his decision, the boy finally expresses a preference to have his mother, although still undesirable and ugly, rather than the *Katheoy*, whom he describes as emotional and frightening. The film ends when the boy decides to restore everything back to its original order, which again demonstrates that individual mobility is not possible. The use in *Remote Control* of an imaginary *Katheoy* to represent a deserving punishment for the boy's incessant discontent affirms that the *Katheoy* is positioned in the social stratum even below the ugly. This assumption is confirmed by Peter Jackson, who remarks that *Katheoy* are "occasionally the objects of highly vituperative criticism" and are viewed as "disgusting" by "some sections of the Thai population" (1999, 230). The outrage which prompts such disapproval, as represented in both films, is the practice of a muscular man habitually choosing to wear women's apparel. Buchbinder observes that "for a man publicly and unmistakably to give up his claim to masculine power and privilege may be to invite not only the disapproval of other men but also their violence" (1994, 18). And this is the case in both stories.

Tasting the Forbidden Fruits: Pleasure of the Rebels

It can be puzzling to Western world thinking to try to comprehend that the unique *Thai-Thai* organization of hierarchical social structure and its immutable intrahierarchy can be significant features in children's films. Such a system conceptualizes and develops the relationships between the characters so that all live in an imaginary society where there is a sharp distinction between the members of different hierarchical orders: to societies in which social mobility is an everyday occurrence, the Thai conception of intrahierarchy fixity may seem surprising. However, to say that this conceptualization constructs zero mobility on the basis of the karmic law of causation so as to cause discrimination among members of society is not wholly correct. It is also too rigid to assume further that zero mobility forecloses any individual ability to formulate choices or actions which might have consequences in the cycle driven by the karmic law of compensation. A superficial reading of either assumption underestimates the Thais' critical understanding of the phenomenon within the karmic cycle. The specified positions of an individual within an order vary—as illustrated in Figures 8.1 and 8.2—in accordance with the varying degree of three variables, namely, karmic law, degree of power, and degree of well-being. To put this relationship more simply, some viewers may argue that the common plot development in this film collection makes a strong reference to the karmic law of compensation in that it determines (and restricts) individual order—often overtly so—and also predetermines, to varying degrees, individual socioeconomic conditions in matters of dominance and life satisfaction. As seen quite often in the films, the superiors within or across divisions in the hierarchy desire to maximize their dominance, towering above their subordinate counterparts whose socioeconomic condition is less fortunate. Given this very nature, the designated order is in accordance with the conceptualization of materialistic society wherein social status is associated with an interplay between power, authority, material wealth, and individual subjective well-being. Because individual social status is shaped specifically by the varying degree of these worldly comforts, those who assume that the power of the karmic cycle functions to offer material rewards or punishments (or some may consider it a payback for so-called merits or demerits) find they lack any form of agency because it is not possible to achieve higher status as a consequence of increased quality-of-life measured by material wealth. This situation explains why this film collection brings every story to closure when the principle characters admit that their ascribed status in the hierarchy is immutable and accept the status into which they have been interpellated.

Within the rigidity of karmic-based social order, the same karmic law both maintains the position of individuals as a constant and also discloses a way in which the capacity for choice allows individuals flexibility and mobility of their position. In answer to the question of how such contradictory concepts can exist under the same concept of a law of compensation, especially when the latter concept allows for variation and mobility alternatives whereby individuals can negotiate their wants and needs, Figure 8.3 below illustrates how the social status of individuals, while still dependent upon the same key aspects, can move toward a higher position in the order.

The relationship in the figure below holds that individual status is subjective, as is well-being. That those subordinates who rebel against their superiors in the films all resume the original order in the end is the significant key that mediates individual desire and the consequences of social comparison on socioeconomic conditions—when measured by worldly comforts (ABC). Further, if the new measure relative to social status (DE and F) is taken into the equation, there is a promising trend which represents a shift in the status of individuals and their worldly comforts (socioeconomic conditions). This new measure acts in

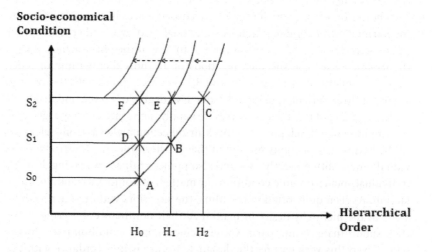

Figure 8.3 Relationship of hierarchical order and socioeconomic condition.

favor of each individual advancing their life in terms of, say, self life satisfaction. This line of thought supports the view that individual status all depends on the mindset of the individual, and hence agency may be possible in the form of mental orientation toward one's world. Both measures have been debated in the films and are most evidently portrayed in *The Little Prince*. Although the title of the film can be related to Antoine de Saint-Exupéry's "Le Petit Prince," the film's narrative is not a reproduction of the original pretext. Rather it favors this *Thai-Thai* thought by concluding that *Saen-dee (A)*, after redefining his life satisfaction (accepting the immutable nature of life as it is), is a rich boy already and is recast as *a prince*, the term denominating a member of a stratum of people who are wealthy or influential at the highest order *(F)*.

This *Thai-Thai* organization suggests that although much of well-being is visible and takes priority in measuring individual status within the order, it is also the degree of an individual's self-mirroring that enables the individual to feel or accept the rich or strong as superior and the poor or the weak as subordinate; and it is only by redefining their life satisfaction subjectively that the subordinate can consider themselves to be higher than their superiors. This new measure as articulated in the films suggests that subordinates whose development of identity and self life satisfaction is encouraged could be able to shape a more individualized hierarchy and acquire upward mobility.

But the *Thai-Thai happiness* does not end here. This recasting of the hierarchy wherein the subordinates could place themselves on top of the stratum of a hierarchy now made favorable to them now permits them to become the superior. In this endless cycle, the Strong is (still) beautiful after all.

Works Cited

Amnuay-ngerntra, Sompong. "King Mongkut's Political and Religious Ideologies through Architecture at Phra Nakhon Kiri," *Manusya: Journal of Humanities* 10.1 (2007): 72–88.

Barea, Milagros. "From the Iron to the Lady: The Kathoey Phenomenon in Thai Cinema," *Sesión No Numerada: Revista de Letras y Ficción Audiovisual* 2 (2012): 190–202.

Buchbinder, David. *Masculinities and Identities*. Melbourne: Melbourne University Press, 1994.

Butte, George. *I Know That You Know That I Know: Narrating Subjects from Moll Flanders to Marnie*. Columbus: Ohio State University Press, 2004.

Cook, Nerida, and Peter Jackson. *Genders and Sexualities in Modern Thailand*. ChiangMai: Silkwork Books, 1999.

Jackson, Peter. *Male Homosexuality in Thailand: An Interpretation of Contemporary Thai Sources*. New York: Global Academic Publishers, 1989.

Kirsch, Thomas. "Complexity in the Thai Religious System: An Interpretation," *The Journal of Asian Studies* 36.2 (1977): 241–266.

Morris, Rosalind C. "Giving up Ghosts: Notes on Trauma and the Possibility of the Political from Southeast Asia," *Positions* 16:1 (2008): 229–258.

Phradhammapidok. *Freedom: Individual & Social*. Bangkok: Buddhadhamma Foundation, 1990.

Phradhammapidok. *Good, Evil and Beyond: Kamma in the Buddha's Teaching*. Bangkok: Buddhadhamma Foundation, 1993.

Phongphit, Seri. *Religion in a Changing Society: Buddhism, Reform and the Role of Monks in Community Development in Thailand*. Hong Kong: Arena Press, 1988.

Pramoj, Kukrit. "Faith and Science" in *Dharmacaksu. 89 (7)*, 2005.

150 · Salinee Antarasena

Puntarikawat, Taweewat. "Bhikkhu Buddhadasa in Thai Context," *The Chulalongkorn Journal of Buddhist Studies* 4.2 (2002): 5.
Rakthonglor, Pinit, ed. *Dhammanukrom Dhammakosa.* Surat-thani: Dhammathan Foundation, 1997.
Reynolds, Frank E. and Mani Reynolds. *Three Worlds According to King Ruang: A Thai Buddhist Cosmology.* University of California Research Series 4. Berkeley: Asian Humanities Press, 1982.
Satien-koset. *Recounts of Traiphum.* Bangkok: Klang-wittaya, 1975.

Chapter Nine

Subjectivity and Ethnicity in Vietnamese Folktales with Metamorphosed Heroes

Tran Quynh Ngoc Bui

Versions of folktales which exist among different ethnic groups can be seen to be shaped by cultural frameworks particular to that group. Folktale motifs which represent complex embedded cultural codes and ethnic differences convey a particular concept of ethnic subjectivity and ethnic identity. That is to say, to investigate folktale is to explore a path to identify the cultural subjectivity of a group, for folktale is an "important means of expressing group identity as well as, frequently, a symbol of that identity" (Jordan, 1975: 170). In other words, we can say that subjectivity and ethnicity have crucial areas of overlap. Folktale can thus be both a local and global phenomenon. The term 'local' in this sense is normally understood as cultural subjectivity and identity characteristic of a nation as distinct from others. However, it can also refer to the subjectivity and identity among ethnic groups within a nation.

The issue of ethnicity has become a major concern for both anthropologists and folklorists since the 1970s, and the term "ethnicity" is defined in numerous ways. However, rather than provide a list of definitions, I prefer to focus on the basic idea which underpins definitions of ethnicity. Most definitions stress this term on the notion of self–identification, a sense of self, the "social and cultural distinctiveness" (Bell, quoted in Hicks 1977: 3) or the "social organization of culture difference" (Barth, 1969). The distinctiveness "sets one ethnic group off another" (Hicks, 1977: 3), and the notion of ethnic identity is adduced in order to differentiate one ethnic group from others. It means that ethnic identification only appears after members of the ethnic categories join together to construct ethnic groups and ethnic identity "arises out of and within interaction between groups" (Jenkins, 1997: 11).

It is the aim of this chapter, using the concept of subjectivity and identity as well as presenting a cultural source of information, to place the narrative of the metamorphosed character tale type in its historical context and to attempt to understand the worldview, values, and cultural traditions of people in multiple ethnic groups in Vietnam. By mostly drawing upon a comparison between the Kinh ethnic group and other minority ethnic groups, the chapter explores the concept of subjectivity and identity and attempts to understand the local voice or self-cultural trait of peoples among ethnic groups.

In Vietnamese folktale tradition, the metamorphosed character is plentiful and plots of folktales about metamorphosed character are very diverse. One of the major themes pivots on the relationship between abjection and intersubjectivity, so for the purposes of this discussion, I delimit my corpus to the metamorphosed character tale type to focus on the unfortunate fate of a character who is rejected by the community because of his nonhuman appearance and a low status in society. Hence the concept of the unfortunate metamorphosed character depends on the concepts of loathsomeness, repulsion, and abjection. The possibility that the metamorphosis constitutes a traumatic subjectivation that forever precludes the character from a subject position of equality within his community has significant potential to define the nature of subjectivity within an indigenous community in which prevails a collective perspective on any person's communal role. On the other hand, any frustration attributed to the metamorphosed character because of his marginal social position is tempered by a folktale convention that his entrance into the mode of intersubjectivity appropriate to his community is merely deferred by his false shape. His transformation is thus apt to coincide with another rite of passage, especially marriage, which marks maturation and full social acceptance.

An ethnic group is not a self-defined monad but exists in and through its interactions with others (Duara, 1996; Eriksen, 1993: 9–12; Schwartz, 1975: 107–108). The geographical proximity paves the way for communicating and cultural exchanges as well as for sharing common customs and habits between ethnic groups. A number of ethnic groups who share a geographical zone and live under similar ecological circumstances use the same language, believe in the same spiritual culture, and experience the same historical circumstance, political institution, and economic process (Đặng Nghiêm Vạn, 1998: 17–18). Breathing in the same cultural "air" creates the premise for common ideologies and cultural parallels among ethnic groups in the same geographical cluster. Thus, as Caglar explains it, "ethnology and anthropology interpret . . . ethnicity as spatialised cultural differences, ethnic groups as bounded and unified cultural entities and ethnic communities as spatialised localities, as integrated and organic communities" (cited in Modood and Werbner, 1997: 246). Hence, common cultural traits among close ethnic groups are an important premise to consider the common features reflected in folktale tradition in these groups.

The Kinh (Vietnamese) ethnic group comprises the majority in Vietnam whereas the other fifty-three minority ethnic groups comprise only ten percent of the population. However, folktales about metamorphosed characters in minority ethnic groups represent a large number in comparison with the Kinh folktales. Thus of twenty-four tales collected about unfortunate, abjected metamorphosed characters, only three come from Kinh tradition. This may be because the metamorphosed character tale type is very ancient and enduring within Vietnamese folktale tradition because it contains a number of mythic forms and primordial elements; hence the extent to which this tale type is preserved will mostly depend upon the historical, social, and economic development of the particular ethnic group it belonged to. Accordingly, mythic factors within the social environment of minority ethnic groups are easily preserved because most of the minority ethnic groups inhabit the midlands and highlands where social life is enclosed within a community. They themselves hold firmly to their traditions, customs, and beliefs, and these in turn play a key role in social development. Moreover, the ideology of minority ethnic people is grounded in mythic thinking,[1] as well as other kinds of autochthonous cultural activities, and natural phenomena are consequently understood and explained by beliefs in magic, the supernatural, and miracles. Thus the popularity of the metamorphosed character tale type in minority ethnic groups is understandable. In contrast, the Kinh ethnic group was dominated for a thousand years by China, and under the influence of Chinese norms, especially Confucian and Buddhist doctrines, folk narrative has been reshaped to become something more logical and rational to adapt to social and historical patterns. The Chinese hegemony not only involved the imposing of Chinese ideology but concomitantly the erasure of native cultural norms. The subjection to a long history of Chinese domination and to Confucian and feudal ideology caused the disappearance of some ancient beliefs which must have been very fruitful and common in Kinh social life and Kinh mythology. Nguyễn Đổng Chi contends that there was an unceasing and unconscious process of abolishing fabulous and miraculous factors, with the result that the folktale tradition of the Kinh ethnic group was largely subsumed within logical ratiocination and philosophy (1993: 1594). As a result of such historical conditions, the mythic tale type such as the metamorphosed character tales is rare in the folktale tradition of the Kinh.

Structure

The metamorphosed character tale type yields nine episodes that can be further organized into three parts. Part 1 involves two episodes. The first is designated Origin, in which the hero's familial situation is introduced, and the creation of the hero is also explained. Some motifs common to this episode are the motif of miraculous birth and the motif of the character's grotesque corporeality. The second episode is termed Acknowledgment because in it the protagonist's parents are disappointed in their child because of his grotesqueness. They do not want to raise him and intend to throw him into a river or bury him.

In Part 2, there are four episodes. The first episode is termed Desire. The hero desires marriage with a beautiful girl who is from noble status, such as a rich man's daughter or a king's daughter. The second episode is entitled Requirement because in order to gain his bride, the hero has to offer many valuable wedding presents specified and required by the future father-in-law. The third is Magic when the hero miraculously creates exactly what the future father-in-law requires. The last episode in this second part is Marriage; in it the hero marries the beautiful lady and during the nuptial night he sheds his ugly appearance to become a handsome man. This episode contains the motif of marriage and the motif of transformation.

Part 3 is conceived as an elaboration and expansion of the plot structure because the tale could possibly end at part 2 with satisfactory thematic and aesthetic closure. In part 3, Catastrophe is the first episode, when the two elder sisters are envious of the youngest sister's happiness and do harm to her. Popular motifs include the motif of catastrophe and the motif of the elder sister's envy. Escape is the term for the second episode, in which the heroine could escape death by using a knife, a stone, and eggs, things that the hero gives her before he sets off on a long journey that leaves his wife vulnerable to attack. The motif of supplementary things is used to describe this episode. The final episode of part three is titled Resolution which brings about the reuniting of the protagonist and his wife and the punishment of the two elder sisters.

In sum, in its skeleton form, we can understand the pattern of plot actions of this tale type as below:

(1) The hero's misfortune → (2) The hero's test → (3) The hero's triumph → (4) Catastrophe befalls the hero's wife → (5) The escape of the hero's wife → (6) Reunion and punishment

As space does not allow a full analysis of all versions, I have had to be selective. The version used here to illustrate the type, with some comparisons with its analogues in the tales of other ethnic groups, is the popular Kinh version named *Sọ Dừa*.

An old couple lamented their childlessness until one day the wife went into the forest to find firewood and was so thirsty that she drank water contained in a skull, and then she gave birth to a son who was in the shape of a coconut skull. Everybody called him Sọ Dừa.

Sọ Dừa asks to work as a goat-herd for a rich man. From the first day they are in Sọ Dừa's care, the goats become fatter and so the rich man is pleased. Sọ Dừa asks his mother to come to the rich man's house to ask for one of the rich man's daughters in marriage. The rich man demands very many valuable things. Sọ Dừa magically obtains everything requested. The rich man now has no idea how to refuse the marriage, so he calls upon his three daughters to ask if any of them would marry Sọ Dừa. The two elder daughters decline, but the youngest offers herself. The rich man remains reluctant to marry the youngest daughter to Sọ Dừa. On the nuptial night, Sọ Dừa transforms into a handsome man.

Sọ Dừa goes on a trip, leaving with his wife two special objects, a knife and a stone. The two elder sisters ask the wife to go out in a boat. They hide her oar and push the boat far away. This causes her boat to sink, and a big fish swallows her.

From inside the fish's belly, the wife kills it. Then the fish's body floats on the water, and drifts to an island. The wife uses the knife to rip its belly open and escapes. She uses the stone to make fire for food and to warm herself.

Two eggs hatch as a cock and a hen. One day, the cock sees a boat from afar and then crows, "Isn't that the boat of the youngest's husband, bringing her back."

Sọ Dừa and his wife are reunited while the two elder sisters flee forever.

Particular motifs in this tale type point to underlying religious meanings within different cultural and historical contexts of different Vietnamese ethnic groups. The study of motifs in light of cultural practices discloses how certain naturalized ideologies are established. Analyses may also provide insight into the grounding nature of conceptual metaphors which have significant cultural influence. Additionally, an analysis of motifs in this tale type allows us to perceive significant ideological changes in cultural perceptions of different ethnic groups. The central motif is that of grotesque corporeality.

The appearance of the character is not simply a physical phenomenon. It is socially constructed and hence entails social identity. Additionally, it is the symbol and the determinant of the self. According to the popular folktale "rule," the appearance of a character aligns the good with beauty and the bad with ugliness. The metamorphosed character tale type which involves questions of self-definition and identity, image and disguise, recognition and misrecognition, however, subverts that concept because the protagonist here is nonhuman in appearance. Hence, in the case of the motif of grotesque corporeality, the inner-outer contrast raises questions about subjects and objects, and the ways in which culture shifts perspective from the whole body to the physical appearance, and so subjectivity (or identity) becomes fragmented. The grotesque corporeality highlights the social construction of bodies that supposedly matter and bodies that do not matter (and are thus abjected), but its paradoxical otherness attests to positive qualities in strangeness and to a capacity for alteration or change.

This motif can also be interpreted as potentially transcultural when considering the various bodily shapes a character assumes in different variants. The protagonist may be a gourd, a goat, a toad, or a turtle shape. Whatever the bodily shape the character assumes, all tales obviously provide multiform and unsolicited information on the culture and societies in which they occur. There are references to custom, beliefs, and cultural patterns becaues "each ethnic group often had its own independent folk beliefs hidden within folktales, and . . . such beliefs had been preserved until quite recently" (Yanagita, quoted in Kawamori, 2003: 238). What I want to argue in this regard is that the bodily shape described in tales is not an arbitrary choice but has specific significance in the belief of each particular ethnic group, and these significances will need to be taken into account.

Folktale and culture or religion have a close connection. According to Propp, "the origin of many motifs could only be explained by reference to rituals due to the fact that the tale has retained numerous rituals and customs" (1984, 106). Therefore, it is important to consider the folktales in terms of rituals and customs, especially because the bodily shape that the protagonist assumes in this tale type may be the remnant of an animistic view of being wherein humans, animals, and objects share a common origin and ancestry. As Ingold argues, these nonhuman entities are thus not so much objects of worship as a "symbol, idea, or image" (2000: 129). It represents "symbolic indicators of position and transition of humans and cultural constructs" (Wessing, 2006: 206) and is "a sign in a system, a representation, forming the model for a structure of mind and a classification of the natural world" (Ingold, 2000: 129). Such a view has profound implications for subjectivity, because it always implies that the maligned, metamorphosed character embodies the communal subjectivity of the culture at a level that expresses the culture's deepest roots—roots which are apt to have been forgotten at any particular moment at which the tale is retold.

Animal symbols in the metamorphosed character tale type may thus be understood as an illustration of concepts grounded in the broader culture because they are seen as an expression of particular ethnic characteristics. In other words, the animal provides a sign in a local symbolic culture and represents ideas of social structure. Therefore, the variants of character bodily shapes can be read in certain contexts as a metaphor for ritual belief in the sacredness of the animal. Characters in the forms of a toad, or a frog, and a turtle comprise 74% (17/24) of the entire list. The popularity of these animals in folktale suggests that there must be some relation between those animals and the social life and practice derived from animistic beliefs in some particular ethnic groups. The Toad, for example, is highly respected in Vietnamese culture because it is argued to be a spirit of water and rain and is a symbol for the ceremony of rain seeking. The toad appears as a sculptured symbol on the edge of the Đông Sơn drum, a kind of bronze drum which is an important archaeological artifact found in southern China and Southeast Asia. The image of toads on the edge of the bronze drum is not simply a decoration but reflects the social and spiritual life of people who invented and used the drum. The Turtle is likewise a creature of great significance. According to the understanding of the Muong, Thai, Bahnar, Jarai, Katu, and Gie-Trieng peoples, they know how to build a solid house by reproducing the turtle's shape. The turtle's legs are the four pillars of a house, its carapace is a roof, and its abdomen is a floor. These ethnic groups are thankful to the turtle, and they do not kill turtles or eat their flesh. They hang a turtle's carapace in front of an altar, which signifies that the turtle is venerated like their ancestors.

Sọ Dừa (a coconut skull) is distinctive from other stories in that the protagonist does not metamorphose into animal appearance but into a coconut shell. This interesting case can also be found in folktales in neighboring Thailand and Myanmar. The character in these stories always has the same appearance—that is, as a head with no limbs like a coconut. This shape should be explained in terms of geography. In Central Vietnam, which is thought to be the provenance of the Sọ Dừa version, coconuts are grown extensively. The coconut's homeland is in provinces such as Tam Quan and Binh Dinh. Thailand and Myanmar are also major producers of coconuts. Moreover, this characterization can be explained in the light of the increase of brainpower as Sọ Dừa (a coconut skull) in Vietnamese is a word constructed from two components: "Sọ" means "skull" and "Dừa" means "coconut." As the coconut shape is similar to the shape of skull, this symbol may relate to the veneration of skulls in ancient worship.

Throughout human time, skulls have been venerated in many ethnic groups around the world. The skull of a large animal is an important trophy in ceremonies because it proves the preeminence of that ethnic group. In wars, getting the opponent commander's skull is a triumph. According to Crossley-Holland,

> The power of the severed head is of course a familiar motif in both primordial and civilized societies. Earlier this century, headhunters in the Philippines needed heads to guarantee the success of their rice crops; in the Tain, we read how Irish warriors carried off the heads of their enemies, tied to their saddles. (1985: 331)

In the ritual practices of the Katu people and other minority ethnic groups in Vietnam, there are some forms of approved homicide. Where the victim is a headman of a village or someone of equal status, his head is severed and "placed in a special hut that is entered only when the villagers need the help of the spirit associated with the heads" (Hickey, 1982: 27).

Moreover, according to primordial belief, the skull is the place which holds the life and the symbol of the perfect spirit. In the Rig-Veda, the vault of heaven was fashioned from the skull of the first man (Chevalier and Gheerbrant, 1994: 888). In Old Scandinavian poetry, "the head is the sky, the fingers are branches, water is earth's hair" (Gurevich, 1985: 45).

In describing the different ways in which animal veneration is practiced, it is clear that animal worship is a popular phenomenon in many ethnic groups and that many animals did have certain positions and typical images in each particular ethnic group. However, when they become a folktale figure, these holy animals and plants lose some of their wonder, and their position is diminished. Ethnological meaning is replaced by the social concept of abjection. In employing the form of a goat, a toad, or a turtle for the protagonist's transformation, folktales borrow only the outer appearance of the holy animals, and so the toad here is not the noble character it used to be in myth but the ugly, humble one. The turtle in this situation is poor and miserable, neither the turtle which is knowledgeable about everything, nor the turtle which in the legend gives advice about building the citadel. This fact once again manifests the conceptual shift from myth to folktale.

In the metamorphosed character tale type, the threat of abjection is both encapsulated and averted by the test given to the protagonist by the future bride's father (not by any supernatural power), when the future father-in-law enacts his unwillingness to accept the protagonist as his son–in–law and seeks to hinder his hope of marriage to the daughter. Especially, in this tale type, the protagonist is not aided by any supernatural power to complete the test but must use his own resources.

The test given by the lady's father takes many forms in different variants. These can be classified as below:

- *The test of working:*
- *The test of strength:*
- *The test of ingenuity*
- *The test of a valuable betrothal gift*

It is arguable that the test motif in this tale type has its root in social practice because this motif is very close to some specific marriage customs in some particular ethnic groups. Accordingly, this motif can be deemed to reflect a Vietnamese social custom: 'thách cưới' (the custom of requesting wedding gifts). In the metamorphosed character tale type, there are some versions describing this detail.

The Kinh version relates that when Sọ Dừa's mother asks for the hand of a rich man's daughter for her son, the rich man replies that: "In order to marry my daughter, you have to bring us one jar of gold, ten pieces of silk, ten pigs, and ten jars of wine. You also have to build a five-room house with silver tie-beams and bronze girders."

This custom is very popular in Vietnamese wedding tradition. For example, in the betrothal ceremony, the bride's family often requests some special wedding gifts from the groom's family, and the wedding ceremony only happens once these gifts have been received.

However, the custom does not exist in some ethnic groups in the Central Highlands who follow matriarchal social practices. According to matriarchal practice, the woman has active rights in marriage, and in this case, the bride's side will bring betrothal gifts to the groom's family. A man under this custom has to live with his wife's family after marriage. This custom is called 'ở rể' (matrilocal custom). There are two forms of matrilocal custom. The first is that the husband has to live with his wife's family to labor for some years, and the second form is that the wife's family meets all expenses of the marriage, and the husband lives with his wife's family permanently. The husband's condition in this situation is scorned because his children will be given his wife's surname. In effect, he is denied any form of subjective agency.

The situation of a husband in the matriarchal system is so humble and lacking in social status because he is little more than a hired worker in the matrilocal marriage structure. Hence, there is an assumption that 'ở rể' custom is reflected in the 'metamorphosed character' tale type because the situation of the husband living with his wife's family in a matriarchal society is just like the situation of the protagonist as servant in this tale type. Both live within and labor for the bride's family. This status is emphasized in some metamorphosed character versions, where before asking for marriage with the daughter of the rich man or the King, the metamorphosed character asks to become a servant of the lady's house. This will prove to be a temporary state for the metamorphosed character because he will subsequently achieve agency by marriage as it enables metamorphosis to human form.

The notion of metamorphosis has long been associated with the notion of subjective agency as metamorphosis entails more than a merely physical change. Because the appearance of the character changes, it changes the self and the social concept of identity as applied to the character. Ideologically, the motif of metamorphosis metaphorically expresses concepts of change and otherness, representing maturation as a process of becoming someone other (and superior to what existed before).

The process of abandoning the previous status and moving to a new one, with new rights and obligations, is a transition which shares a common pattern with initiation rites. Propp asserts that the classic form of fairytale centers on the rituals of initiation. Meletinsky, in contrast to Propp, contends that the detachment of magical powers from the folktale hero created new motifs for elaborating initiation rites. Hence weddings are "the ritual equivalent to the classic folk tale," although the wedding is "both more recent and more individualized than the initiation ceremonies from which it is derived" (1998, 240).

In the case of the metamorphosed character tale type, marriage represents a transitional status because the metamorphosed character by marriage transforms himself to a handsome man and changes his social status to another, higher level. In this process, the derivation of folktale from myth seems evident, although now it conveys mythic notions and mythic motifs on the level of the imaginary. Also, it takes up and continues reflecting religious experience but now in a secular form. In this respect, the depiction of a character shedding his skin in a variety of ways may be seen to reflect ritual customs which used to exist in many ethnic groups.

In versions of the Kinh ethnic group, the shedding is cursorily described, and on the nuptial night, the protagonist simply transforms himself into a handsome man. In other words, the fact of achieving the marriage is the only necessary catalyst for transformation, and no further process or ritual is required. In the tales of minority ethnic groups, however, this motif is detailed and manifold. The protagonist can shed his skin by bathing in a stream with his wife, or the protagonist dies because his wife burns his skin when he was not ready to transform into a human.

The motif whereby the protagonist sheds his skin by bathing may proceed from water ritual beliefs because water is a powerful metaphor for the ritual of community. In some ethnic groups in the Vietnamese Central Highlands, there is a rite of passage whereby in order to be accepted as an official member of the community, a youth has to wake up early to bathe himself in the stream and bring back a bottle of pure water. There also exists a belief in many Central Highlands' folk narratives that after bathing or face washing, a young man is endowed with an extraordinary strength by a water spirit.

Some tales, however, mention that the protagonist dies because his wife burns his skin before he is ready to transform into a human. This incident is argued to reflect a punishment consequent upon breaking a taboo. Breaking a taboo means violating the rules of society because taboo is seen both as expressing social obligation and creating social continuity (Lambek, 1992: 247). In a version of the H'Mong ethnic group, thirteen days is the exact duration of the test for the protagonist prior to becoming a human forever, but his wife becomes impatient and burns her husband's skin before the proper time has passed. The number thirteen is not an arbitrary choice but has its root in H'Mong social practice, in that thirteen days is the duration for burial rites. After thirteen days, there is no more mourning because H'Mong people believe that dead people transform into another life at the end of that period. Not only in this tale type but also in other tales about metamorphosis, the number thirteen is used to indicate the prescribed term required for metamorphosis. For example, there is a story about a man who is captured by a tiger and becomes her husband. After he has lived for a long time with the tiger, he becomes a tiger also. Hence, in order to come back to his human life, he buries himself in a tomb (presumably to manifest that he dies), and after thirteen days, he transforms into a human.

Although the foregoing analyses show that there existed initiation rituals using fire in some foreign cultures, it is impossible to reach a definitive conclusion about the relation between the detail of shedding skin by burning in metamorphosed character tale type and the initiation ritual of primordial people, because no Vietnamese documents mention this custom. However, according to the theory of cultural diffusion, the assumption for this relation is still worthy of consideration and needs to be teased out by readers and scholars.

Conclusion

In order to deeply understand a community, there is no better way than to approach it through its folk cultural tradition, of which folktale is a part. By doing this, ethnic subjectivity and ethnic ideology may be explored. In this study, by bringing different cultural theories to approach the metamorphosed character tale type, we can gain considerable insight into some of the beliefs, rituals, and customs which are in operation among the fifty-four ethnic cultures in Vietnam.

Nevertheless, although folktale is a product of a particular culture, social life does not come directly into fiction, and folktale is not a perfect correspondence to reality. As the real world is described in fiction under symbolic forms and the embedded culture is read symbolically, it is not easy to identify social evidence reflected in folktale. Moreover, although some cultural practices are very obvious and still popular in certain ethnic groups, various primordial rituals and beliefs have disappeared or been transformed into other kinds. Therefore, in order to fully investigate folktale, it is necessary to take into account a variety of theoretical disciplines because "no single outlook or approach offers a final answer to the mystery of this genre, because the wonder-tale at its best is multi-faceted in depth and meaning, always open to a new breath and breadth" (Stone, 2008: 233).

For this study, I have selected a number of motifs which can reasonably be assumed to be the kernel motifs of the metamorphosed character tale type, and I have drawn upon a variety of cultural theories to explore how different culture frameworks may shape various versions of different ethnic groups. When these motifs represent complex embedded cultural codes and ethnic difference, they convey a particular concept of ethnic subjectivity and ethnic identity. Hence, the study concludes that all subjects are just that—subjected to their culture—and the metamorphosed character in fifty-four ethnic groups in Vietnam is shaped and determined by its particular social context.

Notes

1. Bernard Dauenhauer usefully defines myth, as the basis for "mythic thinking," as "the unitary meaning of an ensemble of symbols, and these symbols can be of any kind e.g., words, gestures, natural phenomena such as rainbows, etc." (1971, 173). "And a symbol is here taken to be that perceptible figure which makes present to our attention a non-perceptible or 'absent' order of being and meaning. . . . It is the non-directly evident

foundation of that which is or comes to be evident" (179). "It is that to which no more than an allusion can be made" (180).

Works Cited

Barth, Fredrik. *Ethnic Groups and Boundaries*. Boston: Little, Brown and Company, 1969.

Chevalier, Jean, and Gheerbrant, Alain. *A Dictionary of Symbols*. Oxford: Cambridge, 1994.

Crossley-Holland, Kevin. *Folk-tales of the British Isles*. London: Folio Society, 1985.

Đặng Nghiêm Vạn. *Ethnological and Religious Problems in Vietnam*. Hanoi: Social Sciences Publishing House, 1998.

Dauenhauer, Bernard P. "Thinking about the 'World' as Mythic Thinking," *Kant-Studien* 62.2 (1971): 172–184.

Duara, Prasenjit. "Historicizing National Identity, or Who Imagines What and When." In *Becoming National: a Reader*, edited by S. Eley and R. G. Suny. Oxford: Oxford University Press, 1996.

Eriksen, Thomas Hylland. *Ethnicity and Nationalism: Anthropological Perspectives*. London: Pluto Press, 1993.

Gurevich, A. J. *Categories of Medieval Culture*, translated by G. L. Campbell. London: Routledge and Kegan Paul, 1985.

Hickey, Gerald Cannon. *Sons of the Mountains: Ethnohistory of the Vietnamese Central Highlands to 1954*. New Haven: Yale University Press, 1982.

Hicks, George L. "Introduction: Problems in the Study of Ethnicity." In *Ethnic Encounters: Identities and Context*, edited by George L. Hicks and Philip E. Leis. North Scituate, Mass.: Duxbury Press, 1977.

Ingold, Tim. *The Perception of the Environment: Essays in Livelihood, Dwelling and Skill*. London: Routledge, 2000.

Jenkins, Richard. *Rethinking Ethnicity: Arguments and Explorations*. London: Sage Publications, 1997.

Jordan, Rosan A. "Ethnic Identity and the Lore of the Supernatural," *The Journal of American Folklore* 88 (1975): 370–382.

Kawamori, Hiroshi. "Folktale Research after Yanagita: Development and Related Issues," *Asian Folklore Studies* 62.2 (2003): 237–256.

Lambek, Michael. "Taboo as Cultural Practice among Malagasy Speakers," *Man* 47.2 (1992): 245–266.

Meletinsky, Eleazar M. *The Poetics of Myth*, translated by Guy Lanoue and Alexandre Sadetsky. New York: Routledge, 1998.

Modood, Tariq, and Pnina Werbner. *The Politics of Multiculturalism in the New Europe: Racism, Identity, and Community*. London: Zed Books, St. Martin's Press, 1997.

Nguyễn Đổng Chi. *Kho tàng truyện cổ tích Việt Nam*. Hanoi: Nxb Khoa học xã hội, 1993.

Propp, Vladimir. *Theory and History of Folklore*. Minneapolis: University of Minnesota Press, 1984.

———. *Tuyển tập Propp*, tập 1 [Propp's Collection, Vol.1]. Hanoi: Nxb Văn hóa dân tộc, 2003.

Schwartz, Theodore. "Cultural Totemism: Ethnicity Identity, Primitive and Modern." In *Ethnicity Identity*, edited by George De Vos and Lola Romanucci-Ross. Palo Alto, CA: Mayfield, 1975.

Stone, Kay. *Some Day Your Witch Will Come*. Detroit, MI: Wayne State University Press, 2008.

Wessing, Robert. "Symbolic Animals in the Land between the Waters: Markers of Place and Transition," *Asian Folklore Studies* 65.2 (2006): 205–239.

Chapter Ten
All Is Relative, Nothing Is Reliable
Inuyasha and Japanese Subjectivities

Mio Bryce

The popularity of Japanese manga and anime has been steadily increasing in the Western world, and it is intriguing to speculate about the kind of understanding these Japanese genres receive. Mediated through different linguistic and cultural frames, these texts are inevitably remade. It can also be assumed that a less obvious, but more profound, process of refashioning constantly occurs as Japanese constructions of subjectivity, which underpin manga and anime products, are implicitly reinterpreted in terms of Western assumptions about subjectivity. Because many manga narratives involve a quest and characters who change and develop, they can be readily interpreted as if they conformed to multiple conventions of Western children's literature, especially character development from self-regardingness to other-regardingness, from solipsism to intersubjectivity. An example from my focus text in this chapter, Takahashi Rumiko's popular manga *Inuyasha* (1996–2008), is the demon Sesshōmaru (older half brother of the male protagonist, Inuyasha).

Sesshōmaru is self-contained and independent, calm, and aloof but bears ill will toward his half brother because he thinks their father favored Inuyasha, and is locked into conflict with him over the possession of their father's sword, *Tessaiga*. Over the course of the series, Sesshōmaru gradually develops a capacity for intersubjective relationships through two narrative streams. First, once he has freed himself of the desire for Tessaiga he develops an identity independent from his late father and accepts Inuyasha as his brother and a worthy individual. Second, Sesshōmaru initially appears to lack empathy with others. This coincides with the Japanese view that empathy is an essential quality for being human.[1] Sesshōmaru's change toward altruism begins when he is defeated and

163

badly wounded in a battle against Inuyasha and receives the care of an orphan girl, Rin, who had become mute when she witnessed the murder of her family (Chapters 1–2 in Volume 14, hereafter 14:1–2). When Rin tries to steal food for Sesshōmaru, she is beaten and her face is bruised, but when Sesshōmaru asks her about her injured face, she feels happiness and smiles. The moment touches Sesshōmaru's heart, and his transformation into a hero who primarily acts on behalf of others has begun. In a much later episode (48:1–2), Sesshōmaru enters the world of death in order to strengthen his own sword, *Tenseiga*, and Rin accompanies him. When she dies there, Sesshōmaru realizes that nothing is more valuable than her life and throws Tenseiga away. Once he does so, the sword shines and attracts numberless, wandering dead in search of salvation. Feeling empathy, Sesshōmaru picks up the sword again, purifies their souls, and returns to the world. The intense grief he feels at Rin's death and relief when she is revived by his mother is a new and important experience on his path toward empathic intersubjectivity. The particular twofold evolution of Sesshōmaru's subjectivity seems quite compatible with Western concepts of subjectivity, in that empathic intersubjectivity exists in symbiosis with the self-relating, self-present consciousness of a self-present individual.

We as humans share a strong interest in ourselves, our lives as individuals, and we frequently and diversely talk about it, using terms and concepts such as subjectivity. According to Robyn McCallum, "Subjectivity is that sense of a personal identity that an individual has of her/his self as distinct from other selves, as occupying a position in relation to other selves and to society, and as being capable of deliberate thought and action, and of self-reflection upon that action" (1999, 3). Subjectivity emerges through encounters with others, from a play of similarity and difference. Although, as Jonathan Culler puts it, "subjectivity is not so much a personal core as an intersubjectivity" (1975, 140), it is still based on the premise that an individual is allowed to exist as a unique, independent, and integral entity whose agency is a product of individual choices and decisions performed within an intersubjective sphere of relationships. This Western perspective is not a universal understanding, however, and its terms and concepts do not effectively transfer from one culture to another.

Japanese subjectivities manifest themselves as fluid, ambiguous, and precarious. They are penetrated and pushed around by a society which is highly contextual and empathy-orientated and which embraces ambivalence and fleetingness within a homogeneous yet hierarchical structure (see Lebra, 2004; Sugimoto, 1997). Within the society exist numberless, varied, small, insular groups and subgroups or, in Maruyama Masao's figurative term *takotsubo* (a round ceramic pot for catching an octopus), tied with a rope in isolation with limited security and freedom (1961). In each group or situation, the participants' normative role-playing is required to maintain harmony, generally based on their external attributes (for example, status, gender, age), and an individual's integrity of being and individual preferences are suppressed (for example, Lebra, 1976: 2004; Nakane, 1967; Sugimoto, 1997).

Likewise, individuals' expressions are dictated by the Japanese language and the assumption of inexpressibility. Having evolved from the aforementioned circumstances, Japanese language is poetic, metaphoric, and emotive, and favors value judgments that are implicit rather than overt. Toyama Shigehiko calls it an 'indoor' language (1976). It does not establish the premise that language is "a neutral and lifeless tool" to articulate an object but rather signifies or symbolizes the object along with the speaker's feelings about it according to each varied situation. As soon as it is uttered, it loses the essence: the truth. It is like an egg in which a life is evolving. This indicates the critical significance of metacommunication (for example, postures, gestures, and facial expressions) in Japanese where within an interaction the force of phatic elements to constitute harmonious conversation may exceed the factual content of the message. A perfect intimacy may be communicated in silence, whereas subtle discords may produce abrupt, hostile miscommunication and disconnection.

The idiosyncrasy of Japanese language highlights manga as a most effective apparatus to represent and explore Japanese subjectivities and intersubjectivities. Manga are symphonic texts made of diverse iconographic illustrations, written texts, and frames to create stories with psychological depth. Graphics are focused, exaggerated (as typified by the huge starry eyes of female characters), and shifted swiftly from the normal to the super deformed to reflect situational and emotional changes. Frequent focuses on characters' eyes (as well as hands and postures) visualize their perspectives and sentiments. Language texts, largely monologues and dialogues, project multilayered voices, thoughts, and feelings. Different fonts and shapes of speech bubbles endow utterances in the texts with emotional intensity. The wide range of frames constitutes temporality and spatiality, connecting present and past as well as dreams and memories (see, Yomota, 1999). These elements are integrated to set the stage for storytelling, with characters and situations focalized with distinct atmosphere (Takemiya, 2001). Things, characters, and their emotions are generally captured in fluid and ephemeral motion.

Through an analysis of Takahashi Rumiko's popular manga *Sengoku Otogi-zōshi* (literally Sengoku fantastic narrative) *Inuyasha* (1996–2008)[2] and its representation of fragmented and transmutative selves, this chapter examines the representation of subjectivity in a Japanese context and by doing so affirms the importance of sensitivity toward and awareness of cultural diversity in constructions of the self.

Inuyasha: The Chaos of Wars and Desires

Inuyasha is a fantasy set in the alternative world of Sengoku, overshadowed by magic and supernatural powers. Humans and *yōkai*[3] (that is, mythic beings, monsters, demonic phenomena) in diverse forms, powers and personalities, coexist and continue to battle one another. The Sengoku period (literally, warring nation period) roughly refers to the second half of the 16th century in Japan, when the whole of Japan was in chaos because of continuous battles and intrigues. Numerous individual and collective desires clashed and intertwined, often leading to ironical outcomes. The period setting effectively epitomizes the profound and ubiquitous ambivalence and uncertainty of the human psyche, interactions, and societies as a whole. Nothing is definite and reliable but relative, and therefore the struggle for power becomes endlessly fierce. This also means that relationships based on trust are rare and truly precious.

The story revolves around the ambiguous *Shikon no tama* ("jewel of four souls"). This jewel embodies the ambivalent and fragmented nature of the human psyche, representing a human's four essences, i.e., *Aramitama* (harsh spirit), *Nigimitama* (harmonious spirit), *Kushimitama* (mysterious/intellectual spirit), and *Sakimitama* (happy/fortunate spirit), all of which can work positively or negatively (10:6). For example, *Aramitama* can be courage and physical strength but also violence. What is important, and difficult to achieve or maintain, is balance. When the four essences are well balanced, the soul can maintain goodness, but if not, it represents evil.

Just as the ring in J. R. R. Tolkien's *The Lord of the Rings* can either bestow power or deprive its bearer of free will or agency, the Shikon jewel is a magnetic amplifier of desires and is fiercely pursued by humans and *yōkai* alike. It is believed to grant the holder's wishes, and even a piece of the jewel can revive the holder's life and empower his body and weapons. The jewel attracts ambitious *yōkai* and people alike and intensifies their monstrosity, causing numberless disasters. In itself it is said to be neutral, although easily stained by the evil and darkness of souls, even by grief and loneliness. It needs pure souls, such as the powerful *miko* (Shintō priestess), Kikyō, and her reincarnation, Kagome, to purify it. The affinity with darkness is intrinsic, as the jewel was created by an ancient priestess—Midoriko, just before her death—by combining her soul with numerous *yōkai*, her combatants, and casting it out from her body so that her soul could not be eaten by and empower the *yōkai* (10:6). It is later revealed that their vicious battle has continued within the jewel, where Naraku—the primary source of evil action in the series—as his final wish, attempts to trap the heroine, Kagome. The susceptibility to change and the instability and ambivalence of the jewel symbolize human existence, especially the human psyche and human interrelationships. The power exists, but in an unfixed form, so that the jewel only becomes imbued with meaning by the holder. Any consistency or integrity is not expected, as it can be reversed anytime and by anyone. The jewel thus embodies a state of incessant paradox, thereby manifesting the Japanese perception of the world as relative and ephemeral.

The Shikon jewel is introduced at the beginning of the story when Inuyasha, the main male protagonist, who is a half human and half wild dog *yōkai* and marginalized by both humans and *yōkai*, vandalizes a village to steal the jewel which had been entrusted to Kikyō's care. Inuyasha desired to use the jewel's power to become a full *yōkai*. However, he is pierced by Kikyō's holy arrow and pinned to a sacred tree for fifty years. Kikyō herself has been fatally injured by Naraku (disguised as Inuyasha [22:3]), and dies soon after, asking to be cremated along with the jewel. Inuyasha and Kikyō die in anger at one another's betrayal, not knowing that they had both been deceived by the antagonist, the most formidable half-*yōkai* Naraku, who wants to kill Kikyō and possess the jewel himself. At this point of the narrative, time shifts to 1996, to an old Higurashi shrine in Tokyo, and introduces Kagome, the female protagonist who lives a normal life as a junior high school girl without knowing that she is the reincarnation of Kikyō and bears the sought-after jewel inside her body. On the day of her fifteenth birthday, she is pulled into an old, dry well by a centipede-like *yōkai* and transported to Sengoku, where there is nothing familiar except the sacred tree, to which Inuyasha is still nailed by Kikyō's arrow. With the centipede-like *yōkai*'s reattack, the jewel is taken from Kagome's body. Her presence awakens Inuyasha, and with his promise to help her, she frees him from the tree. Later, Kagome recovers the jewel, which Inuyasha then tries to take. However, Kaede (Kikyō's younger sister and the village priestess) curses him to obey Kagome if she uses a restraining word of power. In a humorous irony, the word she thinks of is *Osuwari!* ("Sit!"), generally used for a dog. Kaede identifies Kagome as the reincarnation of Kikyō and tells her to protect the jewel. After fighting with several *yōkai*, Kagome's arrow splinters the jewel (1:1–5). This is how Kagome and Inuyasha's quest to collect the pieces begins, through which they develop a mutual bond, friendships with other characters, and agentic, intersubjective selves.

Being One and the Other

The chaos of human nature is represented in *Inuyasha* by hybridity, ambiguity, and paradox. The key protagonists and antagonists are all hybrid; they are both one and an other, and they want to be "one." With the exception of everyday animals, reptiles, fish, and insects, the inhabitants of Sengoku are categorized as humans or *yōkai*, regardless of whether they are dead or alive. *Yōkai* have diverse forms, powers, and personalities, ranging widely from the tangible to the intangible. Some are typically ugly, grotesque, and cannibalistic as typified by a Noh–mask-wearing demon who constructs her body out of corpses (3:7). However, others, including the main protagonists, have humanlike appearances and are even noble and beautiful. Unlike most Western monsters with fixed, solid bodies, *yōkai* are changeable and amorphous. The *yōkai* in *Inuyasha* are in essence uncanny, inexplicable, and hybrid beings and phenomena, and as such reflect the images of *yōkai* accumulated since the ancient period (Abe K, 1996, Abe M., 1981; Ema, 1976; Foster, 2009).[4]

Yōkai are generally related to the dark side of humans and nature in an animistic way. They are frequently associated with negative feelings such as jealousy and grief, for example. *Yōkai* imageries and narratives are common in various genres (for example, manga, anime, films, popular fiction, and games) in which their transmutability, penetrability, and diffuseness are often visualized as vague, slimy, and shapeless, and they are hence associated with the abject. Often associated with animals, and always with the nonhuman, they lie outside the symbolic order that constitutes humanity. Human subjectivity is often defined in contrast to nonhuman nonsubjectivity, as Colleen Boggs argues: "only [human beings] participate as subjects in the structural and representational schemes that make up the symbolic order. Representational subjectivity sets human beings apart from all other living creatures—it lies at the core of our secular notion that human beings are special, that there is such a thing as human exceptionalism. . . . Any creature who is not deemed human becomes subject to abuse without recourse to ethical standards that would mark such injury as a wrong" (2010, 98–99). Such a distinction has profound implications for the evolving subjectivity of Inuyasha, in whose representation lies a crucial distinction between becoming a unified *yōkai* being and becoming behaviorally human. The difference is spelled out in 3:1–4, when he and Kagome successfully battle to destroy a frog demon that has possessed the body of a lord, and to his astonishment, Inuyasha is thanked for showing compassion, a trait that the text designates as distinctly human. This is a significant episode, falling early in the series, in that it suggests some parameters between the ambiguity of Inuyasha's subjectivity and the clear cut distinction between the human and frog elements of the possessed lord. Ambiguous imageries express an elusiveness that is often more fearful than *yōkai* with clear shapes and personalities. Their monstrosity often lies in their power to take over others' bodies, either the dead or the living, and/or to be able to 'copy' or absorb the power of others, as the demons in Nagai Gō's *Devilman* (1972–1973) take over human bodies and reproduce their behavior. Like bacterial pathogens, the demon's real identity only appears later; mutual suspicion about who has been possessed by a demon results in mass killing among humans themselves.

The fragility of subjectivity under external influence, such as the pressure for normative conformity, is expressed in the prevalence of spirit possession in Japanese texts (either factual or creative). Komatsu Kazuhiko claims that the concepts built around spirit possession are observed even in present day Japan and lie in the pathos—the emotional and the imaginative qualities— that is deep in the Japanese psyche and indicates Japanese perspectives and concepts of value (1984, 12–13). Mori Jōji uses an intriguing metaphor for such a Japanese self as a 'shell-less egg': this shell-less egg has a flexible surface and thus enables empathic collaboration with others to share a common fate, whereas, in contrast, the Western self is 'a shelled egg' with a solid core of self that enables the pursuit of an individual's principles (1977). The shell-less egg entails that the subjectivity of an individual is easily invaded and taken over. The penetrating and possessing power of *Yōkai* thus represents the precarious nature of subjectivity in Japan.

In a travesty of intersubjectivity, *yōkai* in *Inuyasha* gain power by means of absorption or amalgamation, often depicted as 'eating' or 'sucking' their victims.

For example, the grieving Hiten eats his younger brother's heart to absorb his demonic power, after his brother is killed by Inuyasha (4:4).[5] Tōkajin, who was originally human, abuses the powers attributed to a hermit by reducing the size of humans and eating them without remorse (9:1–7). Naraku lends a human arm to Sesshōmaru to deprive Inuyasha of his sword, Tessaiga. When the attempt fails and the borrowed arm is damaged by Inuyasha, the arm begins to stretch tentacles toward Sesshōmaru's upper arm as if taking it over, so it is cut off (7:6). Naraku also implants a tree-like *yōkai* strengthened by a shard of the Shikon jewel into a wolf-like *yōkai*, thus inflicting excruciating pain, to attempt to force him to kill Inuyasha and his friends. The most spectacular and horrific representation is Naraku's method of acquisition of a new body, by cursing and trapping numberless *yōkai* in a cave to fight each other. The winner eats the loser, so the final winner obtains all the powers of those destroyed, which then becomes Naraku's body. An equivalent transfer of power also occurs between things, as exemplified by the development of Inuyasha's sword, Tessaiga. Aggressive violation of bodies and souls is seen everywhere in the narrative, demonstrating the insatiability, biological urges and barbaric behavior of the *yōkai*, as well as manifesting the fluidity of the situation.

When examined from the perspective of its representation of subjectivity, *Inuyasha* is seen to configure its panoply of characters in complementary and contrasting ways which reflect the ambiguity and precariousness of subjectivity under the strong pressure for social conformity in Japan. In the rest of this chapter, I will examine how subject-constitution is produced in the case of a few of the main characters. As remarked above, Sesshōmaru is easy to comprehend by Western concepts of subjectivity. Inuyasha and Kagome represent intact subjectivity, but in a form distinct from that of Sesshōmaru: they are rather characterized by their innate naturalness, lack of artifice, and innate capacity for empathy. Deep emotion, including empathy, is regarded as the essential quality and resilience of individuals, and it is the innateness of such qualities to subjectivity which sets it apart from recent Western paradigms. Naraku, the antagonist, embodies the fragmented self who knows how precious human bonds are, but, alienating himself from them, becomes the vindictive manipulator of human emotions. Naraku's subordinates, Kagura and Kanna, represent victimized characters deprived of autonomy and hence of agentic subjectivity. Kikyō and the high priest Hakushin also represent fragmentation and are double bound by their own hyperconformity, which is a realistic depiction of the experience of many people in Japan.

Subjective and Intersubjective: Inuyasha and Kagome

Inuyasha and Kagome are empathic, sincere, intuitive and spontaneous, emotional, and honest to themselves, and able to express their feelings directly to one another. Therefore, they are represented as reliable. They are immature but have enormous energy and potential for growth. They do their best in each situation and at the end rely on their deep feelings—the voice from their innate insight—to find solutions to the problems that arise.

Inuyasha is hybrid and ambiguous, as engraved in his name Inuyasha: *inu*, dog from his father; and *yasha*, the ambiguous and fierce god/demon from Hinduism (yashk) and Buddhism. In Japan, *yasha* can be male or female but is often visualized as a woman with intense jealousy; hence it may also obliquely refer to his human mother. In this story, Inuyasha is a wild, unsophisticated boy endowed with intense competitiveness and genuine warmth. Despite his apparent hybridity and the dilemma of affections divided between his first love Kikyō and her reincarnation, Kagome, Inuyasha is essentially intact and has no critical subjective conflict. In fact, full release of *yōkai* power overwhelms him and degrades him to simply a red-eyed, fighting monster (16:8–9). For this reason, his father left him his sword, Tessaiga, which seals in Inuyasha's *yōkai*-ness and helps him maintain his self. He soon realizes that if he became a full *yōkai* and thus lost his humanity, he would also lose himself. His experience of losing himself and slaughtering people with a sense of enjoyment frightens him, especially the possibility that he might kill Kagome without knowing (19:7–9). Once he has resolved to stay himself and develop his strength, he begins to accept

Figure 10.1 Kagome/ Kikyō shoots a bow (*Inuyasha* 1:4).
Source: *Inuyasha*, Volume 1, p. 101. © 1997 Rumiko Takahashi/Shogakukan.

himself as he is, that is, his half *yōkai* identity. As a result, he finally realizes that his human/*yōkai* hybridity is in fact the source of his true strength. This is how he overcomes and integrates his fragmented self.

Inuyasha's development is embodied in the evolution of his sword, Tessaiga, as he himself gains increased proficiency and the sword absorbs specific powers from other swords. His proficiency comes not through knowledge but intuitively from his senses and experiences. He respects and follows Tessaiga's will, and his "feel" for the sword is recognized as what enables them to work together (41:1; 44:3). Kagome learns in a similar way: she becomes adept with bow and arrow at the prompting of her feelings, which can touch the indwelling essence of Kikyō, and hence she does not need to undergo training or purification rituals, but focuses on what she can do in each situation.

The first time she holds a bow, she shoots proficiently (even though, aiming at a moving target while in motion herself, she misses her mark). The illustration (see Figure 10.1) depicts her as strong and fluent, while Kikyō appears as an isomorphic figure in the background. Reincarnation here doubles as an expression of inherent skill and power which shape the character's subjectivity. Kagome is Kikyō's desired self, one who can live as a human. Having grown up with an affectionate family and school friends, Kagome does not want, or pretend, to be someone else, nor does she seek powers she does not have. Her most essential and stable power is her inborn ability to see through illusion to the truth, a power she never loses even when her other powers are suppressed by hostile powers (53:8). Naraku is thus unable to trick her with his illusion (13:4). Her unusual name, *Kagome*, may also suggest her intrinsic power as signified by the *kagome*, a hexagram pattern found in ancient Shinto temples, as well as the paradoxes her adventures embrace suggested by a popular children's game.[6]

The strength of Inuyasha and Kagome lies in their frankness and artlessness, which allow them to maintain their trust in their own subjectivities and to develop their strength steadily and intersubjectively. They are both honest to themselves and one another, and share a mutual desire to be together and express it frankly. When Kagome complains that Inuyasha has expressed his desire to be with Kagome but also said to Kikyō that he has never forgotten her, he simply said that both are true, as he is responsible for Kikyō's fate, but at the same time, his relationship with Kagome is independent. Although this makes Kagome uncomfortable, she thinks their mutual desire to be together is important and accepts him as he is, including his love for Kikyō. Such frankness may appear to be natural, but in Japan it is not necessarily so. Where empathy is demanded and individual subjectivities are less respected, an assertion of one's love can be seen as selfish. A common paradigm of Japanese love triangles is thus: character A confides his/her love for C to B (without telling C) who also loves C, and by doing so suppresses B's chance to confess his/her love for C, although B and C may love each other. The story often focuses on B's struggles in the double bind situation between his/her own love for C and sense of responsibility to support A's love for C. One of Naraku's devices, a sticky spider thread, works superbly in such mental contexts, tangling people with their emotional distress in interactions, causing (unnecessary) distress and problems. Nevertheless, because of her ability to accept and express her feeling directly to Inuyasha (for example, in 8:9), Kagome can eventually escape from this labyrinth, even though she feels loneliness and jealousy whenever she witnesses Inuyasha's love for Kikyō.

Inuyasha's relationship with Kagome is distinct from that with Kikyō. It is developed through time and numberless, spontaneous interactions, including trivial yet often playful quarrels. It also involves people around them. With Kagome, he can be himself: natural, at ease, and rather childish and competitive with her. Their love only strengthens their power as individuals as well as a couple. It is evidenced by their maximized power when they try to protect each other. For example, when Sesshōmaru, using a human arm swings Tessaiga at Inuyasha, Kagome without hesitation jumps in front of Inuyasha to protect him (7:3). When Sesshōmaru strikes down Kagome, Inuyasha fights desperately, even letting Sesshōmaru stab him in the back to regain Tessaiga. After that, although he loses consciousness from the injury, Inuyasha holds the sword tight and remains alert, and that makes Sesshōmaru leave (7:5).

Inuyasha and Kagome's mutual trust is the key to the accomplishment of their mission in the penultimate episode (56:9)—the destruction of the Shikon jewel. They are both tested in darkness in isolation. Kagome is urged to make a wish, which can trap her in the jewel. Inuyasha finds himself inside the jewel and is told that Kagome is born to fight eternally, which prompts him to think and conclude, "No! Kagome was born to see me and also I was born to see her." This enables Kagome to hear his voice and say, "I don't wish anything. I believe that Inuyasha will come." United with him, Kagome finally makes a wish for the jewel to disappear (56:9). This again shows their way of solving problems, not by means of premeditated strategies but by being themselves and using their ability—listening to what their souls and emotions tell them.

Fragmented and Bound Subjectivity: Kikyō

Individuals with special abilities are often subjected to a demand that they use these abilities for society, ignoring their own needs and preferences and suppressing their own subjectivities. This loss of subjectivity is in contrast with the path of Western heroes, who are more commonly represented as affirming their individuality through their contribution to society. The Japanese situation is articulated during a conversation between Kikyō and the ghost of the respected high priest, Hakushin, who, having fallen into despair when his attachment to life had prevented him from becoming a Buddha, had been exploited by Naraku:

"There is no one who has no doubt. Is there anyone who is completely free from stains?"

"But, I needed to be so. I tried to be so."

"I was, too, in my life. I tried not to doubt, not to make mistakes. I know now that it is humans who doubt and hesitate. Because of that, they long for the sublime. Attachment to life and shedding tears for losing it are not something you need to feel ashamed of." (28:3–4)

The dialogue expresses the despair, sorrow, and sense of guilt often experienced by people who try hard to conform. The pressure may be others' expectation. To deal with delicate, everyday interactions and conform without experiencing serious inner conflict, individuals may combine the *uchi-soto* dichotomy (intimate and homogeneous inside group versus formal, often hostile, outside group) and the pragmatic double standards *honne* (true voice) and *tatemae* (facade). A problem with such behavior is that the contextual fluidity or instability of each group/situation can intensify endless competition and inner-surveillance among the members, demanding constant adjustment of their role-playing (Masuhara, 1984). People like Kikyō and Hakushin don't have an inner group within which they can be frank and seek help—in other words, where they can be normal humans.

Beneath the trust in such emotion is a longing for purity, innocence, and goodwill as a core quality of humans. With an evident absence of respect for solid and clear principles or (religious) beliefs, but with the egalitarian belief which can entail the refusal of individual differences and instigate endless competition (Nakane, 1967), *empathy* is perceived to be an essential factor to lubricate social interactions. The respect for harmony is enforced through the inculcation of empathy by nurturing sensitivity toward an other's loneliness. Japanese preschool pedagogy is often built on Doi Takeo's concept of *amae* (expressions of dependency needs) (1971) and emphasizes empathy as a means of social interaction (Hayashi, Karasawa, and Tobin, 2009). Such an educational influence on an individual's development of self can possibly place sincere, serious, and relatively inflexible children in a double bind situation, instigating a sense of guilt for their successes or an envy or resentment of others' successes.

Under these circumstances, Kikyō and Hakushin are unable to live their own lives because of their caring natures and vocational commitment to helping others who are weaker than themselves. They have tried their best to carry out their responsibilities, but their professionalism, perfectionism, and the demands of others suffocate them and create an abyss in the unconscious. The deaf, mute, blind, and psychic priestess, Hinoto, in CLAMPs' *X* is a similar example. This is what 'good' children and adults suffer, by trying extremely hard to meet social expectations and becoming exhausted and broken (for example, Miyoshi, 1996; Yoneyama, 1999).

Kikyō is a beautiful and caring priestess with outstanding spiritual power, knowledge, and experience. She is the only person who can purify and protect the Shikon jewel until Kagome appears. She suffers from Naraku's deceit and its consequences, including her death, revival in a body constructed from her bones and soil from her grave, repeated injuries, and her final death/disappearance. Kikyō's tragedy is that she can only live her life after her death, especially after she realizes that her post-life existence is running out. This paradox indicates how thorough the pressure of internalized social appropriateness can be, especially for able and conscientious, but relatively inflexible, individuals, and how difficult it is for them to protect their inner selves, which are suppressed very deeply. Kikyō and Hakushin illustrate that the facade is felt not only as their social identity but their subjectivity. Therefore, even when they face the extreme crisis and start to listen to their almost muted voice in the depth of their soul, they have to overcome their sense of guilt and sorrow before accepting themselves as they are. Kikyō's mistakes indicate her overconfidence and reliance on her ability, knowledge, and logical approach to problem solving. In suppressing her inner self and intuitive feelings, she allows her insight into the true nature of things to become occluded.

How deeply Kikyō's subjectivity is both fragmented and bound by internalized social pressure is signaled by her love–hate relationship with Inuyasha, which causes the initial deterioration of her spiritual power: she is torn between her personal desire to love and live with Inuyasha and her responsibility as a priestess, who should maintain her purity. Her love for Inuyasha begins with her sympathy for him as an alienated and marginalized individual. She says to him, "I should not show any weakness to anyone. I should not hesitate. Otherwise, I will be taken advantage of by yōkai. I am human but should not be a human." Then she continues, "Inuyasha, you and I are similar. So I cannot kill you." Her forlorn smile is unexpected and imprinted in Inuyasha's heart, and his feelings toward her grow (5:9). In opposition to Inuyasha's desire to become fully yōkai, Kikyō makes him a strategic offer: if she uses the jewel to make him fully human, the jewel will be purified and disappear, releasing her from her responsibility to be its protector. The plan requires that both Kikyō and Inuyasha give up the essential part of their subjectivities: Kikyō's spiritual power and Inuyasha's strength as yōkai. If they did such a thing, would it function as a subject-constituting exercise of agency? Can they still live as they are? We may recall Kusanagi Motoko in *Ghost in the Shell*, saying to Batō that her access to cyberspace is an integral part of her; if she quits the job and returns her body to the government, she is no longer herself. Moreover, although Kikyō and Inuyasha are genuine and caring, they are not of equal standing. Her spiritual power and maturity overwhelms Inuyasha. Her desire to heal his hurt with her love puts her in the position of his carer or elder sister, a role with some responsibility, discouraging her from openly showing who she really is and seeking his help. Their relationship is thus reserved, exclusive and socially isolated, in contrast to Kagome and Inuyasha's relationship, and leaves them vulnerable to attack by Naraku who, by disguising himself as each in turn and then attacking and wounding the other, creates enmity between them.

A core concept in which the pressure to conform distinguishes Japanese and Western subjectivities is a paradox of agency in relation to a community's customs, expectations, and ethical norms, and the role of empathy in this relation. The community's norms are not followed simply because they are dictated by an authority external to the subject but because the subject *affirms* them. Put another way, the subject consciously *affirms* and *chooses* a course of action mandated by the culture's structures of ethics and empathy. In principle, the option to choose differently exists, but may be rendered unthinkable under extreme pressure to conform. Further, to pursue the option produces a diminished subjectivity or marks the subject as simply deviant or evil. In the narrative of *Inuyasha,* choices characteristically take the form of moral dilemmas. Kikyō, for example, resolves to defeat Naraku by using a piece of the Shikon jewel that sustains the life of Kohaku, and hence she can only achieve her goal by means of another's death. Instead, in response to the collective desire of Inuyasha and the others, she chooses to give up her own vocational commitment and strategy to destroy Naraku and give life to Kohaku. Later it is revealed that she left her final light/power to Kohaku, which allows him to live without the Shikon jewel. The climactic moral dilemma in the series falls upon Kagome, when, trapped in the darkness inside the Shikon jewel and faced with the possibility of an eternity of solitude, she has the power to make one wish. The right wish will cleanse the world of the jewel forever, whereas the wrong wish will begin a whole new cycle of evil. Kagome's dilemma is two-tiered. First, there is a choice between wishing and not-wishing. Second, there is a choice between her own desires—to return to her own time-space, or to see Inuyasha one last time—and an altruistic wish with unforeseeable consequences. As the framing text makes clear to readers, the latter possibility is "the one right wish": to wish for the Shikon jewel to disappear forever. This wish also enables subjective agency.

Fragmented Subjectivity and Crises of Agency: Naraku

As a half-demon, Naraku stands in opposition to Inuyasha because in his case the disjunction between the human and nonhuman and the continual re-fragmentation of his being makes subjectivity impossible. While in the chaos of Sengoku, evil seems persistent and inevitable: it is defined as such by its relationship to the moral norm demanded by an everyday ethical life framed by altruism and empathy. *Inuyasha* thus constantly moves toward articulating a social world adequate to deal with unethical choices. Naraku, the most formidable antagonist, is hybrid, transmutable, manipulative, and uncanny. He is a half *yōkai,* evolved from the amalgamation of numerous *yōkai* and a malicious human, Onigumo ("Demon spider"). His abject nature is represented by his elusive, gigantic body, whose complex structure enables him to be the outside and to simultaneously exist in separate form within its hollow interior. The profundity of his solipsism is presaged by his name: a bottomless abyss of darkness and despair, or simply hell. It embodies his elastic, elusive idiosyncrasy, suggested by his association with whiteness and elusive darkness. It is not a pure blackness and evil which opposes whiteness and purity, but it insatiably eats and absorbs the latter. Bright lights make darkness darker. Naraku, and his subordinate Akago (literally, 'baby') are skilled at finding a tiny darkness in human hearts possessing a holy spirit, which they then manipulate. Hence, what Naraku fears is not the person endowed with strong spiritual power, but those who are energetic and honest to themselves, as exemplified by Kagome.

The intense fragmentation of self is demonstrated by Naraku's continuous and kaleidoscopic bodily reconstructions by absorbing numberless others and discarding the unwanted, as exemplified by a gruesome pile of infant bodies left in Mt. Hakurei where he successfully detaches Onigumo's humannesss (28:7). His gravest inner conflict is between his *yōkai*-ness and the humanness of Onigumo fueled by his desire for Kikyō. In an attempt to eliminate his Onigumo element, Naraku uses his power to detach parts of himself as separate beings and to project Onigumo's personality into a construct, but the bond is innate. Onigumo's humanness works as if it is Naraku's unconscious, without which his body fragments, thus he has to reabsorb his projections (22:5).

Although he has numerous bodies, Naraku remains faceless because his face is originally his victim's (10:5). This facelessness is another representation of his solipsism and fragmentation, and signals his lack of integral subjectivity. It is also emphasized by his frequent resort to disguise and impersonation, as when he impersonates Inuyasha to Kikyō and vice versa to make them hate each other. He covers himself with the head and fur of a monkey-like *yōkai* (the monkey in Japan represents superficial cleverness and mimicking ability). Likewise, his frequent use of puppets of his monkey-like or humanlike shapes (for example, 10:5) indicates his lack of self-presence.

Naraku's successful manipulations of the human psyche reveals the vulnerability and susceptibility of Japanese individuals, not necessarily because of any intrinsic flaw but because of their (hyper)sensitivity and fixation on their own and others' sorrow and loneliness. Naraku constantly instigates conflicts between intimate people such as couples and siblings, and enjoys exploiting his victims' sense of guilt, grief, and jealousy related to love and friendship. Conversely, he displays frustration and irritation when he witnesses his opponents' commitments to one another or any actions inspired by empathy or altruism, and thus the moral dilemmas he constructs directly assault such qualities. Nevertheless, his malevolent acts lack substantial motivation. Even his relentless attempts to defeat Kikyō and eradicate his Onigumo-ness are only provoked by Kikyō's remark that he is unable to harm her because of Onigumo's feelings for her (18:3–4).

The inherent emptiness of his being is expressed ironically by his asserted mastery of a self untrammeled by any commitment to other subjects or social forms. His desubjectification and social alienation have thus left him without conscience because he has neither a base nor a desire for subjective reflection. They have also left him without a meaningful goal, even in terms of evil. He has strategies and the ability to execute them but has no aim. Kagome pinpoints this emptiness during their final battle, when she points out that Naraku's relentless and sadistic instigation of people's hatred for one another is in fact based on his recognition of the preciousness of human bonds, and hence of the pain and grief felt if they are lost. The absence of an integrated self remains evident in Naraku's final utterances when Kagome asks him to reveal his true wish: one expresses Onigumo's final regret, as he disappears, that he can never be in "the same place" as Kikyō (56:4); the second is a wish to grant the Shikon jewel's own wish to continue the cycle of turmoil and battle, by trapping Kagome within the jewel (56:4). Even the most intimidating antagonist fails to remain independent and becomes absorbed by the Shikon jewel—that is, by the ambiguous darkness which is the other and simultaneously himself. This confirms the volatility of human presence: fluid, relative, and thus unreliable.

Conclusion

Inuyasha illustrates the elusiveness and fragility of individual subjectivities in Japan, under the social demands for individuals to carry out multifaceted and often contradicting role-playing as each particular situation requires, while retaining some sense of a self. The pains and the sense of vulnerability of the self are acute, and hence there is a continual production of, especially, manga and anime which explore quests for 'individual identity' (for example, Fujimoto, 1998, 2001; Schodt, 1996). The instability of the subjectivities of individuals because of the constant negotiation with their fluid surroundings may not be distinctly Japanese, however. Social pressures witnessed in Japanese societies have some commonalities with internet social networks (for example, Facebook) which give the users the (false) feeling of being 'uchi' (an insider) despite their exposure to the larger cyberspace. With the prevailing cyberspace activities, the concepts of subjectivities may require some reconceptualization, with increased cultural sensitivity to diversity and fluidity.

Notes

1. This is exemplified by the image of the Japanese hero, who is typically defeated in his final battle because of his empathy and lack of relentless cruelty, calculation, and selfishness. The most representative character

is Minamoto no Yoshitsune (1159–1189), who helped his half brother, Minamoto no Yoritomo (1147–1199), the first *shōgun*, who then caused his death.

2. *Inuyasha* was first serialized in *Weekly Shōnen Sunday* by Shogakukan and ran from 1996 to 2008. It was republished as 56 volumes of *Weekly Shōnen Sunday* comics from 1997. A television anime series of 167 episodes was broadcast in Japan from 2000 to 2004, then the final 26 episodes between 2009 and 2010. Four discrete films were also produced and distributed between 2000 and 2004. Takahashi Rumiko was previously known for her hilarious manga and anime such as *Urusei Yatsura* (*Lum*, 1978–1987), *Maison Ikkoku* (1980–1987), and *Ranma ½* (1987–1996). Nevertheless, her interest in creating stories of monsters and the darkness of humans began in the earlier period, as seen in her vicious and grotesque mermaids in her *Mermaid* series, compiled in *Ningyo no mori* (*Mermaid's Forest*, 1987) and *Ningyo no kizu* (*Mermaid's Scars*, 1992), which are also set in the Sengoku period.

3. Throughout this chapter, I use the Japanese term *yōkai*, instead of English *monster*, to maintain the wider and more spiritual nuance of the term.

4. Some *yōkai* are vague in shape whereas others are clearly visualized, defined, and named. Gods and ghosts may be included. Lifeless things such as tools and dolls can gain life as *yōkai*. They are visualized as chimeras, ranging from the somewhat comical, pitiful, or grotesque to vague and frightening—as evident in the written and visual depiction of *hyakki yagyō/yakō* (literally, night parade of one hundred demons) since the Heian period (794–1185), in a number of illustrations in the Edo period (e.g., by Toriyama Sekien, 1712–1788), and in popular culture (e.g., by Mizuki Shigeru, 1922–). Diverse *yōkai* imageries are found in the *yōkai/kaii* database from the International Research Center for Japanese Studies, led by Komatsu Kazuhiko (http://www.nichibun.ac.jp/YoukaiGazou-Menu/); and *Mizuki Shigeru no yōkai world* (http://www.top-page.jp/site/page/mizuki/complete_works/list/) by the creator of the popular *Ge Ge Ge no Kitarō* and a wide range of *yōkai* with old Japanese rural ambience, black humor, and soft, rounded lines.

5. The incident was altered in the anime, however, where Hiten only takes a shard of the Shikon jewel from his brother's forehead (Episode 10).

6. In the children's game, *Kagome Kagome*, the "kagome" sits blindfolded while the other children join hands and circle her. When they stop moving, she must name the person behind her, and if she does this correctly, they change places. It may suggest Kagome's ability to see the truth. Takahashi also presumably accepts that the game is a "back-stabbing" game, based on the betrayal of Oda Nobunaga (1534–1582) at Honnō-ji in 1582, because in Episode 3:1 Kagome mistakes a young man for Oda Nobunaga and (in an act of egregious frame-breaking humor) reads aloud from *Japanese History Made EZ* about his victory at the Battle of Okehazama in 1560.

Works Cited

Abe, Kazue. *Yōkaigaku nyūmon*. Tokyo: Yūzankaku shuppan. 1996.

Abe, Masamichi. *Nihon no yōkai-tachi*. Tokyo: Tokyo Shoseki, 1981.

Boggs, Colleen Glenney. "American Bestiality: Sex, Animals, and the Construction of Subjectivity," *Cultural Critique* 76 (2010): 98–125.

Culler, Jonathan. *Structuralist Poetics: Structuralism, Linguistics, and the Study of Literature*. Ithaca, NY: Cornell University Press, 1975.

Doi, Takeo. *Amae no kōzō*. Tokyo: Kōbundō, 1971; *The anatomy of dependence*, trans. by John Bester, Tokyo; New York: Kodansha International, 1973.

Ema, Tsuyomu. *Nihon yōkai henge-shi*. Tokyo: Chuokoronsha, 1976.

Foster, Michael Dylan. *Pandemonium and Parade: Japanese Monsters and the Culture of Yōkai*. Berkeley: University of California Press, 2009.

Fujimoto, Yukari. "Bunshin—shōjo manga no naka no 'mō hitori no watashi.'" In *Manga no shakai-gaku*, edited by Miyahara Kōjirō and Ogino Masahiro. Tokyo: Sekai shisō-sha, 2001.

Fujimoto, Yukari. *Watashi no ibasho wa doko ni aru no?: Shōjo manga ga utsusu kokoro no katachi*. Tokyo: Gakuyō shobō, 1998.

Hayashi, Akiko, Karasawa Mayumi, and Joseph Tobin. "The Japanese Preschool's Pedagogy of Feeling: Cultural Strategies for Supporting Young Children's Emotional Development," *Ethos* 37.1 (2009): 32–49.

Komatsu, Kazuhiko. *Hyōrei shinkō ron: yōkai kenkyū eno kokoromi*. Tokyo: Arina shobō, 1984 (augmented edition).

Lebra, Takie Sugiyama. *Japanese Patterns of Behavior*. Honolulu: University of Hawaii Press, 1976.

Lebra, Takie Sugiyama. *The Japanese Self in Cultural Logic*. Honolulu: University of Hawaii Press, 2004.

Maruyama, Masao. *Nihon no shisō*. Tokyo: Iwanami shoten, 1961.

Masuhara, Yoshihiko. *Tatemae to honne: Nihonjin-teki aimaisa wo bunseki*. Tokyo: Kōdansha, 1984.

McCallum, Robyn. *Ideologies of Identity in Adolescent Fiction*. New York: Garland Publishing, 1999.

Miyoshi, Kunio. *Shissoku-suru yoi kotachi*. Tokyo: Kadokawa shoten, 1996.

Mori, Jōji. *Nihonjin= <karanashi tamago> no jigazō*. Tokyo: Kodansha, 1977.

Nakane, Chie. *Take shakai no ningen kankei*. Tokyo: Kodansha, 1967; as *Japanese Society*. Berkeley: University of California Press, 1970.

Schodt, Frederik L. *Dreamland Japan: Writing on Modern Manga*. Berkeley, CA: Stone Bridge Press, 1996.

Sugimoto, Yoshio. *An Introduction to Japanese Society*. New York: Cambridge University Press, 1997.

Takahashi Rumiko. *Inuyasha*. Tokyo: Shogakukan Inc., 1997–2008. U.S. edition published by San Francisco: Viz Media, 2009–2011.

Takemiya, Keiko. *Takemiya Keiko no manga kyōshitsu*. Tokyo: Chikuma shobō, 2001.

Toyama, Shigehiko. *Nihongo no kosei*. Tokyo: Chuokoronsha, 1976.

Yomota, Inuhiko. *Manga genron*. Tokyo: Chikuma shobō, 1999.

Yoneyama, Shōko. *The Japanese High School: Silence and Resistance*. London: Routledge, 1999.

Chapter Eleven

Strategic Empowerment

A Study of Subjectivity in Contemporary Indian English Children's Fiction

Suchismita Banerjee

An ancient Indian folktale narrates the story of six blind men who hear about an elephant in the vicinity. Not having any idea about the creature, they decide to learn more about it. The first feels the broad, sturdy side of the elephant and pronounces that it is like a wall. His companion grasps its tail and declares the creature is like a rope, whereas the third gets hold of its swinging trunk and is convinced the elephant is like a snake. The fourth man feels the thick leg and proclaims it's like a tree. Another touches the huge ear and announces that the creature is really like a fan. The last, not to be outdone, runs his hand along the smooth and sharp tusk and concludes the elephant is like a spear.

This tale has been variously interpreted through the ages to signify several things: the relativity of truth, the impossibility of comprehending the absolute, and the validity of every point of view. In recent times, Sudhir Kakar, a prominent Indian psychoanalyst and scholar, has cited this fable to illustrate the pitfalls of translating experiences and practices in one society into universal norms for others. I quote this fable as a metaphor of subjectivity, of the multiple positions and processes that determine the formulation of the subject.

Current debate on the question of subjectivity focuses on its differing notions in the West and the East and the questionable imposition of Western concepts of identity and subjectivity on Eastern modes of thought. In her discussion of the construction of the self, Takie Sugiyama Lebra contrasts the unified, transcendental identity of the Western subject with anthropological depictions of the self. She cites Marcel Mauss's research, which "relativizes the Western notion of *moi*, along with that of the individual and *personne*, by going into the ethnographic literature to demonstrate its peculiarity, compared with constructs of self in American Southwest (Pueblo) and Northwest (Kwakiutl) Native American, Hindu, and Chinese cultures, all of which pose the self as a composite of relations, memberships, names, roles, and positions—in other words, personas" (Lebra, 2004). Tu Weiming, in his examination of the relevance of Confucian traditions in East Asian modernity, argues against the notion that only Western forms of local knowledge are universalizable. "Surely, Enlightenment values such as instrumental rationality, liberty, rights consciousness, due process of law, privacy, and individualism are all universalizable modern values, but as the Confucian example suggests, 'Asian values' such as sympathy, distributive justice, duty consciousness, ritual, public-spiritedness, and group orientation are also universalizable modern values" (Tu, 2000: 264).

Several other researchers have pointed out the opposing conceptions of the self in Western/non-Western culture—that is, self as personal fulfillment versus self as a composite of relations within the community. Yukiko Uchida, Vinai Norasakkunkit, and Shinobu Kitayama note that, "Specifically, in European and North American cultures such as the American middle class culture there is a strong belief in the independence and autonomy of the self ... In contrast, in East Asian cultures, there is a contrasting assumption about the connectedness and interdependence of self with others. The self-in-relationship-with-others is believed to be the locus of thought, action, and motivation" (2004, 225).

Similarly, Sudhir and Katharina Kakar cite the findings of the GLOBE (Global Leadership and Organizational Behaviour Effectiveness) research project in their exploration of the nature of "Indian-ness" in their book *The Indians: Portrait of a People*. In the GLOBE project, middle managers in various industries in sixty-two societies were surveyed (2009, 21). They were grouped into ten cultural clusters: Latin Europe, Germanic Europe, Anglo Europe, Nordic Europe, Eastern Europe, Latin America, Confucian Asia, Anglo (outside Europe), Sub-Saharan Africa, Southern Asia, and the Middle East. The study concluded that compared to the other clusters, South Asia stood out in *humane orientation*, that is, the degree to which the culture's people are caring, altruistic, generous, and kind. Germanic Europe scored the lowest in this category. South Asians also scored the highest in *in-group collectivism* (the degree to which people feel loyalty toward family or friends), a category in which Scandinavia scored the least. South Asia was also among the least assertive culture in the group. Sudhir and Katharina Kakar trace this habit of solidarity with the family group to early childhood rearing practices in India. They acknowledge, however, that Indian society is still in a state of transition, and the impact of globalization on modern urban families increasingly exposed to Western modes of thought will change the dynamics of leadership significantly.

The predominant influence of society in personality development has also been the focus of an in-depth examination by Sudhir Kakar. In *The Inner World: A Psychoanalytic Study of Childhood and Society in India*, he traces the development of Indian identity from childhood. He uses the term identity to mean "the process of synthesis between inner life and outer social reality as well as the feeling of personal continuity and consistency within oneself. It refers to the sense of having a stake in oneself, and at the same time in some kind of confirming community" (1981, 2). This could arguably be considered a definition of subjectivity in the Indian context inasmuch as it highlights the pivotal role of the community in the formation of subjectivity.

Kakar explores the formation of Indian identity in the context of social norms and religious beliefs, and contrasts it with accepted Western notions of individuation and personal success as the hallmark of identity. He notes, "Ever since Max Weber's analysis of Indian society, many Western (and Indian) social scientists have interpreted social institutions such as caste and the extended family as oppressive, in the sense of hindering the growth of such personality traits as 'independence,' 'initiative,' 'persistence,' and 'achievement motivation' in the individual. Such interpretations, however, are intimately related to a historically determined, culturally specific *Weltanschauung* of the ideal 'healthy' personality cast in the Faustian mould . . ." (1981, 10). Kakar goes on to observe that ironically, whereas "modern" Indians are breaking with tradition and actively pursuing goals and skills consonant with American and European middle-class values, Western youth are increasingly focusing on the values of continuity and cooperation characteristic of Indian culture as being fundamental to the process of radical change.

Although Kakar's study focuses primarily on the individual psychological development of the child, he places the child firmly within the network of social roles, traditional values, caste customs, and kinship regulations that make up the "Indian-ness" of Indians. Kakar acknowledges at the outset the dangers of perceiving social groups in monolithic, even stereotypical terms, particularly in a country as heterogeneous as India. Yet, for the purpose of his study, he sets down the assumptions and limits of his work, which deals primarily with Hindu India and with the dominant mode of Hindu behavior (1981, 8). The terms "Hindu" and "Indian" are used interchangeably in his text not only in the interest of readability but also because he believes that other religious groups in India have been profoundly influenced by the dominant Hindu culture.

In the Indian context, therefore, the making of the self is influenced by a complex interplay of factors such as caste, class, religion, and community. What impact does this have, if any, on the representation and formation of subjectivity in contemporary Indian English children's fiction? This chapter will explore the construction of identity and subjectivity in contemporary children's literature, specifically drawing on Sudhir Kakar's study of Indian identity, which probes the dynamics of childhood based on ancient Hindu texts, the philosophy of Ayurveda,[1] folk narratives and proverbs, and popular tales from Hindu mythology.

As children's literature in English emerged as a distinct genre in India, implied subjectivities were shaped by colonialist assumptions. In pre-independent India, children's literature in English was published for missionary schools with the specific agenda of indoctrinating the colonial subject. In her analysis of the manner in which cultural hegemony was strengthened in India, Gauri Visvanathan comments on "the relationship between the institutionalization of English in India and the exercise of colonial power, between the processes of curricular selection and the impulse to dominate and control" (1989, 3). She traces the roots of this institutionalization to the passing of the Charter Act of 1813, which resulted in two major changes in Britain's role with respect to its Indian subjects: "one was the assumption of a new responsibility towards native education, and the other was a relaxation of controls over missionary work in India" (1987, 3). She points out that the responsibility of undertaking the education of the native subjects was one that England did not officially bear even toward its own people. British colonial administrators came to realize that the dissemination of English literature was a useful way to maintain control over the natives under the guise of a liberal education. The introduction of English literature in the school curriculum served the dual purpose of extolling the virtues of order and justice in Western society as well as highlighting the inconsistencies and flaws of the native social system: "A discipline that was originally introduced in India primarily to convey the mechanics of language was thus transformed into an instrument for ensuring industriousness, efficiency, trustworthiness and compliance in native subjects" (1989, 93). Such a procedure has significant implications for concepts of subjectivity because, as Visvanathan further argues, the teaching of English literature was designed to separate the material and discursive practices of colonialism, and hence "the rapacious, exploitative, and ruthless actor of history" was progressively rarified to become "the reflective subject of literature" (1987, 23). Literature is thus privileged not only as an expression of subjectivity but as a model of subject positions of a particular kind.

These subject positions were based on the assumption that the native subject was in need of education and uplift, and the best way to do this was through the medium of English literature taught in the school curriculum. As Visvanathan comments, "The 'Indian character' suddenly became a subject of immense importance, as was the question of how it could best be molded to suit British administrative needs" (1987, 11). Ironically, the Orientalist policy of the British government, intended to promote an understanding of Indian culture and character, actually resulted in the accumulation of a body of knowledge of local texts that was later used to justify the necessity of educating the natives. Whereas ancient Indian texts such as Kalidas's *Shakuntala* were deemed suitable for the English reader, who could appreciate its lyrical qualities and pastoral beauty, such texts were not recommended for study in Indian schools and colleges. The implication was that the native subjects lacked the ability to discriminate between decency and indecency, and exposing them to the riotous "immorality" of their native literature without the moral scaffolding innate in the English character would have disastrous social and political consequences.

The ideal subject position envisioned by colonial administrators was that of a rational intellect that functioned on the basis of evidence and logic. Visvanathan refers to the argument forwarded by these policy makers that Oriental literature tended to "lull the individual into a passive acceptance of the most fabulous incidents as actual occurrences; more alarming, the acceptance of mythological events as factual description stymied the mind's capacity to extrapolate a range of meanings for analysis and verification in the real world" (1987, 20).

To address this moral and intellectual deficiency in the native spirit, English literary works were prescribed in the curriculum because they were declared to be the products of inquiring minds trained in the discipline of reason rather than unquestioning faith and because they drew their material from an empirically perceived world. Literature was assigned the task of shaping critical thought and consequently ensuring the proper development of character.

Postindependence, children's literature was fashioned by nationalist discourse and aimed at providing children with a subjectivity that was uniquely "Indian." This postcolonial approach was adopted by many former colonies in their struggle to develop a national identity. In her study of the relationship between glocalization and the formation of national identity, Anna Katrina Gutierrez comments, "Children's literature is one of the areas that strive to battle colonial mentality by retelling old tales and producing new stories that highlight the beauty and individuality of the country" (2009, 161).

Indian children's literature in the early years following independence consisted largely of English renditions of folktales and legends such as *Panchatantra* and *Kathasaritsagara*, which were primarily based on the Hindu tradition, and stories from non-Hindu sources such as the *Jataka Tales*, a collection of stories drawn from Buddhist lore. As Mohini Rao has pointed out, such tales were aimed at fashioning a pan-Indian identity and inculcating in Indian children a consciousness of their rich heritage and a sense of national pride (1995, 68). Original writing in English was negligible in this phase, although there was a significant corpus of literature in regional languages.

Manorama Jafa traces three phases in the development of children's literature in India. The first phase consisted of the transcription of oral and traditional literature into written form. In the second phase, select adult literature was translated and abridged for young readers. The third phase has seen the publication of original creative literature (1995, 34–35).

Contemporary fiction, which deals with the concerns and dilemmas of Indian children in a globalized world, does not attract a wide readership, but an examination of these novels offers significant insight into the ways in which children's subjectivity is shaped by the specific local and institutional contexts within which they are embedded. These novels represent the child as a complex amalgam of tradition and modernity, and their child characters construct multiple identities for themselves based on the traditional ideals internalized from interaction with the family and community (which emphasize social cohesion and commitment to collective goals) as well as notions of individualism communicated to them through the cultural resources of globalization: television, films, books, and the Internet. This construction of identity involves strategically selecting elements from Western culture that they find empowering and combining them with those aspects of their traditional heritage that provide them with a sense of continuity and belonging. This analysis is predicated on the assumption that children's fiction does not merely reflect or represent current realities, but also actively shapes the subjectivity and perception of reality of its readers.

My study will focus specifically on three novels that are representative of contemporary children's literature in India: *The Battle for No 19* (Ranjit Lal), *The Year I Turned 16* (Deeptha Khanna), and *No Guns at My Son's Funeral* (Paro Anand). A brief summary of each of these novels follows.

The Battle for No 19 tells the story of a group of schoolgirls returning from a trip, who are caught in the violent backlash in Delhi following the assassination of Prime Minister Indira Gandhi in 1984 by her Sikh bodyguards. In the riots that follow, bloodthirsty mobs go on a rampage, looting and indiscriminately killing innocent people simply because they belong to the Sikh community. The girls are forced to watch in horror as their Sikh taxi driver is dragged out of the car and burned alive by a mob. They escape in the mayhem and take shelter in an abandoned house. The novel proceeds to recount their adventures as they first outwit and then defend themselves against a bunch of savage hooligans intent on looting the house in which they have taken refuge.

The Year I Turned 16, as the title implies, is a coming of age novel that traces the way the protagonist Vinita's subjectivity is shaped by the influence of her family, her peer group, and the media. The story is set in the early 1990s, when the policy of economic liberalization led to the advent of cable television in India. The impact of globalization in the construction of the hybrid self is most evident in this novel, which makes specific reference to popular American TV programs and their influence on the characters.

No Guns at My Son's Funeral is set in the militancy-ridden state of Kashmir. Aftab, a young Kashmiri boy, and his older sister Shazia are lured into joining a terrorist group by the charismatic Akram. They carry out his plans unquestioningly, secure in their belief that they are fighting for the liberation of their homeland. Aftab's shifting subjectivity as he seeks to emulate and win the admiration of his hero is the focus of the story.

At the start of *The Year I Turned 16*, the subjectivity of the main character, Vinita Sharma, is shaped by her unashamed admiration of Western culture and its material products. She is a carefree teenager who has a crush on a popular TV star and dreams of nothing more than getting married to a wealthy man. Vinita's fantasies are shaped by the Mills and Boon romances she reads and by Hollywood movies: "the climbing of a long stairway to my private boudoir feels very posh. When I make a descent, I always imagine that a camera is trained on me and that at the end of the staircase, a gorgeous guy will be waiting to escort me to an evening of sophistication and seduction" (2006, 3). She has a high opinion of her best friend's mother because "she loved anything foreign, smelled of imported perfume, cooked 'pasta,' and acquired video-tapes of American TV shows in bulk from her sister in the U.S." (17). Vinita's world changes when her father finally agrees to subscribe to cable television "with forty channels to die for! . . . that would, best of all, bring me the glorious, glamorous, psychedelic world of MTV!" (23). The consequences of the invasion of their living room by this best known symbol of globalization are often comical: Vinita is embarrassed to witness a kissing scene while watching an episode of *The Bold and the Beautiful* with her parents (the Indian censor board at the time banned display of physical intimacy in films on state-run television channels), and she is shocked to see a Michael Jackson video on MTV ("he was white! How could this be, I'd just seen MJ's *Thriller* video a few weeks back and he had been quite black!" (26)).

Vinita's subjectivity is fashioned quite clearly by books and films, but as the story progresses, it is the Oprah Winfrey show that has the greatest impact on her and her family. They are amazed at the frankness and boldness with which guests on the show discuss their most private moments and traumatic experiences, and impressed by the stories of empowerment of marginalized women. In a comment that in some ways represents a neat inversion of race relations, Vinita declares: "One thing the show helped me realize was that foreigners, even Americans, are really just human beings like us. They have strange accents and eat some unholy stuff, but like Shylock said, they also bleed when they are pricked" (32). The influence of Oprah's shows is most evident on Vinita's mother who, after being a full-time housewife catering solely to the needs of her family, decides to embark on a career in fashion designing. Her announcement is initially greeted with dismay by her family, who cannot comprehend this sudden assertion of individuality.

In his analysis of feminine identity in India, Kakar notes that the cultural devaluation of women in a predominantly patriarchal society has an impact on the psychology of Indian women. In these conditions, it is motherhood that "confers upon her a purpose and identity that nothing else in her culture can. Each infant borne and nurtured by her safely into childhood, especially if the child is a son, is both a certification and a redemption" (1981, 56). Moreover, in addition to the "virtues" of self-effacement and sacrifice, the feminine role in India crystallizes a woman's connection to others, her embeddedness in a multitude of familial relationships (62). Little wonder then, that Vinita's mother's decision to follow her dream, thereby possibly jeopardizing traditional gender roles, elicits such a strong response from her family. Nevertheless, the impact of globalization, as observed in the way the characters respond to the American TV shows they watch, is by no means homogeneous. Whereas Vinita's mother is inspired by Oprah's shows to announce her desire to have a career of her own, Vinita defensively reacts to this show of independence by citing examples from other shows that highlight the dangers of demolishing the "natural" order: "just look at the plots of a few of the American soaps we watch where there is a clear link between a woman's personal ambition and the destruction of family values!" (2006, 89). This incident suggests that the formation of subjectivity is not always unproblematic and is often fraught with contradictions. Although Vinita is happy to embrace the material products of globalization, she is alarmed at its influence on her mother. She takes refuge in conservative, patriarchal notions of gender roles to resist this threat to her perceived sense of social stability.

The preoccupation with the impact of liberalization and the possible onslaught of cultural imperialism recurs throughout the novel, largely in the form of school debates and dialogue between the characters. In a class assignment on American influences on Indian television, Vinita lists the similarities and differences between American and Indian culture, and concludes with the statement: "So in the final analysis, cable is great, and the extent to which the Western media influences us, probably depends on—us" (36).

This statement echoes my argument that children as represented in contemporary Indian fiction strategically combine elements of Western culture with aspects of their traditional upbringing to create a hybrid identity that is empowering. Yet this nuanced hybridity is not without its tensions, and Vinita's encounter with Western culture follows a trajectory that is similar to cultural responses to globalization: an initial phase of unquestioning acceptance of all things foreign, followed by a rejection of imported values and a defensive withdrawal into the refuge offered by traditional patterns of behavior, and finally a measured, mature, glocalized response that selectively combines elements of both the native and the foreign culture. This trajectory is most evident in Vinita's reaction to the installation of cable TV in her home. She is initially delirious at the thought of being able to watch the latest serials. Then her mother, influenced by Oprah's shows, announces her plan of opening a boutique. Vinita is immediately uncomfortable with this decision. But by the end of the novel, Vinita is able to sort out her priorities in a way that combines the best of both worlds. She accepts that her mother has the right to make choices about her life and that these choices are not mutually exclusive. She also realizes the importance of having and striving to achieve personal goals while acknowledging that her earlier desire to get married and start a family soon after college (as is customary in Indian society even today) is merely deferred, not reversed.

This resolution of the conflict between tradition (represented by accepted Indian social norms) and modernity (symbolized by Western media) is reflected in a comment made by Marcus, one of the characters in the novel. Marcus is an American teenager who comes to India to visit Vinita's friend Ashley. He is drawn to the warmth and friendliness of Indians, overwhelmed by their hospitality, and amused by their curiosity and avid interest in the most inconsequential details of his life in America. He loves the fact that people who barely know him invite him for dinner just because he's new to the neighborhood and intrigued at the way "the girls resolve in themselves such a contradiction of modern ambitions and traditional values" (144).

The novel traces Vinita's growth from a laid-back, fun-loving girl who is content to take life as it comes and who allows her parents to make crucial decisions regarding her life, to a focused, goal-oriented teenager who consciously charts a path for herself that is based on her own interests rather than the wishes of her family. Vinita's decision to take charge of her own life is to a great extent influenced by the impact of Western media and by the attitudes and perspectives of Ashley, her U.S.-returned classmate, and Ashley's friend Marcus. This assertion of individuality in a society that values conformity above all else can be clearly traced to Western notions of the autonomous self.

Vinita's subjectivity is largely shaped by the products of globalization. On the other hand, Puja's subjectivity in *The Battle for No 19* is impacted by her struggles against gender bias born of a centuries-old tradition of dishonoring the girl child. Sixteen-year-old Puja is consumed by guilt because her twin brother died at birth. Her mother regrets that the male child did not survive instead of her, and her relatives nickname her Papiha (cuckoo): "she denied her own brother nourishment in the womb and killed him, just like an imposter papiha starves its rightful brothers and sisters and throws them out of the nest" (2007, 2).

In his study of childhood and Indian society, Kakar has commented on the ancient Indian prejudice against the girl child and her relative invisibility in folktales and religious and classical literature. "The preference for a son when a child is born is as old as Indian society itself. Vedic verses pray that sons will be followed by still more male offspring, never by females" (1981, 57). He points out that the oral tradition highlights the glaring difference in attitude toward sons and daughters, as folk songs celebrate the birth of a male child but are merely tolerant, if not openly lamenting, the birth of a baby girl. "At the birth of a son drums are beaten . . . conch-shells blown . . . and the midwife paid lavishly, while no such spontaneous rejoicing accompanies the birth of a daughter" (58).

Although the urban privileged class of modern Indian society outwardly shuns this prejudice, the bias against daughters still exists covertly in many families, and this bias impacts the subjectivity of the girl child. Kakar argues that the devaluation of girls in a patriarchal culture could in some cases result in the girls turning the aggression against themselves, transforming the sense of devaluation into feelings of worthlessness and inferiority (1981, 59). This tendency is evident in the thoughts and actions of Puja, the main character in the novel. Puja is painfully conscious that she is unwanted. Her father, an army officer, also holds her in some way responsible for the loss of his son. She tries desperately to redeem herself in her father's eyes by becoming an accomplished archer, but he routinely ignores her and disparages her achievements.

In *Ideologies of Identity in Adolescent Fiction*, Robyn McCallum notes that the interrelations between individuals, subjectivity, and society are sometimes explored in narrative through the cultural or psychological displacement of characters. She argues that when a character is removed from familiar surroundings and placed in an alien environment, this displacement of a character "can destabilize and place in question their concepts of personal identity, though it can also be used to assert the idea of an essential self which transcends social or cultural structures" (1999, 104). Puja's identity at the beginning of the novel is shaped by her sociocultural milieu, and despite her outwardly confident and cheerful manner, she is plagued by a deep sense of emotional insecurity. When she and her schoolmates are trapped in the riots following the prime minister's assassination, they take shelter in an abandoned house. This physical displacement into an unfamiliar environment has an empowering effect on her, and she instinctively takes charge of the group. She is a natural leader and displays commendable intelligence and presence of mind as she plans tactical strategies to counter the persistent attacks of the rioters. Her yearning to be the son her father always wanted gives her the courage to fight off her attackers, and in the course of the novel, the siege situation prompts Puja and her schoolmates to construct their subjectivity strategically. When first threatened by the rioters, Puja consoles her frightened friends by saying that perhaps the men would let them go when they saw they were "just girls" and therefore, weak and harmless. Yet, when the threat assumes terrifying proportions, she is ready to fight the rioters and meticulously plans a counteroffensive strategy, instructing the girls to hide behind the huge masks that adorn the walls of the house so that the men cannot see that their opponents are a "mere" bunch of schoolgirls.

Similarly, when the girls discover that the children whose house they are sheltering in have been hiding in an attic, Puja reassures the frightened children by saying, "We're just girls" (2007, 100). Jogi, the eleven-year-old son of the house owner, and his little sister are instantly comforted, because girls are conventionally perceived as nonthreatening. Later, Puja plans to send Jogi to the neighbors for help but fears he would be attacked as his turban would betray his Sikh identity. Puja's friend Seema persuades Jogi to disguise himself as a girl by playing on his male pride: "you are the only man here, to protect us nine girls!" (118). She convinces him by saying that if he goes dressed as a girl, he would not be suspected or challenged.

Such attempts by the girls to deliberately downplay their threat value by drawing attention to their gender comes in handy when they meet their attackers face to face. The men are deluded into believing they are easy prey and are caught unawares by their aggressive counterattack. This strategic appropriation of gender roles plays out again in the climax of the novel. A battalion led by Puja's father arrives to rescue the girls from the house where they are trapped and besieged by the rioters. In the melee that follows, Puja saves her father from being killed by shooting his assailant with a bow and arrow. She takes on the male role of protector and her stunned father reacts with the comment, "No damn son could have shot like that!" (178). Puja's redemption in her father's eyes is problematic in that the terms of reference remain male-centric, and Puja's action gains stature only when compared to the male norm. However, Puja's clever manipulation of gender roles enables her to fashion her own subjectivity within the traditional norms that circumscribe her, and the novel holds out the hope that Puja will now be able to position herself as a more active subject with a sense of agency.

A different form of subversion of gender roles is seen in *No Guns at My Son's Funeral*. Shazia, a teenaged Kashmiri girl, outwardly functions within the submissive role assigned to her gender by society. Yet, when the need arises, she exploits traditional notions of honor to serve her purpose. For instance, when her young brother Aftab is interrogated by an army officer about being seen in the company of a known terrorist, he is nonplussed and cannot find a plausible explanation. A quick-thinking Shazia comes to his rescue by prompting him to say that the terrorist had threatened to abduct his sister if he was not given money, and that Aftab had gone to negotiate with him. This immediately wins him the gratitude of his parents and satisfies the officer. Shazia later comments sarcastically, "you're a big hero now, at home. Saving your sister from evil men—good little, good little boy" (49). Like the girls in *The Battle for No 19*, Shazia has learned early that her culture views the female sex as weak and helpless, in need of protection. Rather than openly contest this mindset, they choose to manipulate it for their own purposes. Although the girls in both novels are much older and physically stronger than the boys, they have no qualms in appealing to the "manliness" of the boys, appearing to seek their protection and exploiting cultural notions of male superiority.

Kakar points out that the period of late childhood marks the beginning of "the Indian girl's deliberate training in how to become a *good woman*, and hence the conscious inculcation of culturally designated feminine roles. She learns that the 'virtues' of womanhood which will take her through life are submission and docility as well as skill and grace in the various household tasks" (1981, 62). In her adolescence, "a time of instinctual turbulence and emotional volatility" (62), Shazia is torn between submitting to her training in service and self-denial in order to maintain her family's love and approval and her desire to rebel against this circumscription and assert her individuality.

This conflict between individualism and conformity plays out in different ways in the novel. B. K. Ramanujam, a practicing psychiatrist, comments: "the social structure does not permit the emergence of a cogent adult role as perceived in Western societies. Subordinating one's individual's need to the interests of the group . . . is upheld as a virtue. Thus, self-assertion become selfishness, independent decision-making is perceived as disobedience. The response from the in-group is tacit disapproval if not outright condemnation. Under such circumstances, it is easier to play safe" (1979, 54).

Shazia and her brother Aftab play safe by outwardly conforming to the traditional patterns of behavior expected of them, while continuing to pursue their personal agenda in private. Shazia's subjectivity is fashioned as much by her milieu as it is by her ideology. Attracted by the rugged, dangerous charm of the militant Akram and influenced by his fiery rhetoric, Shazia chooses to join his group and work undercover. This allows her to construct multiple identities for herself: one, of the meek, dutiful daughter quietly performing household chores while waiting for her parents to fix a match for her; another, of a committed, patriotic freedom fighter seeking to liberate her state from oppressive rule; and a third identity of the devoted lover of the leader of a terrorist group. Consequently, her subjectivity is informed by these multiple ways of constructing identity.

Shazia is well aware of the power of womanly wiles and employs these deliberately when she needs to coax Aftab's friend to reveal if he had implicated Aftab in his account to the army officer. In the climax of the novel, Shazia is persuaded by her lover to seduce the sentry guarding their imprisoned colleague. After her initial horror at the idea, she agrees to the plan and plays the part of the beguiling temptress to perfection, succeeding in her goal of smuggling poison to the prisoner to help him commit suicide.

Shazia's brother Aftab is an impressionable teenager in search of a hero. He finds one in Akram, the charming leader of a fledgling terrorist group. Flattered by the interest Akram shows in him, Aftab allows himself to be drawn into the group and consciously makes Akram his role model. In his analysis of the psychosocial matrix of childhood, Kakar notes that male children experience deep-rooted stress during the critical shift from the "intimate cocoon of maternal protection" to the more conditional affection of the male world, where affection is a token in each transaction (1981, 126–127). He identifies three culturally influenced psychosocial constellations that emphasize the emotional self-absorption of the masculine psyche in India: "first, the length and symbiotic nature of the mother-son relationship; second, the rupture of this connection . . . and third, the little boy's disappointment when he perceives his father as more of an onlooker than an ally in his boyish struggle to cope with his new life-circumstances" (133).

In the novel, Aftab shares a close relationship with his mother but perceives his father as an indifferent, aloof figure, whose parenting role is largely confined to periodically administering beatings to his wayward son. Kakar points out that the identification of the son with the mother in Indian society leads to a resolution of the oedipal conflict in a way that is markedly different from the Western model. In the West, this conflict is usually resolved "as the boy's aggressive stance towards his rival/father triggers anxiety that is in turn reduced by identification with the father" (1981: 134). In India, however, in the absence of a strong father with whom to identify, the boy is more likely to adopt a submissive, apprentice-like stance toward older males and authority figures. Frustrated by his unsatisfactory relationship with his father, Aftab unconsciously turns to Akram for emotional support, and the latter cunningly exploits this dependence for his own ends. When recounting the story of how one of their colleagues became a terrorist, Akram describes the hardships and rigorous training imparted by special training camps across the Kashmir border. Aftab's imagination is fired by this account: "How he longed to be in just such a camp. Rough. Hard. Learning to become a man. Instead here he was, waiting to be served tea in bed by his Ammi" (2005, 27). This unconscious need to repudiate the mother and identify with the father drives Aftab to go to extreme lengths to gain recognition from his hero. Constantly teased by his friends for being a mama's boy, Aftab longs to do something to show that he is a man, capable of committing acts of violence without qualms.

Kakar also notes that the male child's identity development is characterized by "a heightened narcissistic vulnerability, an unconscious tendency to 'submit' to an idealized omnipotent figure . . . the lifelong search for someone, a charismatic leader or a guru, who will provide mentorship and a guiding worldview" (1981, 128). Young Aftab displays all of these traits: he is obsessed with becoming a man and contributing in a significant way to his espoused cause; and dissatisfied with his own father's unsuitability as a role model, he hero-worships Akram and blindly carries out his every command, to the tragic extent of agreeing to become a human bomb at the end of the novel.

Aftab's overweening urge to act in a way that would make everyone sit up and take notice fashions his subjectivity in the novel. Constrained by the submissive role he has to play in his family, he asserts his right to independence by choosing to work covertly for a terrorist group. He manipulates his mother's affection for him, oscillating between childish behavior and adult-like reasoning, allaying her suspicions by appealing to her maternal instincts, and playing on her susceptibilities.

Both Aftab and his sister Shazia strive to construct an identity that stems from their Kashmiri roots, yet echoes the aspirations and frustrations of their generation. The novel is set in the politically charged atmosphere of militancy and opposition to the presence of Indian armed forces in Kashmir. Their mother nostalgically recalls the days of her childhood when "Every man was a brother—Hindu, Muslim, it didn't matter. There was a time when we were just Kashmiris . . . Religion did not matter, you just leaned on the nearest shoulder, wept on it, if you needed to" (2005, 17). The siblings adopt a more polarized stance, influenced by the radical views of Akram. They are, however, careful to conceal their views from their family for fear of disapproval and rejection. Commenting on the difference in psychic structure between Western and Indian culture, Kakar notes: "Much of the individual behavior and adaptation to the environment that in Westerners is regulated or coerced by the demands of the superego, is taken care of in Indians by a *communal conscience* . . . In contrast with the Western superego, the communal conscience is a social rather than an individual formation, it is not 'inside' the psyche. In other words, instead of having one internal sentinel an Indian relies on many external 'watchmen' to patrol his activities. . . . The greater authority of the codes of the communal conscience, as opposed to the internalized rules of the individual superego, creates a situation in which infringements of moral standards become likely in situations 'when no one is looking'" (1981, 135). Aftab's and Shazia's subversive activities, although stemming from their personal beliefs and attitudes, are conducted secretly, away from the watchful discipline of family and community norms.

In all three novels, the subjectivity of the child characters is shaped within the social matrix, but the process of identity formation is unique and follows different trajectories in each. Vinita's exposure to the material forces of globalization ultimately empowers her to make informed choices about her life and her future. Puja's experiences and actions during the riots help her resolve her internal conflict and establish a bond with her father. Her subjectivity is multilayered and complex, and her father's acceptance at the end of the novel is no longer pivotal but merely adds another layer. Shazia and Aftab's subjectivity is shaped by the atmosphere of fear and distrust that surrounds them, and the double lives they lead points to the precarious constitution of such identities. Aftab's and Shazia's covert allegiance to Akram represents a defiant attempt to deny their link with family and community, and an assertion of their right to choose the course of their lives.

It is evident from the above discussion that contemporary Indian English children's fiction constructs child characters as a complex blend of tradition and modernity, and the subjectivity of these characters is simultaneously shaped by notions of individualism and a deep sense of connectedness to the native culture.

Notes

1. Literally, the "science/knowledge of life," Ayurveda is an ancient Indian holistic system of medicine that is based on the philosophy that life consists of body, senses, psyche, and soul. Its healing remedies are aimed at restoring harmony within the being.

Works Cited

Primary Texts

Anand, Paro. *No Guns at My Son's Funeral.* New Delhi: IndiaInk, 2005.
Khanna, Deeptha. *The Year I Turned 16.* New Delhi: Puffin Books, 2006.
Lal, Ranjit. *The Battle for No 19.* New Delhi: Puffin Books, 2007.

Secondary Texts

Gutierrez, Anna Katrina. "*Mga Kwento ni Lola Basyang:* A Tradition of Reconfiguring the Filipino Child," *International Research in Children's Literature* 2.2 (2009): 159–176.
Jafa, Manorama. "Children's Literature in India." In *Telling Tales: Children's Literature in India*, edited by Amit Dasgupta. New Delhi: Wiley Eastern, 1995.
Kakar, Sudhir. *The Inner World: A Psychoanalytic Study of Childhood and Society in India.* Delhi: Oxford University Press, 1981.
Kakar, Sudhir, and Katharina Kakar. *The Indians: Portrait of a People.* New Delhi: Penguin, 2009.
Lebra, Takie Sugiyama. *The Japanese Self in Cultural Logic.* Honolulu: University of Hawaii Press, 2004.
McCallum, Robyn. *Ideologies of Identity in Adolescent Fiction.* New York: Garland Publishing, 1999.
Ramanujam, B. K. "Toward Maturity: Problems of Identity Seen in the Indian Clinical Setting." In *Identity and Adulthood*, edited by Sudhir Kakar. 2nd ed. Delhi: Oxford University Press, 1979.
Rao, Mohini. "Children's Books in India: An Overview." In *Telling Tales: Children's Literature in India*, edited by Amit Dasgupta. New Delhi: Wiley Eastern, 1995.
Tu Weiming. "Multiple Modernities: A Preliminary Inquiry into the Implications of East Asian Modernity." In *Culture Matters: How Values Shape Human Progress*, edited by Lawrence E. Harrison and Samuel P. Huntington. New York: Basic Books, 2000.
Uchida, Yukiko, Vinai Norasakkunkit, and Shinobu Kitayama. "Cultural Constructions of Happiness: Theory and Empirical Evidence," *Journal of Happiness Studies* 5 (2004): 223–239.
Visvanathan, Gauri. "The Beginnings of English Literary Study in British India," *The Oxford Literary Review,* Colonialism and Other Essays 9.1–2 (1987): 2–26.
Visvanathan, Gauri. *Masks of Conquest: Literary Study and British Rule in India.* New York: Columbia University Press, 1989.

Chapter Twelve

Subjectivity without Identity

Huang Chunming's
Fiction in Postcolonial Vein

Suh Shan Chen and Ming Cherng Duh

Two Episodes

On May 28, 2011, Huang Chun-ming, an eminent fiction writer in Taiwan, was invited to deliver a keynote speech at a literary conference in commemoration of the hundredth anniversary of the country, held at the National Taiwan Library of Literature. In the middle of his speech, Huang was interrupted by a protest from an academic who teaches in a department of Taiwanese language and literature. The protester displayed a banner which declared, "You should be ashamed for not using authentic Taiwanese language for your writing!" Taken by surprise by this impolite interruption, the highly respected writer, at age seventy-six, responded with a verbal attack upon the accuser. The young professor, claiming verbal assault, filed a lawsuit after failing to receive any kind of apology from the writer. Underlying this affair is a conflict about the definition of agentic subjectivity and its representations in local cultural products.

On January 14, 2012, Ma Yin-jiou was reelected to serve his second term as the president of Taiwan, Republic of China. Ma's administrative performance in his first service is considered mediocre at best. At the time of the presidential election, the unemployment rate was high and inequity in property distribution had increased. Ma himself is not a native-born Taiwanese. His political inclination is generally believed to be pro-unification with the mainland. His major achievement, although controversial, lay in an economic policy leaning heavily toward the People's Republic of China. Even though issues about sovereignty and subjecthood in a nation-state were raised, which usually cause some tensions among people, and has done so in most major elections, Ma still won a majority vote of fifty-three percent.

These two seemingly unrelated events are connected by the conception of a nation among Taiwanese people. Does national independence remain salient in the age of global economy, or is it even intensified by the tension between subjectivation and agency that these events share? Are Taiwanese subjectivities always constructed in relation to what, in "Can the Subaltern Speak," Gayatri Chakravorty Spivak characterized as the work of imperialist subject-constitution which rendered the colonized inarticulate (1988, 90)? In the quest to define notions of a Taiwanese selfhood in relation to the always ambiguous relationship with Mainland China, a half-century of colonization by Japan, and a further half-century of living under the neocolonial shadow of the U.S., a challenge for Taiwan's fiction writers is how represented subjects are to be *produced* and what kinds of subject positions can be imagined for them. The performance of subjectivity seems to be inextricable from the performance of nationality and the occupation of subaltern subject positions, and hence it is crucial, when considering fiction, to examine the narrative forms and functions out of which represented selves are composed and how such forms reproduce subjectivity as a lived experience. Both of the events referred to above are, in different ways, concerned with power relations. The processes of subject-constitution depend, in Judith Butler's terms, on performativity and the ways in which the self may enact a subjected position, or be subjectivated, under the aegis of exterior forces of power and knowledge (Phillips, 2006: 310). The objection against Huang's literary practice was, in effect, an assertion that his work is produced within, and hence performs (or mimics), a subject position determined by continental Chinese discourse, whereas the employment of specifically local linguistic forms works to undo the fixity of that position and develop a more fluid local discourse.

The first case is particularly striking because Huang has long been considered a so-called Xiang-tu (nativist) writer, a term attributed to those who promote the consciousness of native land through native language and literature. Even if writing in Mandarin Chinese suggests subaltern status, Huang does not deserve this imputation because the language of his fiction artistically assimilates colloquial Taiwanese into an identifiable Chinese composition. Departments of Taiwanese language as such emerged out of an ideological urge for national independence of Taiwan in the past decade. Some of the proponents, sometimes referred to as fundamentalists, advocate a system of writing which can emancipate the people from Chinese mental manipulation—for example, they argue that the sound system of Taiwanese should be translated into written language. Huang on several occasions had criticized these arguments as excessively doctrinal, and this led to the public confrontation. Further underlying the confrontation is the principle that ethnic differentiation is not innate but is constructed and reproduced through sociopolitical processes. As Allen Chun has pointed out, authorial practices are shaped within a larger regime of institutional practices, which are in turn the source of authorial subjectivities, and hence it may be more pertinent to examine those institutional regimes (political systems, university departments, academic discourses, for example) than to focus on simply conceptual representations (2008, 695). In the political sphere, unification and separation are constantly debated from extreme perspectives, and the question of the language of literature is imbricated with questions about what nationalism means to (and for) Taiwanese people. If, for example, a cultural relativist perspective is taken, and hence subjectivity is local and produced within local language forms, and self-awareness and agency are less possible within global or even cosmopolitan discourses, then people need a sense of belonging to a language community distinct from other languages if they are to form close intersubjective relationships. In this sense, subjectivity can be a micro form of nationalism. Citizens who consider the mainland to be the motherland will perforce favor mainland Mandarin, whereas separatists might fervently embrace local forms of language. Others who may consider themselves as both Chinese and Taiwanese may feel no problem with this dual identity. The presidential election highlighted the relationships between national identity and subjecthood, but the result may suggest that a substantial proportion of Taiwanese people do not feel in danger of losing their specific identity. Indeed, as Huang Chun-ming's fiction illustrates as it reflects and refracts the political and cultural mentality of Taiwanese people, the threat of subjective loss has had a long presence in Taiwan.

Historical Sketch

A historical glimpse may be instrumental to the understanding of such mentality. It is widely recognized that Taiwan is a migrant country. The inhabitants consist of four major racial and ethnic groups—the Mainlander, the Hoka, the Fukian, and fourteen groups of indigenous Austronesian peoples—and more recently new immigrants mainly from South Asia and China. Since the seventeenth century, parts of the island have been successively occupied by Spanish, Dutch, and British colonizers. In 1895, Taiwan was ceded by the Ching Dynasty to Japan after the First Sino-Japanese War, which began a fifty-year period of colonization until the end of World War II. The defeat of Japan, followed by the Cold War, gave rise to the hegemonic power of the U.S. Although Taiwan was never physically occupied, American people have exerted unprecedented influence over many aspects of Taiwanese life since the mid-century. Taiwan was safeguarded by the global geopolitical situation and benefited economically from the ambivalent struggle between the U.S. and Communist China, even into the twenty-first century. Both superpowers were conceived by the nationalists as imperialists or neocolonialists. They cast shadows over Taiwan in two senses: on the one hand, they protect and provide certain benefits, but on the other, they constitute a threat.

As this brief sketch indicates, Taiwan is an ethnically diverse society with a complex colonial past, and individual subjectivities may be shaped in quite different ways if people, according to their experiences, feel a strong affinity with Chinese, Indigenous, Japanese, or American cultures. National identity can thus be quite varied, or in the case of literary texts may be embedded only as an implication, in that a concept of cultural (as distinct from national) identity is represented as a social construction based on power and status and both defines, and is defined by, the places to which a person has access and the opportunities available to individual subjects. In ethnically diverse societies, there may be a distinction between national identity and ethnic identity, and hence subjectivity might not incorporate elements of national identity (Li et al., 1995: 343).

At the level of subjectivity, the constantly vexed question about Taiwan's status as a sovereign state can in part be answered by arguing that for Taiwanese people nation is rather an "imagined community," as Benedict Anderson has phrased it. Anderson's well-known formulation seems apposite for Taiwan: "[the nation] is imagined as a community, because, regardless of the actual inequality and exploitation that may prevail in each, the nation is conceived as a deep, horizontal comradeship," although the terms of this formulation are challenged by Huang Chun-ming's fiction (1983, 7). Moreover, national identity fluctuates as the political environment changes, and because ideological "conversion" is not exceptional among political leaders, subjectivity is not a topic of dispute. It is simply taken for granted.

Finding a Voice for the Subaltern

Huang Chun-ming's fiction can be read as a reflection of ambiguity in the representation of subjectivity. Huang's reputation is built on his fictions which are usually considered among the best of contemporary Taiwanese literature—Sung-sheng Yvonne Chang, for example, describes him as "one of the most talented fiction writers and original observers of social reality in Taiwan's post-1949 era" (1993, 154). He began publishing in the 1960s and is still active. He is also one of the few cross-writers in Taiwan, having written picture books and plays for children's theater. His works have been translated into English and French and adapted into films (Haddon, 1996; Huang, 2009). His writing is usually described as realistic, especially because of the empathy shown toward a range of subaltern figures: the aged, children, the weak, the meek, women, and sex workers. However, despite his penetrating observations on Taiwan's evolution into its current state and his succinct delineation of its encounters with other people, the constructions of subjectivity in his works are seldom discussed within a postcolonial reading of Taiwan's history of colonization and subsequent encounters with neocolonialist and global forces (see Chen, "Postmodern or Postcolonial?" 2007). We propose to do that here, focusing in particular on the ways that colonialism has become more subtle, sophisticated, and latent, even as the collective memory of colonization gradually fades away. At the same time, the temporal aspect of the concept of postcolonialism allows us to bring neocolonialism under its umbrella, which seems an appropriate move for the complicated case of Taiwan.

Five of Huang's fictions were selected for discussion which include, in chronological order, "The Taste of Apples" (1972), "Sayonara/Zaijian" (1973), "Young Widow" (1975), "I Love Mary" (1977), and "Cheers, Soldier" (1988). It is not incidental that most of them appeared in the 1970s when the aftermath of the Vietnam War was followed by the visibility of transnational corporations. The economy of Taiwan had at this time proceeded to the so-called take-off stage. International business, foreigners, and the accompanied cultural artifacts flooded into this erstwhile traditional society. American and Japanese are for Taiwanese people ambiguous figures. They are symbols of modernity and wealth and thus became objects of admiration, hate, and envy. On the one hand, Taiwanese resented the uncomfortable invasion of the foreigner. On the other, they welcomed the visitors not just for ostensible economic cause but also for something impalpable in their complicated emotion. The first four stories demonstrate a subaltern position performed by Taiwanese in their encounters with Americans and Japanese. In the fifth, rather different, story Huang elaborated his critique of colonialism at a deeper level by presenting the colonization of Taiwan—by Chinese Nationalists, Chinese Communists, and Japanese Imperialists—from the perspective of the indigenous people.

A Stroke of Luck: Being Run Down by an American's Car

Subject-constitution as subaltern is represented in several ways in these stories, but commonly pivots on economic deprivation and dependence and images the state of the nation by adopting the narrative perspective of subjectivated, subaltern characters. In "The Taste of Apples," an impecunious part-time laborer with six children is run down by an American military officer's car. With both legs broken, he is sent to an American-run hospital. The owner of the car visited the afflicted family, with a police officer as translator, and arranged for them to be taken to the hospital. Huang uses the search for the house and the family's circumstances as a means to depict their utter abjection. The house is makeshift—"The foreigner was a head taller than any of the shacks in the area, so all he could see was a mass of rooftops thrown together with sheet metal and plastic covers, plus some old tires and bricks to hold them down" (2001, 136–137)—and when they stop a little girl to ask directions, she turns out to be mute. The child is from the family they are seeking so knows the way, but they recoil from her and hurry away. Sixteen years before Spivak's discussion of the silenced subaltern, Huang has used this symbol of disempowerment through exclusion from speech. He reduplicates it when the officer and policeman find the house but the wife does not understand Mandarin, and the eldest daughter, Ah-zhu, has to translate.

At this point, Huang further complicates the perspective. Although the story depicts the ambiguous relationship between American and Taiwanese, the family's already abject state is not attributable to America but already existed before the foreigner exacerbated it. Huang develops this perspective in two scenes interpolated before the family goes to the hospital. Ah-zhu is sent to fetch her younger brothers from school, and her thoughts along the way turn on her future: "'If Papa can't work, there'll be no money for the family and Mama will have to adopt me out.' . . . She never wavered from a conviction that she would be a well-behaved, obedient daughter in her new family, accepting any and all hardships that came her way." (139). Meanwhile, her brother Ah-ji stands in shame in front of his class because his parents have failed to pay his school fee. People without support from an extended family are abject in a society without a welfare system, but Huang deploys these micro-level circumstances to define macro-level dependency. Late in the story, when the American officer has given the family an envelope containing more money than they have ever imagined (NT$ 20,000) and established that his organization will pay the hospital fees, support the family until Ah-fa recovers from his injuries, and send the mute daughter to a special school in America, the subaltern position of the family is again emphasized: "since the money was right there in front of them, something had to be said. But what, what should they say? All this indecision gave them the uneasy feeling that they'd done something wrong and offended someone" (154).

A cue for reading the story as a kind of parable about subaltern status is given early in the story in the fragments of a telephone call about the accident. The caller, presumably the officer in the car, is informed by a "junior secretary" that, "This is the Asian country with which we have the closest ties of friendship. Besides, it's the most secure. . . . America has no intention of jumping into the middle of a quagmire. . . . I'll take the responsibility" (136). Historically, Taiwan was not physically occupied by the Americans, but there were air force bases during the Cold War era and Taiwan had been the recipient of massive U.S. aid after World War II (especially 1951–1962). This situation is not only alluded to as an explanation of why the American officer turned out to be kind, friendly, polite, and generous, but is a key part of the story's frame. The story ends with the "lucky" family sharing some apples given to them as part of their lunch. An apple was symbolic of America because it was imported and expensive, and hence beyond the reach of the working class: Ah-fa points out that they could buy two kilograms of rice for the cost of one apple, and this prompts the children to try them:

> The silence of the room was broken by the crisp sound of apples being eaten into, gingerly, one after another. As they took their first bites they said nothing, although they felt that the apples were not quite as sweet as

they imagined; rather they were a little sour and pulpy, and when chewed they were frothy and not quite real. But then they were reminded of their father's comment that one apple costs as much as four catties of rice, and with that the flavor was enhanced. . . . Ah-fa, who hadn't wanted one at first, finally succumbed to the temptation. "Ah-zhu," he said, "hand me one of those."(156)

The taste of apples represents both power and happiness as it enacts the subjectivation of a people 'colonized' by economic and material factors, as power relations are exercised through subtle interactions, as Ah-fa's capitulation demonstrates. Although the characters found the apples to be "sour, pulpy, frothy and not quite real," they cannot but accept them with gratitude. To apply Fanon's perspective, (neo-)imperialism tactically induces a dominated people to psychologically perceive themselves as inferior. Thus, the colonizer conquered the subordinated from within. The process of this inner colonization consequently resulted in the persistence of subservience.

The Subaltern as Mimic

Not all gifts turn out to be a blessing. In contrast to "The Taste of Apples," Huang's parable about slavish adherence to a master culture, "I Love Mary," satirizes subject formation as a reconstruction of personal identity on the basis of an imagined foreign model. In his essay, "Of Mimicry and Man: The Ambivalence of Colonial Discourse" (in *The Location of Culture*), Homi Bhabha argues that, in mimicry, the representation of identity and meaning is rearticulated along the axis of metonymy. Thus in "I Love Mary," the protagonist's determination to become the owner of his American boss's German shepherd dog, Mary, functions as a metonymy of a desire to imitate a colonial "master." Bhabha's observation that such *objets trouvés* of the Western world are erratic and eccentric, "part-objects of presence" (1994, 131), offers a helpful explanation for how Shuen De ("Dave") Chen's fetishization of Mary destroys everyday life and renders him subjectively abject.

Dave, a subaltern employee in an American business outlet, learns that his immediate superior is about to return to the company's overseas headquarters and does not wish to take Mary with him. Aware of Dave's desire, the superior officially makes Dave Mary's new owner. To Dave, Mary becomes a symbol of prestige bestowed upon him. However, the introduction of Dave's prized possession into the home causes severe disruption. A far cry from the children's expectations, the newcomer is a monster, not a pet, and the burden of taking care of her falls upon the shoulders of Yu-Yun, Dave's wife. The situation becomes a source of increasing tension, as Yu-Yun is repeatedly reprimanded for failing to deal with Mary. The tension comes to a crisis when Mary escapes during estrus. Dave lashes out at his wife and declares that he has more affection for Mary than for his wife and family. Yu-Yun, demeaned to a gender exploitation which signifies her as a double-colonized subaltern, leaves with the children, while Dave takes Mary to the veterinary hospital to have her aborted. The veterinarian in charge happens to remark that Mary is not a pedigree dog but an ordinary crossbreed.

Unlike Huang's other fictions, this piece can be read as light, satirical comedy primarily because the protagonist is so absurd and deserves to suffer. It does, however, represent an acute loss of subjectivity, first in Dave's irrational xenophilia and then in his fetishization of the dog as a metonym for what is superior (that is, foreign). In this respect the story goes beyond mere ridicule of self-erasure through mimicry of a supposed superior other and becomes a metonym for the danger posed to a national subjectivity by slavish mimicry. The story thus employs mimicry ironically to demonstrate how the subaltern within a transnational corporation performs and perpetuates inferiority. The final irony is that the dog bestowed upon Dave was unwanted and, as a crossbreed, has no *intrinsic* value, so as Dave's fetish, Mary is not a substitute for the status he aspires to but a sign of what is missing—that is, a sign of Dave's self-fashioned lack of subjective agency.

Yu-Yin, Dave's wife, exemplifies the subaltern status of women. She suffers from what Spivak terms "a double-colonization," insofar as she is oppressed by two layers: by her patriarchal husband and by the capitalist colonizer. Fortunately she was able to assert her own subjective agency and emancipate herself from the double tyranny. In "I Love Mary" and the next two stories to be discussed here, "Young Widow" and "Sayonara/Zaijian," Huang portrays three faces of compradors that may represent different phases of commercial colonization. The first protagonist wholeheartedly traded his national identity as Chinese for a mimic foreignness; in "Young Widow," a particular economic community minimizes and corrupts identity for the purpose of profit making; and in "Sayonara/Zaijian," the protagonist strives to protect and recover a sense of agency placed under threat by his subaltern status.

A Subaltern Country, the Sex Industry, and Spaces for Agency

"Young Widow" and "Sayonara/Zaijian" provide two cases of encounters between Taiwanese people and outsiders visiting the country to take advantage of its sex trade. In the novella "Young Widow," the visitors are neocolonizers, U.S. soldiers on rest and recreation during the Vietnam War; in "Sayonara/Zaijian," they are Japanese businessmen, representing a former colonizing power. The two stories offer a contrast between, on the one hand, the nature of subaltern positions of bar girls and managers, and on the other, the extent to which the exploiters can in turn be exploited.

Huang again plays on the effects of mimicry in "Young Widow," in that a bar manager has employed a friend who works in advertising to devise a concept that will make the bar unique. The advertiser, Ma Shanxing, came up with the idea of the "Young Widow" in order to appeal to a particular Western imaginary about the orient: the bar girls were to be given a basic training in traditional Chinese culture, but emphasizing the core idea that a widow should remain chaste for the rest of her life. This feature of a particular subaltern femininity was devised to accommodate the erotic fancies of the foreign patrons, because an imagined inaccessibility was added to the erotic mix, as Huang adroitly grasps the psychology of orientalism and inverts it. Constructed in the image of young widows and wearing traditional Cheongsam dress, the girls thus needed to be seduced rather than taken. The light in the bar was dimmed to create an atmosphere of love and death, and the room to which a customer was taken included a photograph of "the deceased husband" which the "widow" discreetly covered over. The young soldiers imagined what were to be pitiful oriental women and they acted to satiate their desire, but the bar girls were no longer passive objects of erotic fantasy but active agents collaboratively constructing the postcolonial experience with the consumers. As Hillenbrand observes:

> Ma's presentation of traditional China here deliberately taps into a vein of sensationalist thinking about the 'orient' among Western observers that has a history as long as the East-West encounters itself. The critical difference of course, is that instead of an Orient 'othered' by the Western gaze, Huang's text gives us a Taiwanese protagonist who undertakes this process of erotic Orientalization himself. (2007, 159)

As remarked above, Taiwan has not been occupied or colonized by America, but had been economically dependent. Hillenbrand, in her study of American influence during 1960 to 1990 on Japanese and Taiwanese cultural, urban, and recreational life as shown in fiction, suggested that,

> Huang advances his critique of the sex industry at full throttle. Yet at the same time, his text intimates that the conglomerate of Taipei brothel-operators are, in the end, nothing more than shrewd entrepreneurs: their line of work may be dubious, but their sense of business and work ethic are exemplary. (157)

Nevertheless, they do fail to grasp that their success is based on a neocolonial convenience. When Ma Shanxing, now working in real estate, warns his friend General Manager Huang that the days of the "Young Widow" are numbered ("Any day now, the Pentagon defense budget will leave you in the cold"), Huang cannot understand how "the Pentagon and the U.S. Defense budget were somehow connected with him" (1996, 302), but of course the text here is making an ironical point about the dependency of the colonized. Dependency is temporarily reversed in "Young Widow" in the figure of two very young soldiers—Billy and Tommy—traumatized by their war experience: genuine affection is sparked between two of the prostitutes (Feifei and Cassia) and the soldiers, especially when the girls take the soldiers for a sightseeing tour to Zhinan Temple where they genuinely perform their culture. Watching Feifei in worship, Billy is deeply moved: "Of all the women he had known or had met, the impression he had of Feifei was special. Ever since he had met her, he had the sense of being enveloped by some indescribable, warm feeling. The source of this warmth was Feifei's thoughtfulness" (300). Whereas the text makes it clear that Feifei's behavior is at least in part opportunistic, and that Billy is reacting to his own needs, its alignment with her perspective for substantial segments attracts reader empathy. Billy is subsequently wounded in a Viet Cong ambush, losing his left arm, but is the only survivor of the encounter and attributes his survival to a talisman presented to him by Feifei at the temple. Discharged from the army, he returns to Taipei in search of Feifei, and their meeting constitutes the novella's ambiguous close, as together they leave the doomed "Young Widow" for an indeterminate future. There exists here a reciprocal interaction between the giver and the taker. The binary opposition of an oppressor/oppressed relation is much too simple to define the situation, as it is the supposedly consumed subaltern who realizes her purpose through performance.

In contrast to the depiction of the businessmen who orientalize their own culture for the purpose of profit, an intense patriotic sentiment is still at work in "Sayonara/Zaijian" (Goodbye), which hinges on the protagonist's deprivation and recovery of agentic subjectivity. Since the 1950s, the Kuomingtan (KMT) government of Taiwan had consolidated its dominance by instilling a nationalist ideology. Anti-Japanese sentiment was a part of its agenda because the invasion of the mainland and the colonization of Taiwan by Japan were historical disasters for people who lived on both sides of the Taiwan Strait. School children were taught to hate Japanese and conceived of this hatred as patriotic. The narrator/protagonist of "Sayonara/Zaijian" epitomizes this attitude:

> My position as someone who has a pretty good grasp of recent Chinese history has led me to abhor the Japanese. I was told that my grandfather, whose stories I'd loved listening to, had had his leg smashed by the Japanese as a young man. Then there was my middle school history teacher, an unforgettable man we all respected, who tearfully related to us episodes from the 1937–1945 War of Resistance against Japan . . . Tears flowed as we listened to him, and we hated ourselves for being too young to have participated in the war, searching out the "Jap devils" and avenging our countrymen. (*The Taste of Apples*, 2001: 211)

At the same time such attitudes were being cultivated, students were also erasing memories of political conflict that had prompted a massacre of dissidents and were being educated to recognize themselves as Chinese. The KMT government asserted its orthodoxy and legitimacy by claiming that Taiwan was a Chinese province rather than an independent country, despite its political sovereignty. Despite such propaganda, however, by the early 1970s cooperation between Taiwan and Japan had grown out of their colonial tie, the emerging geopolitics of the Cold War, and the rise of the global economy. For some Japanese, revisiting their ex-colony may satisfy a nostalgia for the exotic, especially when combined with erotic fantasy. It is in such a context that the story "Sayonara/Zaijian" is based.

The story begins as the protagonist is assigned by his employer to escort seven Japanese businessmen on a tour to a hot spring resort. The tourists, long-term friends and business colleagues, described themselves in military language as "Seven Samurai" who had formed a "Thousand Beheadings Club"—that is, their aim was to have sex with a thousand different women in the Third World. As a patriotic person educated in "recent Chinese history" who considered himself to be highly principled, it was with reluctance and resentment that the narrator undertook the assignment, and even considered resigning his position instead. Chiao-hsi, the site of the resort, was his hometown, which exacerbated the problem that he would be acting as translator and pimp for the 'Seven Samurai' and would be implicating his female compatriots. Because he could not afford to lose his job, the narrator accepted his deprivation of agency but subsequently looked for ways to undermine his guests, such as delaying their pleasure and ensuring that the prostitutes are paid five times their normal price.

At the core of the story is language. Because the Japanese have no knowledge of the Chinese language, the narrator gives vent to his resentment by mistranslating the exchanges between the men and the prostitutes (for example, "son of a bitch" becomes "chubby, but cute." Slippage of signification reaches its apex, however, when the narrator is asked to accompany the men on a train trip to Hualien and, on the train, a senior college student approached the Japanese visitors and expressed a wish to study in Japan. The narrator's thoughts again home in on the underlying subaltern attitude—"isn't it all topsy-turvy for a student of Chinese literature to leave Taiwan and go abroad for advanced study?" (245)—and he sets out to use the language gap to misrepresent both parties and humiliate them. The middle-age Japanese are introduced to the student as "a fact-finding group of Japanese college professors" and the student is represented as "a college senior [. . .] writing a thesis on the War of Resistance." By substituting his own questions and answers in the exchange, the narrator induces the Japanese to recall traumatic images of wartime atrocities which made them feel personally implicated and induces the student to feel embarrassed at his devaluing of his own culture.

By means of his game, "the perpetration of a gigantic hoax," the narrator recovers a sense of personal agency and dignity in ways unknown to the guests on whom he took his revenge (209). In the early twentieth century, the notable writer Lu Xun had cautioned his fellow Chinese that this "tactic of spiritual victory" represents the internalization of defeat. But what spaces for agency exist if a harsh reality must be accepted and resentment stifled? It seems a common destiny for a postcolonial nation to set aside conscience and national self-consciousness because a once colonized people remain in a position of disadvantage. But they are not always victims of oppression. They find a way, dubiously and subtly and at times ungraciously, to offer resistance. National identity, which evolved out of a binary opposition of oppressor and oppressed, has become an ideology less effective for dealing with the complexity of economic reality and necessarily becomes more pragmatic, as Allen Chun argues: "In contrast to both ethnicity and culture . . . identity is essentially a pragmatic, or subjective, relationship. . . . Identity is also less about the fact of who one is than about the perception of those facts. Because we are dealing with the perceptions, we should emphasize, as well, that they are selective and strategic by nature" (1996, 126). Huang's story perhaps oversimplifies this process in order to represent the narrator's uneasiness and the feeling of subordination, as the sentiment between the once colonized and the colonizer is something more ambiguous and sophisticated. Nevertheless, the space for agency located in "Sayonara/Zaijian" identifies how national subjectivities come into being as the Taiwanese assimilate and digest historical experiences, remembered or educationally constructed, to economic and political reality.

"Concrete Learning over Wishy-Washy Theorizing": Embodied Representation

By 1988, when Huang wrote "Cheers, Soldier," multiculturalism had emerged as a salient subject for public discourse. In the fictions discussed above, Huang vividly caught the postcolonial posture through various dialogues and interactions between Taiwanese, American, and Japanese peoples. However, the scope of each was restricted to the viewpoint of the Taiwanese majority. "Cheers, Soldier" complements the group by sharply delineating Taiwan as a *settler society*, which, to adopt Clare Bradford's definition to a new context, is an invaded country in which colonizers "exercised racial domination over the autochthonous inhabitants of the lands they invaded" (2007, 4). The story thus addresses the complexity of the postcolonial situation through an encounter with some of the indigenous people who are the authentic native inhabitants of the island. One means whereby the subaltern may speak in fiction is to attribute a voice through either first person narration or character focalization, but this may simply reproduce a dominant discourse in which the subaltern is appropriated and spoken for. Representation of subjectivity is thus an illusion. Huang strives to get around this problem by constructing a first person narrator who is engaged in making a documentary film about Taiwan, under the title *Fragrance Island*, and thus the issue of representation is immediately identified. Having embraced the principle that mental information has to be blended with on-the-spot experience—that concrete learning is superior to wishy-washy theorizing—the narrator embarks on a journey with Xiong, an indigenous youth, to the remote mountain village of *Haocha*, home of some Lukai tribal people. It is dark when they arrive, and the narrator becomes bewildered in his host's dim, candlelit hut. These representational strategies problematize any assumption that the subjectivity of an other, and particularly someone ethnically other, can be made accessible.

The crux of the story occurs when the narrator inquires about some photographs of soldiers in different uniforms displayed on the wall. The first "was clad in the uniform of Japanese soldiers dispatched to southern China during the Pacific War," and Xiong identifies him as, "My mother's husband." A second died fighting in the Japanese army in the Philippines. A third, whom Xiong identifies as his father, was one of many villagers sent by the Nationalist Army who were rumored to have been "caught by the Eighth Route Army and made into bandit troopers by the communist bandits," and not heard of again. Xiong's eldest brother died fighting with the Nationalists; his second brother was also recruited, but survived. In a matter-of-fact way, Xiong reports further that his grandfather fought against the Japanese when they annexed Taiwan (after the 1895 Treaty of Shimonoseki), and his father before him had fought against the Han-Chinese settlers. When asked if this family history made him angry, Xiong reacted with surprise and related an analogy told to him by another family warrior, his maternal grandfather. The narrator quickly sees its allegorical import:

> The story about his grandfather took me by surprise. Total aggressive extermination was its embedded message. There was no denying that, historically, the lot of these mountain folk was to be attacked. The flip side to this philosophizing was resistance; there would be hope for them if just one of their soldiers remained. In an ideology of negation of the individual, with national and racial consciousness as its sole focus, sacrificing individuals appears as nothing in the bigger picture. Did Xiong understand this form of thinking or had it become a social grammar of their aboriginal culture, causing them to act before they understood? That explained how Xiong could appear so calm emotionally when he talked about those framed photographs and their ill-fated subjects (2011, 58).

Left alone, and befuddled by too much unaccustomed wine, the narrator can only find an inadequate response:

> I still remember, on the top of the notebook wet with my tears, grabbing my pen, the pen that had trouble listening to my summons, writing crookedly the slated words: "On earth, where could be a history more disheartening than this? Where would there be an ethnic minority with a fate more heartbreaking." . . . I was still able to pick up the glass that

was empty except for a few drops and mumble repeatedly in my heart: "Cheers, soldier!" (61–62)

In pondering what he interpreted as "a social grammar of their aboriginal culture"—that is, a basis for a common, embodied subjectivity that had evolved in a visceral way—the narrator offers an explanation for what he knows is inexpressible. Subjectivity was evolved from the experience over generations of living as a subaltern people in extremity with no voice to speak and no temper to be furious. They were deprived of their own nationhood and disseminated around the globe by the colonialists, imperialists, and capitalists for the purposes of war and labor. Xiong's family was simply an epitome of the collective fate of indigenous people in Taiwan. It is with "Cheers, Soldier" that Huang established himself as a postcolonial writer. His scope stepped outward to the global scene as he reached inward to the deep mountain recesses of his native land. For the first person narrator, the visit to the village was an experience of becoming haunted by the phantoms which loom from the crimes collectively committed by outsiders. On the other hand, it was also an enlightening experience, as the process of journey and dialogue symbolize that awareness has to be acquired in the dark, through hard labor and sought from within.

Subjectivity of /for Whom?

As the title of this article has suggested, subjectivity can be separated from identity. A postcolonial reading may cast doubt on the assumptions of nationalism. From the outset, we provided two episodes to illustrate the ambiguous and yet ambivalent atmosphere in Taiwan. In the political sphere, people divided themselves into two opposing camps, but they also opted for something beyond politics. National identity was blurred and at times fluctuated. Nation may mean differently even within the same ethnic group. Thus, even a highly acclaimed nativist writer can be accused of a lack of loyalty to the land. But was the accusation groundless? Was the writer aware of what his works meant to nationalism? Or does it imply that the young scholar just raised an anachronistic question which was no longer of any significance?

In his *Imagined Communities*, Anderson indicated that national identity derived from language, rather than race (1983, 46). Huang was criticized for the language used in his fiction. His supporters were willing to endorse his mixture of Chinese language and Taiwanese dialect as a respectable performance. For Huang, Chinese language can never be a problem. He mastered it, enriched it, expanded it, and hybridized it with Taiwanese dialect. But for the fundamentalists, Chinese is Chinese. It is imbued with an ideology that can invade the unconscious with an imperialist virus, whereas the separatist ideology of national identity might be realized by altering language according to genuine Taiwanese expression. Conscious or not of his personal ideological bent, Huang may conceive the controversy as neither an issue nor agenda to intentionally take up in his writing. Contrarily, it may seem to Huang that the national identity propagated by the fundamentalist was just a 'false consciousness.' If subjecthood is not an issue for most Taiwanese inhabitants, the urge for national identity inevitably loses its ground. Again the presidential election of 2012 seems to confirm this truism.

Huang's writing goes beyond political questions of subjecthood and identity to exemplify a postcolonial condition of subjectivity and establish him as a forerunner of postcolonial writing in Taiwan. In "The Taste of Apples," though the family may be collectively represented as subservient people in the colonized past, no hostility could be felt against the colonizing counterpart given their "noble" arrangement for the accident. The apples symbolize the colonial encounter, not simply as sweet or sour, but something more complicated to be handled, digested, and comprehended. "I Love Mary" lays bare the psychological submission of the colonized in the domain of global business. By portraying the abhorrent personality of the organizational man, it enabled the subaltern woman to become conscious of her condition of double-colonization by patriarchy and capitalism. In "Young Widow," readers witness an extraordinary form of colonialism in historical contingency, as "Orientalism" is appropriated by the presumed oppressed for monetary profit but is thematically overthrown by a young woman whose performance of a native subjectivity attracts reader empathy. In "Sayonara/Zaijian," anti-Japanese sentiment was real yet delineated in sarcastic manner, as the narrator's role-playing exposes how attitudes and assumptions are endemic and held unthinkingly. An irony that emerges from this text is that his unwilling participation in a distasteful event prompts him to refashion his own subjectivity as a struggle to find a space for agency. The significance of postcolonialism finally becomes clearer and adds a last comment on the issue of language in "Cheers, Soldier" when the narrator comprehends for the first time that he himself belongs not simply to a colonized people, but to a people that has itself begun its local history as colonizers with a bent for genocide. "Cheers, Soldier" surpasses narrow national and racial boundaries and provides a thought-provoking reflection that those who considered themselves as oppressed can be simultaneously oppressors.

Therefore, what Huang perceived as postcolonial was multidimensional. He was sensitive enough to grasp the very elements of complexity with penetrating observations on diverse encounters and dialogues among receptive insiders and intrusive strangers. He exhibited, not instructed, the abundant facets of postcolonialism in that subjectivity was conceived as fluid, contingent, and ever-changing. And given its ambiguous meaning to each individual, national identity has to give way to a more comprehensive conception of subjectivity.

Works Cited

Primary Texts

Huang, Chun-ming. "Cheers, Soldier." In *Taiwan Xiangtu Writer Huang Chun-ming: Three Short Stories, With A Critical Introduction*, edited by Willy Chenja Du. Master's of Fine Arts thesis, University of Iowa, 2011.

Huang, Chun-ming. *The Complete Work of Huang Chun-ming*. Vol. 1–6. Taipei, Taiwan: Unitas Publishing Co., 2009.

Huang, Chun-ming. *The Taste of Apples*, translated by Howard Goldblatt. New York: Columbia University Press, 2001.

Huang, Chun-ming. "Young Widow." In *Oxcart: Nativist Stories from Taiwan 1934–1977*, translated by Rosemary M. Haddon. Dortmund: Project Verlag, 1996.

Secondary Texts

Anderson, Benedict. *Imagined Communities*. London: Verso, 1983.

Bhabha, Homi. *The Location of Culture*. London: Routledge, 1994.

Bradford, Clare. *Unsettling Narratives: Postcolonial Readings of Children's Literature*. Waterloo, Canada: Wilfrid Laurier University Press, 2007.

Chang, Sung-sheng Yvonne. *Modernism and the Nativist Resistance: Contemporary Chinese Fiction from Taiwan*. Durham, NC: Duke University Press, 1993.

Chen, Fangming. "Postmodern or Postcolonial? An Inquiry into Postwar Taiwanese Literary History." In *Writing Taiwan*, edited by Wang David Der-wei and Carlos Rojas. Durham, NC: Duke University Press, 2007.

Chen, Kuo-wei. "Fight Fire by Fire: The Switch of Modernism and Nationalism in Huang Chun-ming's Novels." In *The Taste of Earth: Collected Papers on Huang Chun-ming's Literature* (泥土的滋味：黃春明文學論集), edited by Bau-chai Chiang and Jenn-Shann Lin. Taipei, Taiwan: Unitas Publishing Co., 2009.

Chun, Allen. "Fuck Chineseness: On the Ambiguities of Ethnicity as Culture as Identity," *Boundary 2* 23.2 (1996): 111–138.

Chun, Allen. "The Postcolonial Alien in Us All: Identity in the Global Division of Intellectual Labor," *positions* 16.3 (2008): 689–710.

Haddon, Rosemary. "Introduction: Taiwanese Nativism and the Colonial/Post-Colonial Discourse." In *Oxcart: Nativist Stories from Taiwan 1934–1977*. Dortmund: Project Verlag, 1996.

Hillenbrand, Margaret. *Literature, Modernity, and the Practice of Resistance: Japanese and Taiwanese Fiction, 1960–1990*. Leiden: Brill Academic Publishers, 2007.

Huang, Yi-kuan. "Imagined Nation and Homeland Images: The Film Adaptation of Huang Chun-ming Novels and Representation of Taiwan New Cinema." In *The Taste of Earth: Collected Papers on Huang Chun-ming's Literature* (泥土的滋味：黃春明文學論集), edited by Bau-chai Chiang and Jenn-Shann Lin. Taipei, Taiwan: Unitas Publishing Co., 2009.

Li, F. L. N., A. J. Jowett, A. M. Findlay, and R. Skeldon "Discourse on Migration and Ethnic Identity: Interviews with Professionals in Hong Kong," *Transactions of the Institute of British Geographers: New Series* 20.3 (1995): 342–356.

Phillips, Kendall R. "Rhetorical Maneuvers: Subjectivity, Power, and Resistance," *Philosophy and Rhetoric* 39.4 (2006): 310–332.

Spivak, Gayatri Chakravorty. "Can the Subaltern Speak?" In *Marxism and the Interpretation of Culture*, edited by C. Nelson and L. Grossberg. Basingstoke: Macmillan Education, 1988.

Chapter Thirteen

Scrivener's Progeny
Writing the Subject

Robyn McCallum

"Is that you, Fever?" she asked. "You are not thinking that you're Godshawk again?"

"Oh, I'm me," said Fever. "I think I'm more me than I have ever been."

Philip Reeve, *Scrivener's Moon*

A grounding premise with which this collection begins is the idea that "the acceptance of theoretical approaches across cultures has taken place without interrogation of the political implications of social and epistemic formulations that are profoundly ethnocentric and Eurocentric" (Sakai, 1997: 118). In order to redress such impositions, "it is becoming increasingly desirable to seek a basis for dialogue about the crucial concepts of subjectivity across Western and non-Western cultures," a dialogue which this collection thus enters into with the question, "if subjectivity is truly dialogic, then, what does this imply for its representation across different cultures?" (Chapter 1, this volume). The various contributors raise a number of questions and issues related to the representation of subjectivity within and across specific cultural contexts, but a key common problem is the issue of how to speak of subjectivities across cultures and across languages. As Mio Bryce asks in her chapter: "in discussion of subjectivities . . . are we always talking about the same thing?" (Chapter 10, this volume). Potentially, the answer to this question is going to be at best "maybe" even within an academic community which shares native-speaker fluency in the same language; across culturally diverse academic communities which perhaps share a language with varying degrees of fluency, the question becomes more difficult to answer in the affirmative. If we set aside language difficulties for the time being, the key term which is reiterated throughout this volume is 'dialogue,' implying the exchange of ideas within discourse, that is speech and/or writing.

A 'dialogic' construction of subjectivity implies, among other things, the construction of the subject within and through language. This was an idea that I wanted to suggest when I decided to borrow from the title of Philip Reeve's third volume in his *Fever Crumb* series, *Scrivener's Moon*, for the title of my own chapter. In Reeve's futuristic post-disaster series the Scriven are a race of northern nomads; their main visible physical difference from other human races is their pale skins which are "blotched and dappled with markings like leopards' spots" (Reeve, 2009: 9). It is believed by the Scriven that these markings are "sacred ideograms" and that "they had been written on by a god called the Scrivener who had inscribed the future history of the world on their skins" (9). By the close of the third volume, it has been disclosed that the Scriven, and another northern race called the Nightwights (or the People), are in fact the result of a human mutation, a genetically engineered human subrace called "Humanity 2.0" whose DNA codes had been rewritten to create a race of human beings adapted for survival in a post-nuclear war world— their skin markings, designed to ensure that they only mated with their own kind, are the trademark of the corporations making up *The Scrivener Institute*. Other genetic modifications included increased resistance to radiation, physical adaptations to enable the survival of a nuclear winter, reduced aging and a longer reproductive life, and "nanotech upgrades" (Reeve, 2011: 240) making "brain functions compatible with . . . mnemonic harvesting technology to aid the exchange and retention of group knowledge" (242). As readers familiar with Reeve's *Mortal Engines* quartet will recognize, the last characteristic makes the Scriven comparable with Reeve's stalkers, or "resurrected men," cyborg figures designed originally as remembering machines but later used as soldiers (Reeve, 2009: 248, 2011: 236, 2006: 533).[1] In a sense, the Scriven belief in a Scrivener god is not so far from the truth, except that the god is in fact humanity itself taking on a god-like function in rewriting and reproducing its own identity. The image of a group of human beings who write upon and inscribe the bodies and minds of their own race has analogies with the idea of the subject as spoken, or written, into being, the subject whose subjectivity is enacted through a (genetic) language which predates that subject but also enables its coming into being. The "Scrivener's progeny" in this sense are the ideas about and representations of the subject which are brought into the conversation through successive dialogues about that subject across cultures and across languages.

John Stephens begins his introduction to this book with a reference to what he terms "two positions" which he contends have been "naturalized" within academic discourse about the representation of subjectivity in children's literature. Those two position statements are quoted from a book, *Ideologies of Identity in Adolescent Fiction* (1999), and both have been widely cited and quoted within children's literature criticism since 1999. The first is relatively unproblematic:

> [I]deas about and representations of subjectivity pervade and underpin adolescent fiction. Concepts of subjectivity are intrinsic to narratives of personal growth or maturation, to stories about relationships between the self and others, and to explorations of relationships between individuals and the world, society or the past—that is subjectivity is intrinsic to the major concerns of adolescent fiction. (3)

These kinds of thematic concerns have continued to have a central place in English-language fiction for young people, and in the critical discourses around that literature in part because, as John suggests, "the literature and criticism are informed by the same cultural metanarrative. The literature . . . is about subjectivity to the extent that the producing culture is preoccupied with it" (Chapter 1, this volume). Childhood and adolescence are both seen as transitional stages—that is, age-determined periods of physical, psychological, social, emotional, and cognitive growth and development. And fiction for young people is always offering its readers representations of how characters evolve a sense of identity as some sense of themselves in relation to the world they inhabit. "The educational and domestic structures of Western societies aspire to encourage children to be reasonable, creative, autonomous, and achieving human beings, and these ideals are furthered by the ideological positions implicit in the literature produced for children" (Stephens, 1992:120). In this sense, then, the position is one which was already naturalized before its restatement in *Ideologies of Identity*, although that book has perhaps furthered its acceptance.

The second "position" statement, however, I now think, can be quite problematic, and I quote here two slightly different versions of it:

> [S]ubjectivity [is] that sense of a personal identity an individual has of his/her self as distinct from other selves, as occupying a position within society and in relation to other selves, and as being capable of deliberate thought and action. (3)

> [Subjectivity] is an individual's sense of a personal identity as a subject—in the sense of being subject to some measure of external coercion—and as an agent—that is, being capable of conscious and deliberate thought and action. And this identity is formed in dialogue with the social discourses, practices, and ideologies constituting the culture which an individual inhabits. (4)

These are loose definitions which encompass and to some extent conflate various theoretical approaches to subjectivity, but what is being suggested here is an essentially Bakhtinian conception of subjectivity comprising three interrelated and dialogic processes: subjectivity involves a sense of personal identity which is formed within and through relationships with others (in relation to social processes), structures and discourses which position and coerce subjects, and a degree of agency (that is, a capacity for independent thought and action within a negotiated social world). A key assumption is that the three systems of relationships, between self and other, subject and social process, agency and sociality, are to be thought of as dialogical and intrinsically interconnected.

This second position statement is not inherently problematic, but its complexity can lead to simplification and misappropriation, and my language choices are, in retrospect, misleading. In particular, the phrases "personal identity" and "conscious and deliberate thought and action" in isolation might be read as a reinstantiation of the unique, unified liberal humanist self, as Mio Bryce appears to do in her chapter in this collection, where she quotes the first version of the definition and goes on to assert that "it is still based on the premise that an individual is allowed to exist as a unique, independent, and integral entity whose agency is a product of individual choices and decisions" (Chapter 10, this volume). The problem, here, lies in a binary thinking which opposes self and other, subject and social process, and agency and sociality, rather than seeing each of these as dialogic and as inextricably intertwined. In fact these binaries form a starting point for many of the chapters in this collection (see Gutierrez, Banerjee, Hisaoka, Bryce, and Lee). The imposition of a Western binary logic onto a comparison of Western and Eastern conceptions of subjectivity runs the risk of polarizing a Western "unified autonomous subject" and an Eastern "self-in-relationship-with-others." As Anna Katrina Gutierrez astutely suggests, "[t]he challenge is to move away from Western theories of subjectivity by focusing on the useful negotiation between East and West," rather than polarizing them. Certainly this collection represents inroads in making that move toward "useful negotiation," but to limit Western subjectivity to the liberal humanist unique, unified autonomous subject, in order to define how Eastern subjectivity is different, is to also limit the possibilities of dialogue and negotiation, and run the risk of falling back once again into a Western binary logic. As I argued in *Ideologies of Identity*, the idea of a universal individualized unique and essential self which underwrites Western humanist ideologies, has been systematically undermined since its invention; humanist traditions have always been more or less implicitly aware of the constructedness and hence a fictionality of that self (1999, 5; see also Howe, 1992; Booth, 1993; Hutcheon, 1989; Bullock, 1985). This is in part what makes Bakhtin's concept of dialogism so attractive, as it would seem to provide us with pathways out of binary systems of meaning toward a theory of subjectivity which posits intersubjectivity, rather than self, at its heart. Identity is thus to be thought of as differential and correlational, or to quote Bakhtin:

> I am conscious of myself and become myself only while revealing myself for another, through another and with the help of another. The most important acts constituting self-consciousness are determined by a relationship toward another consciousness (towards a *thou*). (*Problems of Dostoevsky's Poetics*, 1984)

Bakhtin's conception of the self is thus intrinsically intersubjective, encapsulating the idea of "self-in-relationship-with others" which would seem to lie also at the heart of concepts of Eastern subjectivity underpinning so many of the essays in this collection. Furthermore, Bakhtin's image of intersubjectivity is inherently fluid, not so much a state of being as a continuous process of becoming. Thus, subjectivity is not fixed but always shifting, subject to change as relationships shift and change. The idea of the subject as fluid can be problematic, however, when it is mapped onto a trajectory of childhood and adolescent development or growth. As Kerry Mallan and Sharyn Pearce suggest in their introduction to *Youth Cultures*,

> As a defining age category, 'youth' is often regarded as a state of becoming, as a necessary (and often tortuous) pathway to adulthood. The reward of adult status carries with it the *mythical* virtues of maturity, independence, stability, and above all a secure identity: one which is whole and not troubled by the uncertainties that characterize the transience of youth [emphasis added]. (2003, ix)

On the one hand, adolescence is thought of as a process of becoming and hence of moving from a state of fragmentation and alienation to a state of stability and wholeness; whereas on the other, the idea that adulthood entails a "secure" identity, a state of stability, or wholeness, is a myth. It is, however, as many of the essays in this collection demonstrate, a myth which is frequently sustained by the teleological narrative structures common to Western children's and adolescent fiction which, in mapping the development of subjectivity onto a trajectory from childhood to adulthood, imply that adulthood constitutes a point of unified closure, which of course it does not.

There is a danger that in attempting to dismantle the binary logic which opposes Eastern and Western conceptions of subjectivity, and in asserting points of interconnection, that it will seem that I am seeking to universalize concepts of subjectivity and as a Western English-speaker, reimpose a Western paradigm. As John Stephens suggested in the introduction, subjectivity, like ideology, "inheres in texts as something immanent in narrative forms and language" (Chapter 1, this volume). A dialogic approach to representations of subjectivity across cultures needs to pay attention to the nuances of language, as Mio Bryce implicitly suggests in her comparison of Japanese with Anglo-European languages, and as I suggested of my own language choices above. There is never a direct transparent correspondence between words and things, signifiers and signifieds, in any language, nor can there be a direct translation from one language to another. So, as I suggested earlier, in discussions of subjectivity across cultures and languages, we can never be sure we are talking about the same thing, particularly if that subjectivity is conceived of as constructed within sociality and language. *Ideologies of Identity* was recently translated into and published in Chinese. As I had no input into the translation and cannot speak or read Chinese, I was interested to know what "sense" had been made of the book in a language which I had been told had no single character for the English word "subjectivity" and asked a Chinese international student to translate some key passages back into English for me.[2] The differences between my English and the translated Chinese/English are subtle but interesting. The two definitions of subjectivity quoted above, for example, translate back into English as follows:

> [S]ubjectivity is an individual's personal identity distinct from other selves; it occupies a position in the society in which other selves also exist; it makes an individual think well and behave discreetly.

> [S]ubjectivity is an individual's cognition of a personal identity as a subject that suffers from some measure of external oppression and as an agent, capable of consciousness and initiative thinking and action. The identity is gained in dialogue with the social discourses, customs, and cultural ideologies that an individual inhabits.

The changes are slight, and I think the basic "sense" of the definitions has been retained, but the differences are telling. "It makes an individual think well and behave discreetly" and "capable of consciousness and initiative thinking" would certainly seem to imply a more limited and diminished sense of agency than "capable of conscious and deliberate thought and action." The qualifiers "well" and "discreetly" along with the replacement of the noun "action" with the more concrete verb "behave," implies a concept of subjectivity much more along the lines of cultural advocacy than I had in mind.

Language is central to how subjectivity is represented and articulated because language offers the subject the (elusive) possibility of control over meaning, the possibility, in other words, of fixing meaning and identities. Language offers individuals meanings and forms of subjectivity that they can assume and live as if they were true and in the process become subjects. The processes involved are perhaps more clearly articulated by Terry Pratchett in a passage early in *The Amazing Maurice and His Educated Rodents*:

> He'd [Maurice] realized something odd that day, just after lunch, when he'd looked into a reflection in a puddle and thought *that's me*. He'd

never been *aware* of himself before. Of course, it was hard to remember *how* he'd thought before he became amazing. It seemed to him that his mind had been just a kind of soup. (Pratchett, 2001: 17)

In Pratchett's novel, a group of rats eat the remains of an experiment left on the rubbish tip outside the Unseen University—the Wizard's University in Pratchett's Discworld—and undergo a "change," one effect of which is the capacity for language and speech. In turn, Maurice, a cat, becomes "amazing" after eating one of these talking (or "educated") rats. In the passage quoted, with its obvious allusions to Lacan's "mirror phase," Pratchett is making a connection between cognition, self-consciousness, and language. The exact nature of "the change" which the rats and Maurice undergo is a little vague, and the passage blurs the line between self-consciousness (looking in the reflection in the puddle and being self-aware), cognition ("he thought"), and language acquisition (and hence the capacity to be self-reflective through language and to be able to say, "that's me"). An implication of all this blurring is that all of these capacities are mutually dependent upon each other. The passage continues:

He'd realized there was something educated about the rats when he jumped on one and it said, "Can we talk about this?" and part of his amazing new brain had told him you couldn't eat someone who could talk. At least, not until you'd heard what they'd got to say.

The attainment of self-consciousness, language, and thought, is thus (at least according to Pratchett's version of the mirror stage) tied up with the recognition of the selfhood of others. The idea of subjectivity represented here is again, at heart, intersubjective.

Language, as I suggested above, offers individuals the possibility of control over meanings and forms of subjectivity, the possibility that through becoming a speaking subject, an "I" in other words, an individual might become the source of the meaning he or she speaks. Likewise, the idea that we might also write that subject offers the possibility of fixing subjectivity within discourse. Language, however, always preexists the individual speaker or writer; it is, after all, learned rather than innate. Hence, the first person subject speaker is the subject rather than the author of the language he or she writes or speaks. And language can be an inherently ambiguous and unstable signifying system, governed by infinite play and deferral, rather than stability, of meaning. The epithet for this chapter (like the title) comes from Philip Reeve's *Scrivener's Moon*. Coming toward the close of the novel, Fever's assertion, "I think I'm more me than I have ever been," sounds ostensibly like a restatement (albeit playful) of the Cartesian subject (*cogito ergo sum*), the basis for the Western liberal humanist unified coherent subject. Read in the context of Reeve's sprawling now seven volume series, a series populated by fragmented and contingent subjects, however, Fever's assertion is ironic. Fever, the central character in the prequel series, is a racially mixed subject, part Homo Sapiens, part Scriven (or Homo Superior): her father, Dr. Crumb, is a London engineer and her mother, Wavy, is a Scriven, daughter of Auric Godshawk, the last of London's Scriven overlords. Furthermore, Fever has a cranial implant containing the memories and knowledge of her grandfather, Godshawk. The "nanotech upgrades" made to Scriven DNA (2011, 240), which I referred to earlier, it would seem have made her brain functions compatible with such "mnemonic harvesting technology" (242). Having realized that the time of the Scriven would soon be over with the Scriven population's gradual decline, Godshawk had performed surgery upon an infant and ailing Fever, implanting a stalker brain containing his consciousness in her brain. The effects of the implant, however, do not become apparent until Fever approaches adulthood when Godshawk's memories and emotions surface as dreamlike visions and Fever begins to experience selfhood as a split subject (2009, 255). The implant is disabled by the magnetic pulse from a Magneto gun (a gun used to disable stalkers) toward the close of *Fever Crumb*, and the novel closes with Fever saying "the one thing about herself that she was certain of: My name is Fever Crumb" (321).

The prologue of *Scrivener's Moon* opens with a passage (apparently) narrated from the viewpoint of Auric Godshawk and which echoes the close of the first book:

> He forded the river as daylight died and blundered into thick undergrowth between the birches on the far bank. Sobbing with fright and pain he raised his hand to his chest and felt the hard point of the arrow sticking out through his coat. . . . He was a stranger in that country; an explorer; a scientist; a soldier of fortune. His name was Auric Godshawk. (2011, xiii)

For the reader who has read the first two volumes in the series, the prologue, it would seem, is either an analepsis, or this book is yet another prequel. As the prologue continues, however, Auric's self-assured focalization begins to flicker, as his memory "seemed to be missing vital chunks" and his hands do not seem to belong to him, "frail, girlish things they seemed" (xiv). The clues as to the identity of the focalizing character become more obvious with a conversation between him and Cluny, the mammoth-girl who has rescued him and is nursing him back to health, when she tells him he is "*not a dying man*" and that he is "feverish"—Auric replies, "Yes! I am feverish . . . I am *Feverish*." Later that night, Auric wakes up and sees a girl in the shadows watching him:

> She was not his mammoth-girl. In his confusion, he thought for a moment she was Wavey, and he started up, and she rose too, but as they walked towards each other he saw that she was a stranger; a

Scriven-looking girl, watching him with wide-set mismatched eyes, one grey, the other brown. *Poor mite*, he thought, for she was a Blank; the Scrivener had put no markings on her flesh at all. There was an angry star-shaped scar above her breast and as she reached up to touch it he reached up too, in sympathy and understanding, and felt the same scar on his own flesh. Then lost memories started rushing past him like snow and he stretched out his fingers to the girl's face and touched only the cold surface of a looking glass.

His own numb fear looked back at him out of her widening eyes.

"No!" he shouted. They both shouted it; him and the girl in the mirror, but the only voice he heard was hers. "I am Auric Godshawk! . . ."

But he wasn't. . . . What remained of him was just a ghost inhabiting the mind of this thin girl, his granddaughter. Her name, he suddenly recalled, was *Fever Crumb*. (2011, xvii)

In Lacanian terms, the episode presents the mirror-phase as initially a moment of misreckoning as Auric perceives the image in the mirror as an other, utterly separate from himself, but there is no corresponding moment of recognition, that is of Fever's recognition of herself as a "me"—as there is in the passage I quoted above from *The Amazing Maurice and His Educated Rodents*. Instead, that Auric shouts his own name, but hears only Fever's voice, foregrounds the extent to which Fever/Auric remains a fragmented subject; with Auric, the ghost inside the "tiny machine" inside Fever's brain, Fever's subjectivity can only be asserted as a "name" for the body he and she inhabit. Fever's later assertion, "I think I'm more me than I have ever been," then, is ironic insofar as it appears on the one hand to assert a relation between cognition and identity (through its allusion to a concept of a unified Cartesian subjectivity) but at the same time, problematizes that relation through the idea of being "more me"—it is a statement which leaves the reader asking "who (and what) exactly is Fever?"

As I noted at the outset of this chapter, the two position statements with which John Stephens opened his introduction to this collection are quoted from my book, *Ideologies of Identity* (1999), which was based on my PhD thesis (1994) that coincidentally was supervised by John, the editor of this book, who is now a colleague. I wrote those statements as a young, Anglo-Australian woman just entering the world of academia, with no children and very little practical knowledge or experience of children or adolescents, but I was fairly well-read in English literature and I had a reasonably good knowledge of theories of subjectivity and narrative. Were the latter adequate credentials to be making position statements? Certainly, as I have noted, those two quotations have been both widely cited and quoted since 1999, a phenomenon which I find flattering but often also puzzling; and my feelings about being involved in this current project have been of a similar nature. The project had its genesis in a series of conversations between John Stephens and a young Filipina doctoral

222 · Robyn McCallum

student, Anna Katrina Gutierrez, back in late 2009, and as time went on, other international doctoral students, Asian scholars, and myself joined this conversation. In a discussion of Filipino folktales, Anna Katrina had suggested that John was perhaps imposing Western paradigms of subjectivity on Asian textual representations. I in turn suggested that he was imposing paradigms which were not only Western, but also patriarchal—now a middle-aged academic and mother of two boys, I certainly could not see myself in the mirror of the unique, individualized, coherent subject that he seemed to be asserting was the dominant paradigm of Western children's fiction. In retrospect, that was perhaps because I was finding myself increasingly drawn toward fiction by English writers such as Philip Reeve, that is, writers whose work implicitly interrogated that paradigm and in doing so confirmed my own sense as a parent as being a contingent self and of my children as contingent selves, or "selves-in-relationships-with-others." This is not to suggest that Reeve reflects any more accurately the "lived experience" of real children or adults than any other writer; rather he interrogates the taken-for-granted ideological assumptions of the dominant mainstream and offers alternatives. From these conversations, the project gradually began to take shape, and as John recruited the various contributors to this volume, the dialogue continued. It was quite some time, however, before I realized he had in mind that I write this final chapter. Why me? All of the other contributors were either from an Asian country or had substantial knowledge of an Asian culture and language. Was there perhaps something about me that John had not noticed in twenty-seven years— the native-speaker fluency in only one language (English), the blue eyes, white skin, once reddish (now greying) hair, or perhaps it was my height?

Hence, it was with some trepidation that I found myself "book-ending" this collection of essays about Asian subjectivities, particularly as the other "book-end" is a white, male academic. Is this a problem? Given one underlying premise of the collection, that some concepts of subjectivity, in particular the idea of a unified, unique individualistic subject, "are arguably specifically Western constructions, not portable, and do not simply transfer to the narratives of non-European cultures," then, initially, I thought that maybe it was. To return again to Mio Bryce's question: "in discussion of subjectivities . . . are we always talking about the same thing?" The answer here, I think, ultimately, has to be "no." If subjectivity is truly dialogical, that is "formed in dialogue with the social discourses, practices, and ideologies constituting the culture which an individual inhabits," then we can never be sure that we are talking about the same thing across different cultures and languages. But are Western subjects, such as myself, always so utterly interpellated by Western paradigms as to not be able to think and speak outside of them? And is Western culture such a unified monologic entity so as to not allow difference and variation, and hence dialogue in other words? Again, the answer has to be "no." If that were the case, this collection could never have been conceived of at all. Collections such as this are rarely read from front to back. Instead, they tend to be read from the inside out; we may start with the introduction but then read the rest according to our own interests and preoccupations, so perhaps the "book-ending" is not a problem anyway. Further, and perhaps more fundamentally, an underlying purpose of this collection is to continue the conversation begun by John and Anna Katrina, invite dialogue from other scholars and to leave it open to further dialogue.

Notes

1. The *Fever Crumb* series comprises *Fever Crumb* (2009), *A Web of Air* (2009), and *Scrivener's Moon* (2011), and forms a prequel series to another of Reeve's major series, the *Mortal Engines Quartet* (published in the U.S. as the *Hungry Cities* chronicles), comprising *Mortal Engines* (2001), *Predator's Gold* (2003), *Infernal Devices* (2005), and *A Darkling Plain* (2006). The *Fever Crumb* series is set in a postapocalyptic England after 'the Downsizing' which followed on from a catastrophic 'sixty minute' war between the American Empire and Greater China and the Traction Age (the setting for the *Mortal Engines Quartet*); a key character appearing in both series is the stalker, Shrike. For discussions of the *Mortal Engines Quartet* see Bradford et al. *New World Orders in Contemporary Children's Literature* (2008) and McCallum (2009).
2. I am very grateful to Wei-wei Xu (Macquarie University) for her thorough English translations of passages from the Chinese edition of my book.

Works Cited

Booth, Wayne C. "Individualism and the Mystery of the Social Self; Or, Does Amnesty Have a Leg to Stand on?" In *Freedom and Interpretation*, edited by Barbara Johnson. New York: Basic Books, 1993.

Bradford, Clare, Kerry Mallan, John Stephens, and Robyn McCallum. *New World Orders in Contemporary Children's Literature*. Basingstoke: Palgrave Macmillan, 2008.

Bullock, Alan. *The Humanist Tradition in the West*. New York: W. W. Norton & Company, 1985.

Howe, Irving. "The Self in Literature." In *Constructions of the Self*, edited by George Levine. New Bruswick, NJ: Rutgers University Press, 1992.

Hutcheon, Linda. *The Politics of Postmodernism*. London: Routledge, 1989.

Mallan, Kerry, and Sharyn Pearce. Youth Cultures: Texts, Images and Identities. Westport, CT: Praeger Publishers, 2003.

McCallum, Robyn. *Ideologies of Identity in Adolescent Fiction: The Dialogic Construction of Subjectivity*. New York: Garland, 1999.

McCallum, Robyn. "Ignorant Armies on a Darkling Plain: The New World Disorder of Global Economics, Environmentalism and Urbanisation in Philip Reeve's *Hungry Cities*," *International Research in Children's Literature* 2.2 (2009): 210–227.

Pratchett, Terry. *The Amazing Maurice and His Educated Rodents*. Doubleday, 2001.

Reeve, Philip. *A Darkling Plain*. London: Scholastic, 2006.

———. *Fever Crumb*. London: Scholastic, 2009.

———. *Scrivener's Moon*. London: Scholastic, 2011.

Sakai, Naoki. *Translation and Subjectivity*. Minneapolis: University of Minnesota Press, 1997.

Stephens, John. *Language and Ideology in Children's Fiction*. London: Longman, 1992.

Contributors

Salinee Antarasena, Assistant Professor at Ramkhamhaeng University, holds a BA (English) from Chulalongkorn University, Bangkok, then MA and PhD (both in Creative Writing) from Macquarie University. Her recent research has focused on color perceptions and color categorization in advertising created by the blind. She received a Young Alumni Award for an outstanding Thai alumnus who has made a significant contribution to relations between Thailand and Australia in 2009 through to 2010.

Seemi Aziz has a PhD from the University of Arizona (Tucson) and is an Assistant Professor at Oklahoma State University. Her interests are in reading and literacy, visual culture, and cross-cultural representations. She is author of *Teaching Islamic Religious Art as an Aid to the Understanding of Islamic Culture* (2008).

Suchismita Banerjee is enrolled in the PhD program at Jawaharlal Nehru University, New Delhi. The focus of her research is the idea of childhood in contemporary Indian English fiction for children, specifically the impact of globalization on the construction of the child and the formation of childhood identities as represented in Indian English children's literature. In her attempt to gain visibility for contemporary Indian English children's literature in academic circles, Suchismita has published an article titled "Contemporary Children's Literature in India: New Trajectories" in the *Journal of Children's Literature*, a publication of the Children's Literature Association of India. She has also presented research papers at children's literature conferences at Coimbatore (India) and Frankfurt.

Christie Barber is a lecturer in the Department of International Studies at Macquarie University, where she teaches Japanese language and history. She is also a PhD candidate, and her research focuses on representations of masculinity in contemporary Japanese film and literature for young people.

Mio Bryce is Senior Lecturer and Head of Japanese Studies in the Department of International Studies at Macquarie University, teaching Japanese language, literature, and manga related units. She has a PhD in Japanese classical literature (*The Tale of Genji*) from the University of Sydney. Research interests include historical, sociocultural, and psychological issues depicted in literature and in youth cultures.

Tran Quynh Ngoc Bui, PhD in English Literature, is a lecturer in the Department of Literature at Ho Chi Minh City University of Education, Vietnam, where she specializes in literary theory. Her recent research has focused on folktales in which the principal character has the role of an "Unfortunate," and explores how these tales reflect concepts of a social contract and the extent to which changes in or breaches of social contracts shape the tales' attitudes toward the "Unfortunates" and how apparently familiar plots and motifs may signify in specific ways in local cultural contexts and in conjunction with historical, cultural layers contained in these tales.

Suh Shan Chen is a lecturer in the Department of English Literature at National Taitung University, Taiwan, where she teaches Introduction to Western Literature, Western Novel, and Film. Her recent research focus is on the comparative study of Chinese classic fiction and Western literature with similar themes.

Ming Cherng Duh is an Associate Professor at the Institute of Children's Literature in National Taitung University, Taiwan. He holds a PhD from the University of Southern California. His current academic interests include sociology of literature, fairytale, popular fiction, and children's fiction.

Anna Katrina Gutierrez gained her BA in Psychology at the Ateneo de Manila University in the Philippines and an MA in Children's Literature from Macquarie University. She is currently enrolled in a PhD in Children's Literature at Macquarie University and has taught there as an Associate Lecturer. Her research interests include Eastern and Western representations of themselves and one another in folktale, film, comic books, anime, and manga, and how these representations interact with one another in children's fiction to create glocal spaces and subjectivities. Her publications include articles in *The International Journal of the Humanities* and *International Research in Children's Literature*.

Miyuki Hisaoka completed an MA in Children's Literature at Warwick University in England. She has worked for many years as an editor of children's books with publishers in Tokyo. Her research interests are in picture books and cross-cultural studies.

Sung-Ae Lee, PhD in English Literature, lectures in the Department of International Studies at Macquarie University, Sydney, Australia. Her current research interests are in Asian cinema, colonization in Asia, trauma studies, Korean fiction and film depicting the Korean War and its aftermath, and in the fiction, poetry, life-writing and popular media of the Korean diaspora. She has published her research in *Remaking Literary History* (2010); *Asian Ethnology*; *Diaspora*; *Journal of Asian American Studies*; *Children's Literature in Education*; *International Research in Children's Literature*; and *Feminist Studies*.

Lifang Li, PhD in Literature, is an Associate Professor in the College of Literature, Lanzhou University, Gansu, P.R. China. She has been involved in children's literature research for more than ten years and has published one research monograph (on the indigenization progress of Chinese children's literature theory in the occurrence period) and more than sixty research articles on children's literature. She participated in the thirtieth IBBY Congress held in Macao, 2006; ninth Asian children's literature convention held in Taiwan, 2008; nineteenth biennial Congress of IRSCL held in Frankfurt am Main, 2009; and twentieth biennial Congress of IRSCL held in Brisbane, 2011.

Robyn McCallum is a Lecturer in English Literature at Macquarie University, Australia, and a member of the advisory board for International Research in Children's Literature. Her research deals with the impact of cultural forms on children's texts, with a particular focus on adolescent fiction, and visual media, especially film. Her publications include, *Retelling Stories, Framing Culture* (1998), with John Stephens, and *New World Orders in Contemporary Children's Fiction* (2008), with Clare Bradford, Kerry Mallan, and John Stephens. Her book, *Ideologies of Identity in Adolescent Fiction* (1999), was the 2001 IRSCL Honour book.

John Stephens is Emeritus Professor in English at Macquarie University, Australia. He is author of *Language and Ideology in Children's Fiction* and *Retelling Stories, Framing Culture* (with Robyn McCallum), and editor of *Ways of Being Male: Representing Masculinities in Children's Fiction and Film*, along with about a hundred articles and two books on discourse analysis. *New World Orders in Contemporary Children's Literature*, a study of the impact of the concept of "new world order" on children's literature since the end of the Cold War, coauthored with Clare Bradford, Kerry Mallan, and Robyn McCallum, was published by Palgrave in 2008. He is a former President of the International Research Society for Children's Literature and currently Editor of *International Research in Children's Literature*. In 2007, he received the 11th International Brothers Grimm Award, in recognition of his contribution to research in children's literature.

Index

CPSIA information can be obtained
at www.ICGtesting.com
Printed in the USA
BVOW11s0628201117

500892BV00021B/882/P

9 781138 108981